MW01644167

FROM MINK SLIDE
to
MAIN STREET

by

Charles Byron Arnette

Also by C.B. Arnette

The Saga of the Lu-Cee-Bee

History of the East Main Street Church of Christ

Second Printing 1992

Typsetting & Composition By B & E Graphics, Murfreesboro, TN
Printing & Binding By Williams Printing Co., Nashville, TN

Library of Congress Catalog Card Number 91-92241

ISBN 0-9621673-5-5

ACKNOWLEDGEMENTS

The writer of *"From Mink Slide to Main Street"* has had much pleasure in writing his memories about the Square, its buildings and its people. The manuscript has undergone more than twenty-one months of preparation. These months have been filled with many, many enjoyable hours of interviews and recollections held in parlors, kitchens, dens, front and backyards, front and back porches, offices, restaurants, via local and long distance telephone calls and in nursing homes. The story could not have been written without the assistance of the many who supplied data and their recollections about the Square. The writer began a list of the people interviewed but discarded it when the list grew into several pages. Those who helped in this effort know who they are and C.B. Arnette has expressed to them his grateful appreciation.

The writer owes much gratitude to those who supplied pictures of the Square and its people. Special thanks are extended to Charlotte Smotherman, wife of recently deceased Dr. Bealer Smotherman. She offered whatever pictures that could be used by the writer from the huge repository of pictures that had been collected for many years by Dr. Smotherman. Bealer was a lover of history and delighted in preserving pictorial records of scenes and people. Fortunately, his and most of the other pictures on these pages were within the time frame of the story—1923-1991.

Others who supplied pictures were Joe Lovell, Robert "Tee-Niny" Scales, Peggy Westbrooks Cranker, Mrs. Jesse Messick, Tony and Vincent DeGeorge, Mrs. Horace Welchance, Herschel Mullins, Lacye Welchance, Dr. Ernest Hooper, Scott Edwards, Harold West, Mrs. Tommy Farmer (Daughter of Ed Bell), Karen Elrod Dismukes, Lillian Johnson, and Sam Lasseter.

Much appreciation is due Sidney Adams for his expert craftsmanship in drafting the several maps of the Square and surrounding area. The maps are exact representations of the Square as it appeared in 1923. The reader will note that the tour follows the arrowed lines shown on the maps.

Many thanks are extended to Cindy Flatt Phiffer for her diligent research of the past and present owners of the properties around the Square. Most of her work required title searches in the Rutherford County Archive Section at the courthouse.

The writer again expresses his gratitude to Bernice Burns for her professional typing abilities and for wearing the hat of assistant editor. Her help is always valuable.

If former Mayor Hollis Westbrooks needed any accolades or merit badges, the writer would have dedicated this book to him. Many pleasurable hours were spent with him in his room at Murfreesboro Health Care Center. His alert mind and extensive recollections supplied much needed information for this book. Hollis was there on the stage and on the scene during most of the sixty-eight year period that is covered by this record. Without much fanfare and perhaps more than anyone else, he helped bring the Square from Mink Slide to Main Street.

Old buildings are not ours. They belong, partly to those who built them, and partly to the generations of mankind who are to follow us. The dead still have their right to them: That which they labored for ... we have no right to obliterate.

What we ourselves have built, we are at liberty to throw down. But what other men gave their strength and wealth and life to accomplish, their right over it does not pass away with their death.

John Ruskin

Foreword

From the earliest agora of ancient Greece to the town squares of today, it seems that the town square is a fitting symbol of the aspirations which move modern society to create that focal point of community life without which there can be neither individual nor collective self-fulfillment. Given the English language connotation of the word "square," it may be that this term does not do full justice to the notion of what the French call "place," the Italians "piazza," the Spaniards "plaza," and the Germans "platz."

These terms go beyond the mere geometric definition of a certain site, while they emphasize that the site is of special importance as a focal point, center, or gathering place. Relatively new by European standards, the Murfreesboro town square, for about one and three-quarter centuries, has been the focal point, the shopping center, the record keeping repository, the administrative center, and the gathering place of Rutherford County. During the majority of those years, the Public Square has been the center of economic activity in the county and a showcase for private enterprise in action. Unique among the town squares in Middle Tennessee, the Murfreesboro square was a prominent center for shoppers from surrounding counties for at least half a century. Its merchants, especially the ladies' clothing and ready-to-wear stores had been most aggressive in obtaining inventories of the latest styles and fashions from the New York and international fashion centers. On these pages, thumbnail sketches of those merchandisers will be given.

In the middle of the present century, a brief retreat from the town square concept occurred. With the advent of Jackson Heights Shopping Center, followed by Mercury Plaza Shopping Center, the Public Square began a decline. The new shopping centers had new stores, and, above all, the parking was plentiful and unmetered. This near-demise of the Square as an economic center was not unique to Murfreesboro but was representative of America's attraction and influx to the new shopping centers. There was even talk and serious planning of demolishing the Court House to make way for a modern and more functional county administrative building.

This neglectful and blatant disregard for the historical significance and architecture of the Court House was a serious affront to the ladies of Murfreesboro. They were soon up in arms and began a concerted action to squelch even the very thought of such a dastardly destruction.

The ladies' efforts were more than successful, inasmuch as they prevailed upon the county squires to remodel and restore the venerable and historical centerpiece of Rutherford County. Gordon Lynch, who had recently founded Lynch Construction Company, was granted the contract. At about that time, it was decided that the large lawn surrounding the Court House should be diminished in order to construct an inner drive and additional parking spaces.

Ed Bell wrote a column in the *Daily News Journal* during the 1930s and 1940s. The by-line for that much-read column was "From Main Street to Mink Slide." The articles dealt usually with the humorous and sometimes mundane characters whom Ed would encounter in his daily walk around the square. That gifted writer could take a humble and least-noticed person and turn him or her into an admirable individual of no low esteem. Since Ed was highly individualistic, he regarded his characters as separate and apart from the masses. Naturally humble himself, his people were at least on his level or slightly higher—not too high, for Ed was not beholden or ingratiating to any man.

Ed Bell was a big man, not only in stature but in character. He was cynical and also humorous, two traits not too often companionable in newspapermen and writers. To him, everyone and everything was singularly deserving of being perceived on the upside rather than the downside. Ed wandered about the Square in a seemingly unpurposeful manner. This writer's frequent meanderings brought us together often. His notice of me and cheerful greeting made me feel a bit taller. It was somewhat less than usual for a kid to receive much attention from an adult around the Square in those days.

Ed was tall, thick-necked, muscular, and broad-shouldered. He was shaggy looking with tousled honey-colored hair and fair complexion. His ever-present smile seemed to be heartfelt, rather than a fixture that would either be turned on or off according to his mood. For his jaunts around the Square, he wore a blue coat with the right upper pocket supplied with sharpened yellow pencils. If the occasion ever demanded a necktie, one had a suspicion that he was nurturing a desire to remove it.

In his quiet, unassuming, and unobtrusive manner, Ed pursued his profession. Story writing was such a natural inclination and so instinctive to Ed that it could never be conceived that he would ever do or want to do anything else but write. Much like a dedicated and avid fisherman, Ed searched and contrived for stories. Most of his characters were little people in society, people for whom he felt a deep respect and compassion. His artistic strokes could portray the deep innermost wants, whims, thoughts, and vagaries of those ordinary and less-than-ordinary people about whom he wrote.

Ed courted and married a lass whose name was Sara McGuire. His tale about their courtship reveals his true romantic feelings for her. The story becomes almost poetical and a thing of beauty, as he wafts the reader through their trysts. Sara was a beautiful girl with auburn hair, who won at least two beauty contests, one at Central High, and the other on the stage of the Princess Theatre. She is most remembered as being slightly freckled, outgoing, continually smiling, and wearing a tartan skirt.

The children of that marriage were Emily, now Mrs. Thomas Farmer of Murfreesboro, Jeanne Grigsby of Clemson, South Carolina, Susan Graham of Mesquite, Texas and Linda Bryan of Houston, Texas.

Whereas Ed Bell wrote "From Main Street to Mink Slide," this writer proposes to reverse that title in an attempt to describe the progress and development of the Square "From Mink Slide to Main Street." Hopefully, "Main Street" should symbolize the new and handsome countenance which the Public Square presents at the beginning of the 1990s. "Mink Slide" should represent the Square as it appeared through the eyes of a five-year-old boy. Mink Slide in 1923 is where and when the story begins. Ed could have written the story better, but Ed is no longer around, and there seems to be no one else on the scene with vivid close-up memories with a yen to write about them. However, it is encouraging to know that Ed Bell would applaud the effort. To his friends and admirers of his writing skills, this writer would like for them to know that no pretensions are made or implied that the story is being written in a manner even approximating literary skills that Ed would have employed.

Apologies are also extended to those who remember those great teachers: Eliza Ransom, Rachel Sanders, Bessie Smith, Mrs. W.E. Reeves, Josephine Ralston, Lenora Stockard, and Katherine Clark. Sincere appreciation is also extended to Frances Allen Hobgood, that superb Latin teacher who unknowingly caused me to have a deeper respect for language. Latin was not one of my subjects, but it was my privilege to sit in the back of her classroom during study period. Also, many thanks are due Baxter Hobgood, who expanded and enhanced my love of history. Those teachers gave me what skills I have by which to write this account.

This story is about people. People make history and this account is about the individuals who made history around the Square from 1923. The bard, Shakespeare, appropriately stated that "All the world's a stage, and all the men and women merely players." The stage in this drama was and is the Public Square.

Ed Bell, gifted Murfreesboro author and *News-Journal* columnist during 1930s and 1940s.

PREFACE

The very first in my frame of memories remains vividly etched in my mind, almost exactly sixty-nine years later. It is a still frame with the exception of Santa Claus, who walked into the room and stopped in front of my two sisters and me. Other people were sitting in front of the burning fireplace. Santa was tall and slim, wore a dark hat, did not speak, and wore a white paper mask over his eyes. He probably had candy and fruit, but that is not in the picture.

My parents had moved in the early part of 1920 to Silver Hill, which is eight miles from Murfreesboro. The house and forty acres were owned by my maternal grandfather, Jeptha Hall, who served as Chief of Police of Murfreesboro until 1928. This first memory frame occurred on either Christmas Eve or Christmas Day of 1920.

The next three frames are also indelibly etched on my memory screen, all of which flickered on the same day. In either January or February 1921, my father was to take me to town. The day was cold, and the sky was overcast. A horse and buggy with folding top were near the house, and I was on the seat almost covered with a heavy wool lap rug. The picture does not show my father, but he was either already on the seat or preparing to climb into the buggy. My mother was standing on the ground holding a hot rock wrapped in newspapers. That warming device was about eight inches in diameter and would keep the area underneath the snugged lap rug warm practically all day. The journey to town had probably been planned for several days, and I am sure I had looked forward to the day with much anticipation. The memory frame flicks off with this scene. I recall nothing of the trip to town.

The next picture of that day shows a scene located on what I later knew to be West Main Street. The street at that time had a tree-planted and lamp-lighted median strip down the center. This was quite a thoroughfare for Murfreesboro, especially since it provided an attractive entry to the Square for the newcomers who had just disembarked from the passenger trains at the depot. The picture here is rather blurry, since the scene is mixed with much pandemonium and horrible, deafening sounds, all of which were absolutely foreign to a child not yet three years of age who had heard nothing louder than a barking dog.

The horse and buggy with its father-and-son occupants had just passed the county jail and was proceeding toward the rail depot about two blocks farther. Suddenly the air was rent with such ear-shattering, earth-shaking, clanking, clattering, and tumultuous sounds that I was almost irretrievably struck with never-to-be-forgotten terror. The horse which evidently had also never been to town began whinnying and rearing while trying to extricate himself from the harness and shafts. Instead of falling forward on one of his rearings, he arose almost perpendicular to the street and toppled to the left, breaking the shaft on that side. Meanwhile, I had fallen to the floor of the buggy, hiding under the seat, screaming and crying, with hands over my ears. The second memory frame ends here on this terror-stricken scene. The culprit of all that pandemonium was a steam-driven locomotive, with either passenger or freight cars, braking at the railway station.

The third and final scene on that memorable day illuminates the screen of my memories. The horse was subdued but probably apprehensive. Somewhat calmed by the example of the horse's more peaceful behavior, but still unforgiving of the fate that had put me in such terrifying circumstances a short while before, I had crawled from underneath the seat. Probably no more than an hour had elapsed since the last scene. The picture portrays the father and the boy in the buggy. The horse was drinking thirstily from a concrete trough located on a corner of the inner portion of the Square. The immense court house formed a backdrop immediately in front of us. My peripheral vision showed activity and buildings. There was a dime in my mouth. My mother had probably given it to me for spending money on that, my first trip to town. Alas! This was not to be. The ten-cent piece was to be removed from the regulated channels of trade. While the horse was gulping the water, I swallowed the dime, thereby invalidating the Law of Conservation and Creation of Energy. The picture fades from the memory projection screen. This is the final memory frame of the day and for several months thereafter. That was my introduction to the Square of the town of Murfreesboro, Tennessee. For an inexplicable reason or for several complicated reasons, I have gained and nurtured an affinity for the Square, its people and its history.

The employment of a Public Square in town and city planning was quite innovative in 1811 when Capt. William Lytle donated sixty acres to be used as the permanent seat of justice for Rutherford County. Fortunately, the early settlers of the lands west of the Allegheny Mountains were presented with large areas from which they could choose town locations and could use a more modern design in street, lot, and municipal planning. The erstwhile explorer-settlers would not be restricted and hampered by the many centuries-old streets and buildings that were common to the Old World places whence their not-far-removed forefathers had come to the New World.

The cities and towns of the early civilizations had generally evolved from a good defensive point on an established road convenient to water and forests. An advantageous site on a navigable river or on a sheltered bay or inlet would enhance the selection of a location to build a town. As the towns grew in size and population through decades and centuries, the former paths converging at the town center from other towns or roads became streets that had no advantage of prior long-range planning. Many of the towns became large cities. The streets radiated from the hub or city center, conforming to the well-worn and winding paths initiated centuries before. Consequently, a traveler to the great cities remaining today from early civilizations will note directional signs stating "City Center" at convenient places along the streets that eventually lead to the municipal buildings.

The architect who was charged with laying out the streets of Washington, D.C., near the end of the eighteenth century, adopted the city center or hub feature but had the enabling advantage of letting his streets radiate in straight lines from the capitol, much as the spokes of a wheel.

Capt. William Lytle's donation of sixty acres was designated as land north of "Murfree's Spring Branch" (a site immediately south of the present Coca Cola Bottling plant). Lytle's only reservation was that one lot be redeeded to him. The Commissioners agreed, and he was given a lot on the southeast corner of the Square. That lot will be more specifically defined in a later chapter.

Hugh Robinson, a member of the County Seat Selection Committee, was Murfreesboro's first surveyor. He was chosen to survey, plan, and lay out the new town. The present Public Square was set apart for the courthouse and stocks. Without the doubtful benefit of long-established procedure in planning a town and with the absence of existing roads into the tract, the surveyor was able to choose a grid system with the Square in the center. The principal streets—North and South Maple, North and South Church, East and West Main—emanated from the Square. The additional streets comprising the grid-system layout ran parallel to each of the four sides of the Square and were staked out at about 1,000-foot intervals along the principal streets. (See original map of Murfreesboro, p. xii.)

After the stages of surveying, planning, and staking of lots by Robinson, an auction of the lots was to begin on June 12, 1812. It was reported that the disposal of the lots went quite rapidly. Thus, the town of Murfreesboro was formed, and the Public Square came into being. In retrospect, the location of the town and its Square was a judicious choice. Evidently, Hugh Robinson chose the site of the Square because it was the highest elevation within the sixty-acre tract. Also, importantly, a fine stream of running water flowed from Murfree Spring Branch from the southeast along the southern and western boundaries of the new town. Possibly the commissioners also considered the fact that the town

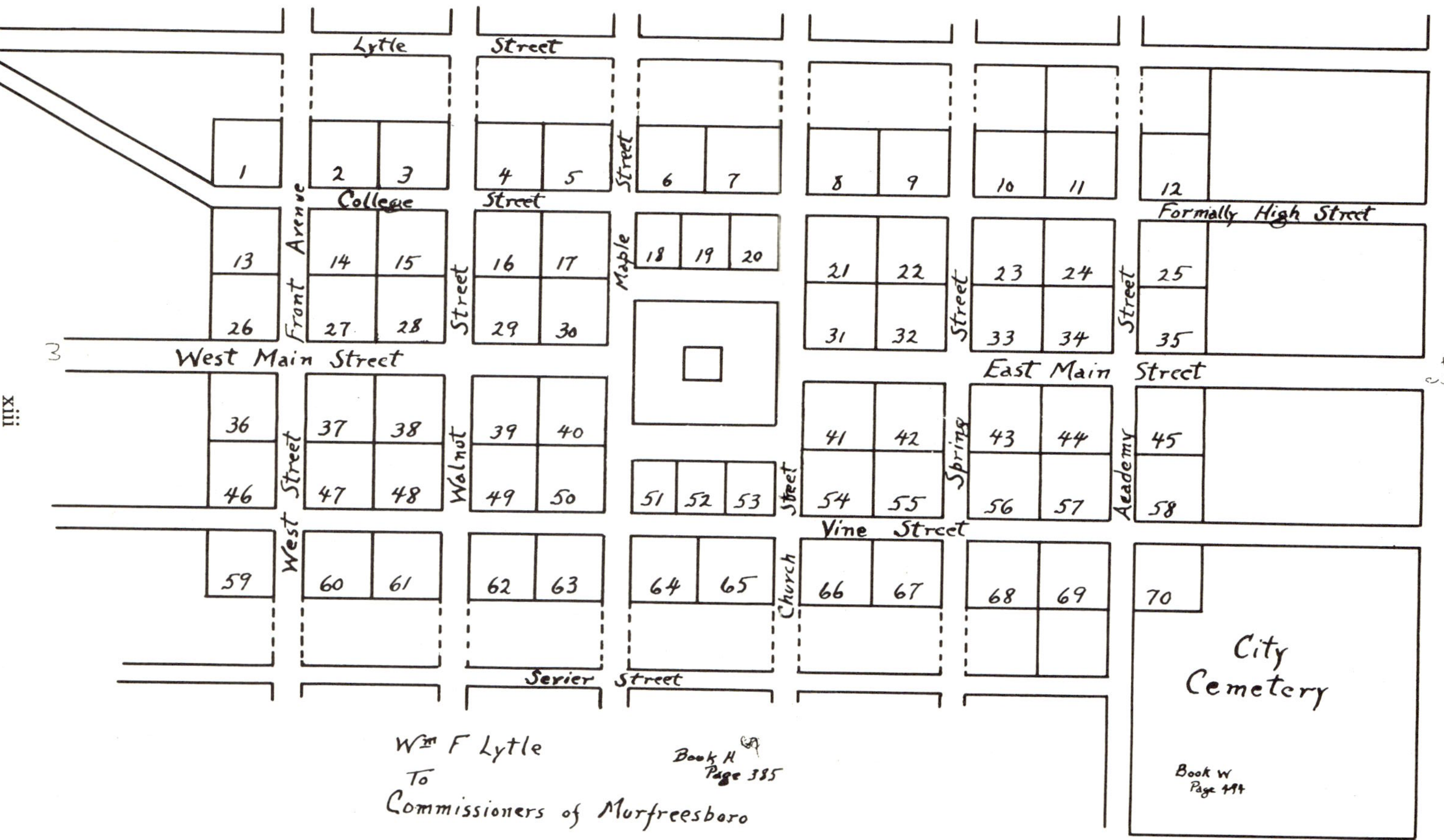
Wm F Lytle
To
Commissioners of Murfreesboro
Book H Page 385
City Cemetery
Book W Page 494
Lytle Street
College Street
Formally High Street
West Main Street
East Main Street
Vine Street
Sevier Street
Front Avenue
Walnut Street
West Street
Maple Street
Church Street
Spring Street
Academy Street

would occupy a location that was almost in the exact center of both Rutherford County and the sixteen-year-old state of Tennessee. The commercial advantages of the convergence of the main arteries of travel from north to south and east to west in the town have been most significant in the development of Murfreesboro. The far-sighted commissioners could not have foreseen the greatest transportation catalyst of the nineteenth century which would result in the Nashville-Chattanooga Railroad passing only four blocks west of the Square. The first railroad train rolled into Murfreesboro July 4, 1851, with 1,500 passengers, and became the occasion for one of the town's greatest celebrations.

The people in free democratic societies tend to stratify themselves in three undelineated groups—the lower, middle, and upper classes. The only positive advantage to this tendency is that it inspires a person on one of the lower levels to better himself or herself through education and whatever else is required to rise in social acceptance, considering that this acceptance is based on good manners, morals, and deportment. Until the 1960s, such social stratification was more pronounced in Murfreesboro than in most of the surrounding towns.

In the 1920s, 1930s, and 1940s, that class demarcation was quite distinct. The lower class, for the most part, inhabited the Bottoms, Depot Hill, and substandard black neighborhoods. The upper class consisted of the families who lived on or near Main Street. The middle class, which was the major group, lived in the other neighborhoods, which also included many blacks.

With few exceptions, the shops, stores, banks, and professions on the Square were occupied by the middle class which was also an entrepreneurial class. Those people put all of the money they had or could borrow into ventures which offered no guarantees or assurances that they would succeed. However, their dreams, visions, and self-confidence outweighed the gamble with their futures at stake. Some were not successful. If they failed, the losers faced a bleak future, for jobs were hard to find. Almost unbelievably, the common wage for many householders was seven to $10 per week. The standard wage for a skilled carpenter in those days was $1.50 per day for six days per week. It was a great night at my carpenter-uncle's house when he arrived home to announce that he had been selected for a job at a new house construction on what is now Southeast Broad Street. He was to be earning $2.50 per day. The year was 1932, and the house was to be owned by State Senator Andrew L. Todd.

The early settlers of Murfreesboro were for the most part of Scottish descent. Most of the business owners and professionals around the Square one hundred years later were the progeny of those intrepid people. Now, during that period of momentous transience—the 1920s, 30s, and 40s—there were other nationalities represented on the Public Square. There were Jews, Italians, blacks, and at least one man of German descent. All of those will be portrayed on our armchair visit around the Square from Mink Slide to Main Street.

Adolf Hitler, in his *Mein Kampf*, foretold that the greatest thorn in his flesh, in his struggle for supremacy, would be the bourgeoisie or middle-class people. The shop owners would be a cantankerous, independent lot who had neither the will nor mind to conform or to be regimented.

Almost immediately after the sale of the lots on the Square in 1812, a courthouse was built, followed by stores and houses. Gradually, the house sites gave way to commercial enterprises. Over the next hundred years, the commercial area expanded to embrace most of the four streets parallel to the equilateral Square, i.e., Vine, Walnut, College, and Spring streets. Spring Street was the exception. Its two blocks between College Street and Vine were void of commercial buildings in 1923. Therefore, the metes and bounds of the area which will be discussed in this narrative will be confined to that area bounded by the aforementioned streets with a few departures.

Maps are provided which give the numbered address of each store or building with which this account deals. An arrowed line is shown which denotes the progress of the tour around and about the Square. A sectional map precedes the chapters that deal with the businesses, owners and other pertinent information contained within that particular section. A master map is shown on p. i.

Although this writer has endeavored with careful research and his best recollections to give the names of the businesses, the store operators and the building owners of each address, there will undoubtedly be several names that are not mentioned. For any omissions that may have occurred, the author apologizes. It is hoped that the reader realizes that the nature of this undertaking has required the writer to depend to a great extent on his and the memories of many contributors—memories which at best are not infallible.

CONTENTS

ILLUSTRATIONS

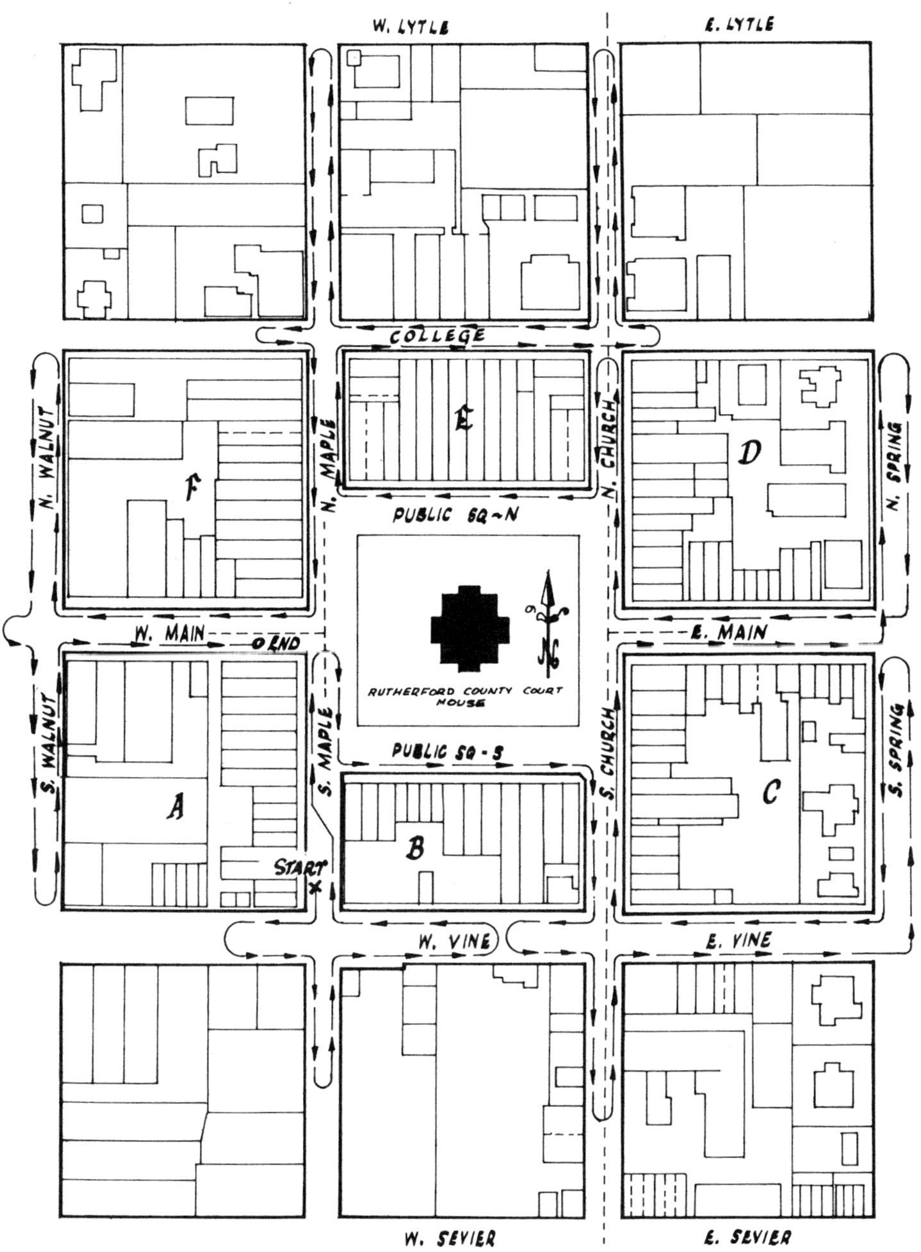

Murfreesboro, Tennessee -----1924

N
W. MAIN
221 219 215 213 211
201
GENERAL FEED
GRAIN & LIME
SALES
COBBLER
ELEC. MOTOR
S. WALNUT
115
123
FLETCHER & SON
WHOLESALE GRO.
BAND RM 2ND
POOL
RESTAURANT
GRO.
UNDERTAKING
MEAT
OFF.
102 104 106 108 110 112 114 116 118 120 122 124 126 128 130
S. MAPLE
216 214 212 210 208
224 218
206 202 200
W. VINE
223 221 217 213 211 201
BOTTOMS

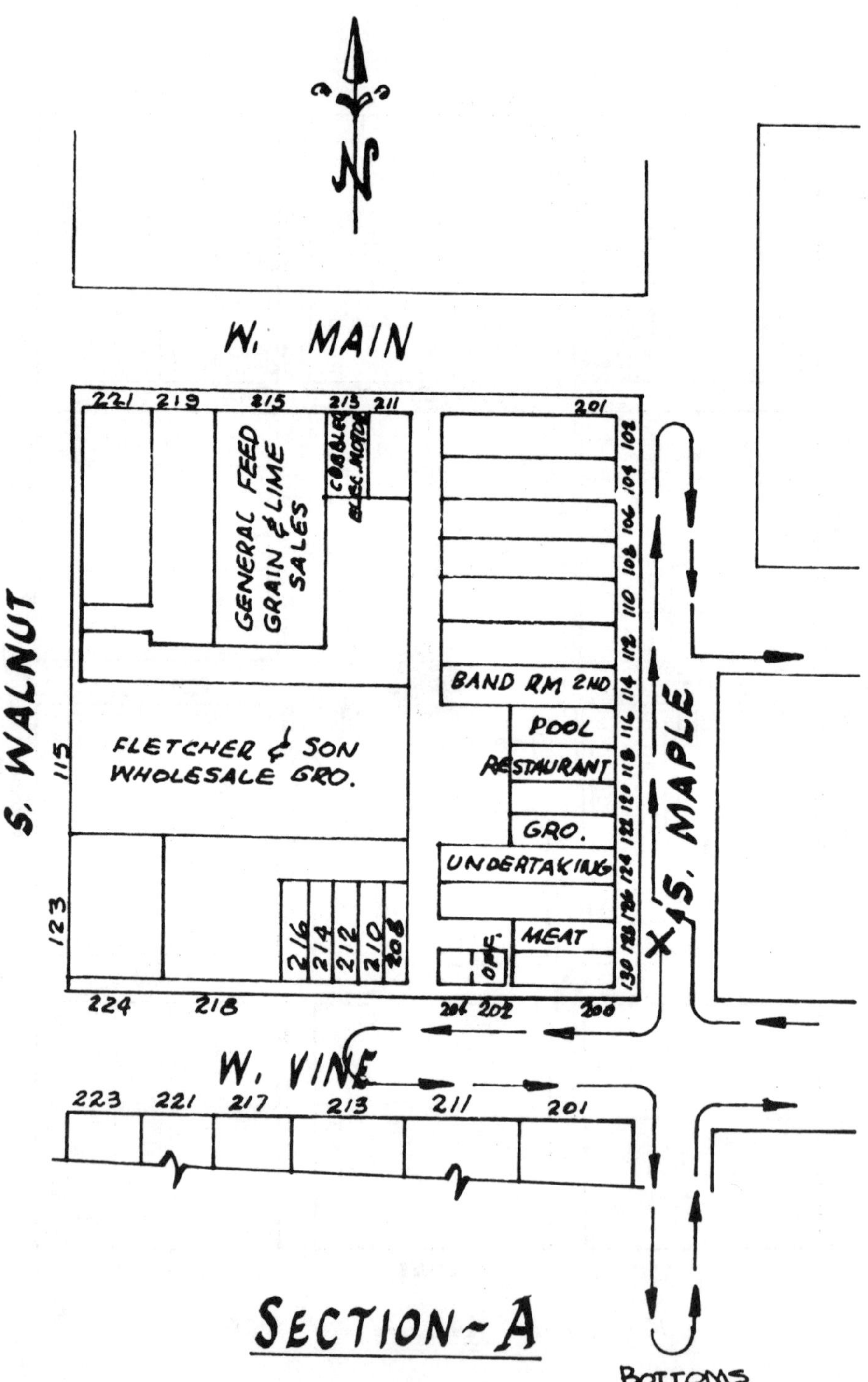

SECTION ~ A

Chapter I

South Maple (Mink Slide)—West Vine

Since the title of this account is "From Mink Slide to Main Street," and since I began my sojourn upon the Square on Mink Slide, it is only fitting that the story should begin there. Mink Slide was that short portion of South Maple Street that extended from Vine to what is now Holden's Hardware. Several reasons have been given as to why that area was named "Mink Slide." Two reasons seem most plausible to me. Before 1940, there was a vacant lot on the northeast corner of South Maple and Vine. It was about one and one-half acres in size. During weekdays, the lot was used sparsely for hitching horses or for horses pulling buggies and wagons. On Saturdays, the lot was filled with fur traders and farmers who augmented their income by trapping mink, oppossum, raccoon, fox, weasel, and muskrat. Prime mink furs were bringing $20-$25, oppossum $1-$3, raccoon $2-$4, fox $5-$10, and muskrat $2-$3. Other popular trading items on the lot were knives, guns, horses, and mules. Mink was the most valuable and sought-after fur on the lot.

The 250-foot length of sidewalk across South Maple from the trading lot sloped from the present Holden Hardware Store to Vine Street. About midway of that slope in the walk was a perceptible downward gradient about twelve feet in length. For some reason, that section of pavement was almost glassy smooth in finish and was, consequently, a very slippery pavement, even when it was not wet or icy. Of course, the pesky piece of sidewalk was the recipient of many posteriors. Therefore, a combination of the prize mink furs and the slippery section of sidewalk resulted in the name "Mink Slide." Ed Bell described the predominantly black business district called Mink Slide as a "little piece of street which slants down from a bent corner of the Square like the neck of a funnel and ends at the rim of the Bottoms."

In 1922, my parents moved into town. With little or no money, my father began his butcher business by peddling fresh meat around town. My memory is vague about that phase of his business, but I do remember often accompanying him in the wagon. In 1923, my father managed to borrow $300 from E.P. Leach, who had a buggy shop and money-lending business on the corner of Vine and South Church streets. That $300 enabled my father to start in business about and on the

Square, a business that grew and lasted thirty years. His first location was on Mink Slide, a location (A-128) that was next to the last store on the Slide approaching Vine. Today, in 1990, that site is vacant.

A combination meat and grocery store was unheard of in Murfreesboro in those days. The repertory of a butcher shop was usually limited to fresh beef, veal, pork, lamb, goat, salt pork for boiling, rabbit in season, and, occasionally, poultry.

As yet in 1923, mechanized refrigeration had not appeared in Murfreesboro. That great development for a butcher shop occurred around 1927-1929. My father managed to find a custom-made meat and ice storage room which was insulated and had a floor dimension of six feet by eight feet. It was 10 feet in height, with the upper portion used for ice storage. Usually, 300 pounds of ice were required every day. This arrangement had to suffice for the modern meat market then. The only other necessary fixtures were a table or counter on which to wrap meat and support a cash register, a meat block on which to cut and saw meat, and a sausage mill mounted on a table. The meat block was of paramount importance, since everything evolved from that station. The block was usually 18 inches thick, diameter 32 inches, and was cut from the trunk of a sycamore tree. It was supported by three oak legs cut to make the work surface of the block 30 inches above the floor.

Besides the fixtures, there were three other requirements necessary for a successful business on the Slide in those days. They were hard work, long hours, and, probably most important, good judgement. The hours were 5:00 a.m. to 6:00 p.m. Monday through Friday, 5:00 a.m. to 11:00 p.m. Saturdays, and 4:00 a.m. to 8:00 a.m. on Sundays.

Delivery boys played an important role for the businesses around the Square. Most were black boys. They were called porters, and they used bicycles to make their deliveries. That was a function that I could handle, so my assistance was required from age seven until about sixteen. Some of the names of the black porters who worked for my father were "Ruck," "Huse," "Mutsie," and "Mouse-man." "Huse" was cross-eyed and had six fingers on each hand. The sixth appendage on the opposite side from the thumb was exactly like the small toe on each foot.

When my father began his butcher shop in 1923, he was most fortunate in hiring a black youth whose name was E.J. Daniels. He became a superb butcher and knew the customers and their requirements so well that often they would ask for E.J. when they called. My parents placed much dependence upon him, and it was a sad blow for the family when he died in 1938.

★ ★ ★

As stated earlier, the stroll about the Square begins at the butcher shop on Mink Slide. A turn to the right leads to Vine Street only thirty feet away. Immediately out the door and to the right was a hole-in-the-wall place that was used as a tiny walk-up sandwich joint on Saturdays.

The operator was Charlie Spray. He was about 60 to 70 years of age, low in stature, had twinkling eyes, and sported a silvery mustache. Next to Charlie Spray, on the corner of Vine and South Maple Street (A-130), was a restaurant operated by Ernest Dowell. Later, William Ferrell operated a grocery store at that place. The tenant who probably was there the longest was Lou Lucinski, who operated a popular short-order restaurant during the 1950s and 1960s.

Mink Slide possibly had more pedestrian traffic than any other section on the Square. On Saturdays and holidays, the walking traffic was so congested that a child would have to walk through and past legs to go anywhere. Most of the shoppers were black people who had come to town on Saturday dressed in their finest. On Decoration Day (May 30) and on Saturdays during harvest time, the Slide could not accommodate the huge crowds which had to spill into the street. My job on those busy days was to stand in front of the shop with two wood half-barrels filled with ice and bottled soda pop. The popular drinks then were Coca-Cola, Nu-Grape, Nehi, Bluebird, Orange Crush, and Cream Soda. Most of those drinks were bottled in Murfreesboro.

Memorial or Decoration Day was the most boisterously celebrated day of the year. During most of the 1920s, there were still several Civil War veterans who would don their Confederate uniforms, come to town, and join the parade around the Square. There would be blaring bands with an occasional rebel yell. Speeches would be made from a raised platform on the east side of the court house. Finally, the crowd and the exhausted old soldiers would retire to the site of a former Civil War gun emplacement where old Highway 41 intersected Stones River. From early morning, joints of hogs and goats had been barbecued over long, shallow pits in the ground. A wire fence had been stretched flatwise between two trees, and from there the people would help themselves to a grand feast. After more speeches and several encores of "Dixie" by the two marching bands, the day would end. For some of the old gray veterans, that would be their final attendance.

While the Memorial celebration was in progress, there was an even larger observance in Murfreesboro. It was the annual Decoration Day that was observed by almost every black person in Rutherford County. The central meeting place was on Mink Slide; and, as the crowds multiplied, people would spread onto the adjacent streets and sidewalks. Many had brought lunches while others bought sandwiches and drinks from the several vendors around. After midday they went out to the various black cemeteries in the county. There, they had singing, praying, and preaching. Then the graves of their departed would be decorated, usually with fresh flowers.

During the 1920s, 1930s, and most of the 1940s, Independence Day, or July 4th, received scarcely any recognition and never any display of fireworks. Those were in abundance during the season before Christmas and New Year's Day.

Around the corner of Mink Slide and Vine there was the office of Dr. George Calvert Harden. That building is still standing (A-202). In the upper section toward the floor line, a plaque recognizing his ownership of the building, remains.

Westward beyond Dr. Harden's Building in 1945 was the location (A-214-216) of the genesis of what is now the very successful Haynes Lumber Company and Haynes Candy Company. The four brothers Haywood, Charlie, Fayne, and Grady Haynes formed a partnership for the sale of candies and related items. While continuing this business, the four brothers formed Haynes Brothers Construction Company on Front Street in 1948. In 1951, the name was changed to Haynes Brothers Supply Company. In this year, the embryo lumber supply company was grown enough to move to its present location on Broad Street. The author considers this account as another prime story of the many examples of private enterprise in action as one travels from Mink Slide to Main Street.

Chapter II

Down the Slide and across Vine Street, there was a two-story frame rooming house operated by Mollie Brown. She also served sandwiches from a side window. In the early 1930s, her house was demolished and supplanted by Joe and Frank's Market. That was one of the earliest combination meat and grocery markets in the town. Joe Fulghum and Frank Robinson were the proprietors of the enterprise. The present progeny of that business is Frank's IGA Supermarket on Bradyville Road, owned by Woody Robinson.

★ ★ ★

Just past the vacant lot on South Maple Street was a framed two-story house occupied by a black undertaker. My only memory of him was that he liked fresh opossum and that he would pay me fifty cents for a fresh carcass. That would lend extra impetus to my trapping ventures during the winter. Southward past the undertaker's house was the beginning of the "Bottoms." That was an area two blocks south of the Square and at a much lower elevation. It occupied about eight square blocks through which Lytle's or Town Creek flowed. Frequently, during rainy periods, Stones River would back into Lytle's Creek, causing the "Bottoms" to be flooded with depths of water that often reached four feet. That, of course, called for the evacuation of the residents and their scanty furnishings. Those occasions gave the other residents of Murfreesboro plain and visible reasons as to where and how they could display their charitable virtues.

★ ★ ★

On the threshold of the "Bottoms," turn around and walk one block up the hill to Vine Street and turn left past the vacant corner lot of the late 1920s that became Joe and Frank's Market in the 1930s. About one hundred feet down the street there was a tall wood and wire fence which enclosed a large junk yard. A two-story frame house was in the center of the lot. The house was used as an office and store rooms for the more valuable junk items such as copper, aluminum, etc. Around the house and against the fences were huge piles of cast iron and steel items that would soon be returned to the foundry. The owner and operator of that business, which had no competition in town, was Mr. Paul Legora. The title "Mr." is used here because it helps to describe that unusual man. Paul was always dressed in a dark suit and a white shirt with a starched collar. A freshly knotted tie was above his buttoned vest which had a gold watch in the right pocket and a gold chain crossing the middle of the vest. A silvery, well-trimmed mustache matched his silvery hair, which was always covered with a Homberg hat. It seemed a paradox that such a gentlemanly attired man was a junk dealer.

Inexplicably, Paul Legora was not the junk dealer's original name. His great-grandson, William Soffiantino, reports that his great-grandfather's real name was Leopaulus Soffiantino. Why did Leopaulus change such an heroic Roman name to Paul Legora? The man, as I remember him was fair complexioned, suggesting that his ancestry hailed from north Italy. This enigma as well as the man remains a mystery all of which contributes to the stories of the interesting personalities on and about the Square in those years.

One day when I was about ten years of age, I was pulling my coaster wagon along the railroad tracks between the old freight and passenger depots. There at my feet, and up and down the tracks, was a bonanza of iron spikes that I was sure Mr. Legora would want to buy. Soon my wagon was loaded with so much iron that I could barely pull it up West Main Street, across Front Street to Vine, and up Vine two blocks to the junk yard where I just knew Mr. Legora would gladly pay at least one dollar or maybe more for my fortunate find of iron spikes.

The man walked over to my wagon, took one glance at my hard-earned treasure and asked where I had gotten it. I whispered the secret location since I was anxious to hurry back for another load. Mr. Legora shattered all of my hopes when he said, "Boy, don't you know the railroad people own those spikes? Don't you know that the police will get you if you are caught with them? Boy, you take those spikes back and drop them where you found them!" Out of the yard to the street, down Vine, across Front Street to West Main and furtively down that street, then back to the railroad tracks went that early venture into business.

Paul had a daughter with red hair whose given name was Rose. Her brother was Bill Soffiantino. As for Mr. Paul, there is probably an interesting story somewhere in the past of the Beau Brummel of the junk yard.

★ ★ ★

There was a small brick building (B-123), about 18 by 20 feet, on the corner across South Church. It was a barber shop operated by a gray-haired black man whose name was Sam Woods. He was about six feet tall and had a demeanor that commanded respect. Most of his customers were white people. His charges were twenty-five cents for a haircut and fifteen cents for a shave. My mother insisted that I visit his barber shop every other Saturday night.

Contrary to present-day custom, Saturdays and Saturday nights were busy times in Murfreesboro. The stores around and off the Square remained open until at least 10:00 p.m. Parking was at a premium around the Square, since many people came merely to park in their cars and watch the passers-by.

★ ★ ★

Next to the brick barber shop was a vacant lot which was occasionally used by medicine and minstrel shows. The medicine shows were usually unheralded. The pseudo doctor would drive into town, set up on the lot early Saturday morning, and begin haranguing the crowds. Some of the doctors claimed to have a painless method of pulling teeth. After an attention-getter of banjo, guitar, or French harp music, the good painless doctor would begin his spiel, ending with the statement that his normal charge was $5.00, but today he would relieve the patient for $2.00. In those days, there were always several people in the audience who suffered from toothache. They would pay the doctor $2.00, go behind a screen, and then would exit in a moment or two, extolling the painless doctor.

The old-fashioned herb and medicinal doctor was another kind of physician who claimed to adhere to the oath of Hippocrates. He would have a larger wagon or van and one or two additional people to entertain the crowd. The more threadbare doctors had to use a well-trained monkey. Another doctor might have a real Indian dressed in traditional costume. After the crowd was sufficiently entertained, the great man, who, after many years of study and research, had finally discovered the elixir that would cure or relieve just about all of the world's ailments, would appear. First and foremost, his panacea would cure all liver-caused diseases. Bad backs, arthritis, ague, rheumatism, gout, and even laziness would go away after his magic potion was administered. People usually clamored to pay eight dollars for his sure-fire fantastic remedy, but since the good people of Murfreesboro had shown such hospitality to him, he would generously sell the first fifteen bottles for three dollars each. Also, the first fifteen people who stepped up would receive a free bottle of a rare tonic guaranteed to drive away the blues and restore vitality.

A minstrel show came to that lot on Vine Street at least twice per year. It was advertised as "Silas Green from New Orleans." An advance scout would appear in town about a week before the scheduled performance. He would post flyers and circulars in the stores around the Square and on the utility poles in the vicinity. The *News Banner* and the *Daily Home Journal* would advertise the great minstrel show. A tent, about 75 by 100 feet, would be erected in the morning before the night show was to be held. Kids who loitered about during the tent erection would often be given a small task in return for a free pass. On one occasion, a minstrel show worker sent me after a gallon of striped paint. I fairly flew on my bicycle to all three hardware stores—Spain and Hudson, Braswell and Mullins, and Haynes hardware stores. Each store clerk would send me to the next store. All were out of striped paint. I had to tell the show man the bad news. He expressed his disappointment but gave me a free admission ticket for my efforts. Some days later, I found that there was no such thing as striped paint.

The scent of carbide lamps was a familiar smell at all of the traveling shows. The smaller ones did not carry the large portable electric generators. But the bright carbide lighting gave a fair illumination. The format of the shows was similar. Each had about eight black-faced performers sitting in a semi-circle around a straight man on the stage. They would bandy jokes that today would seem corny, but then they were comical. There would be tap dancing, quartets, duets, solos, and banjo picking. The main act of the show was a skit in which there was an innocent maiden, a villain, and a handsome hero with a black mustache.

Those were some of the attractions at the vacant lot on Vine Street. Another event at the lot remains impressed on my memory. It was the first balloon ascension in Murfreesboro. It was on a Saturday. Eugene Guill, a captain in World War I and also in the local National Guard was in charge of preparing the balloon for its aerial journey. He and his staff built a fire in a pit at the center of the lot. When the fire was at its maximum heat-producing efficiency, a large electric fan was placed near the hole. The fan would suck the heated air from the pit into the collar of the huge balloon. After a while, the balloon would begin to take shape and rise from the ground. W.W. Raub was the balloonist. He and his wife operated a grocery story in Westview. When the inflated balloon began to tug at the ropes that were held by several fellows, Mr. Raub climbed into the basket and began his ascent. That particular flight did not last very long. The balloonist landed at the fairgrounds, only about two miles south on the Shelbyville Pike. Still, it was a sensational sight for first-time spectators.

During the early 1930s, Carney Handley moved a dog wagon to the vacant lot and operated there into the 1950s. A dog wagon was usually a portable short order restaurant mounted on wheels. Its dimensions would be approximately thirty feet long and ten feet in width. The menu would consist of hot dogs, hamburgers, barbeque, ham, eggs, coffee, and cold drinks.

★ ★ ★

Eastward past the vacant lot on Vine Street was a brick building (B-117) that was already showing signs of age in the early 1920s. The building was occupied by the Tennessee Rubber Company, which was in the business of recycling automobile tires. The company, organized in November 1922, manufactured the Ezy-On-Lace-Boot, which it claimed was the only boot for automobile tires on the market that would cover a rim cut and that could not blow out. The company further claimed in 1924 that its boots were sold all over the United States and that the demand was so great the company expected an immediate increase of capacity. A by-product of the business was the clincher rims of the tires. The short lengths of the hard rubber were put into bundles and sold to local people for fire kindling.

Howard Dill began operation of a machine and welding shop in that building during the early 1930s. Later, in about 1936, R.H. Smith and Roscoe Brown operated a tinsmith business there. Eventually, Mr. Smith was instrumental in forming the present-day Murfreesboro Supply Company. Roscoe Brown continued the enterprise, moved to East Vine Street, and eventually to the corner of Spring and Sevier streets. His son, Gary, operates the business today in a new building at 841 Commercial Court.

★ ★ ★

The old brick building in the middle of the block on Vine Street was demolished in the late 1940s. The established firm of Harrison and Alexander erected a large new yellow brick building at that location. The firm had been on the Square for many years and elected to expand its operation.

Robert Hatton Harrison was born in 1900 and died in 1956. During his business sojourn on the Square (F-107) and on West Vine Street (B-117), he epitomized the image of a good business man and a true gentleman. During the years of his involvement in business (1922-1956) his firm was one of the most successful stores in the area.

The name of the firm was Harrison & Alexander and was probably better known to the rural trade of Rutherford County than the local townsmen. The firm dealt in feed, seed, fencing, hardware, and related items. One of the main thrusts of the business was that they bought in such large quantities that their prices were lower than most of the competition. It was remarkable that the business grew even during the Depression Years. It was even more remarkable when one realized that Robert Harrison extended credit to his customers from one crop season to the next during those hectic economic years.

A most appreciated attitude of Mr. Harrison was the sincere greeting that he extended to every customer who walked into Harrison & Alexander. If one was rich or poor, great or small, white or black, young or old, that person received the same treatment from the person of Robert Harrison.

Robert's father, Hatton Harrison, began business with a partner, Ellis Alexander in the first decade of this century. Hatton and Ellis were brothers-in-law. When Hatton died, his son retained his half of the partnership. When Mr. Alexander died, Robert bought the estate's share of the partnership. However, the firm continued to operate with the same original name, Harrison & Alexander.

Henry Clay Alexander was the son of Ellis Alexander. Henry Clay graduated from Vanderbilt and also graduated from law school at Yale. This Murfreesboro native reached the very zenith of national and international finance when he became president of the House of J.P. Morgan in 1934. He retained this position for several decades and died in approximately 1980.

When Robert Harrison died in 1956, the large yellow brick building was leased to the Farmer's Co-op. The Greer Stop Nut Company came

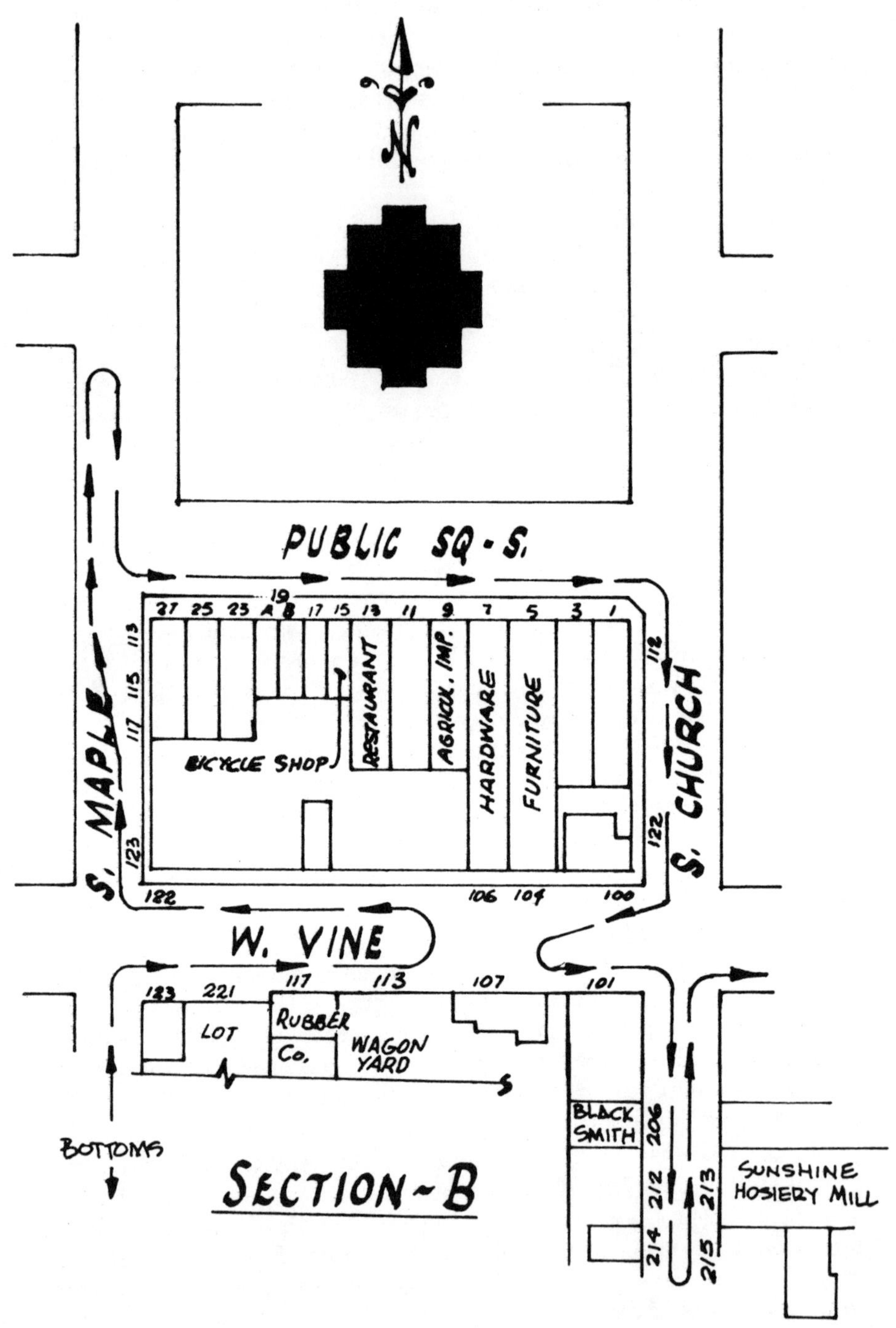
PUBLIC SQ - S.
S. MAPLE
S. CHURCH
W. VINE
27 25 23 A 19 B 17 15 13 11 9 7 5 3 1
113
115
117
123
122
112
122
106 104 100
BICYCLE SHOP
RESTAURANT
AGRICUL. IMP.
HARDWARE
FURNITURE
123 221 117 113 107 101
LOT
RUBBER Co.
WAGON YARD
BLACK SMITH
206
212
214
213
215
SUNSHINE HOSIERY MILL
BOTTOMS
SECTION - B

next and was followed by Penuel's Surplus Sales in 1968. Howard Penuel and his two sons, Hooper and Lou, operated the business until 1979. Howard was elected trustee of Rutherford County in 1978 and disposed of the store the following year. The next tenant was Larry Sims who conducted antique auctions here for awhile. Troy's Gym followed Sims with an exercise and fitness business. Troy's was here until the building was demolished along with the other buildings in the block in 1990.

★ ★ ★

There was a vacant lot east of B-117 in 1924. Mr. Harrison erected another yellow brick building east of his place of business. Leon Schklar's wife, Edith, operated a surplus store here in the fifties. Greenfield's Sporting Goods Company came next with a large variety of fishing and hunting goods. Olen Bell came to the store as manager in 1959. He later became part owner of a marine and boating business near Berry Field on Hi-way 41. The next occupant of the store was L.D. Agee with his Agee Sporting Goods which remained here until the City of Murfreesboro demolished those buildings.

Those properties remained in the ownership of Robert Harrison's heirs until 1984 when they were sold to the city. His heirs were Mrs. Robert Harrison Jr., Sarah Harrison Parker, Mary Keeble "Kib" Harrison Huddleston and Betty Harrison Hester. The city continued collecting rents from the buildings until they were demolished.

South Maple

Across the street at that point and along the north side of Vine Street was the horse, mule, and fur trading lot already mentioned.

John Valley White came back to Murfreesboro in about 1928. It was said that he had been operating a concession with a traveling carnival. His mother lived in a large yellow two-story frame house on the corner of Vine and Academy at the present location of the First Baptist Educational Building.

Mr. White was a true entrepreneur. He rented the northeast corner of Vine and South Maple streets. There, he erected a tent that was about 30 by 25 feet. He covered the dirt floor with red cedar sawdust. A wood counter, two wooden half barrels for drinks and ice, and a cooking stove were the only fixtures. White was interested in a low-price, high-volume business, so he installed no chairs or benches. His idea was to hustle the people out to make space for the next customers. Every item cost a nickel.

Hot dogs, sausage, hamburgers, ham, eggs, and cold drinks comprised the menu. With the awnings up around the tent, the aroma of the cooking onions and meat would waft over the Slide and to the farthest reaches of the Square. On Saturdays, the customers spilled out into the street and onto the back lot. John Valley White set a record for the most customers served at any restaurant in Murfreesboro. The word went out up and down the Slide that Mr. Henry was mixing sawdust in his sausage and hamburger patties. His patties were extra large, so large that they more than covered a bun. Possibly his critics did not want to give the man credit for his generous attitude. Shades of modern times! Remember in 1983 when a well-known restaurant chain was accused of mixing worms in its burgers.

Mr. White called his joint "Po Boys." More than fifty years later the town has a Po-Folks restaurant. "Po Boys" was an immediate success, but more about that later when the "Po Boy" moves to the fire hall, hires a flagpole sitter, serenades the town on Sunday morning, and incurs the wrath of the city fathers.

After the tent was taken down, the lot remained vacant for several years. There was less and less horse, mule, and fur trading. An imposing yellow brick building was erected on the corner of Vine and South Maple (B-123). Forrest Paschal Furniture Company was the new business. Forrest and his wife, Nell, began the operation in the early 1950s and remained there for about thirty years. Forrest was an avid collector and restorer of old carriages. Every parade held in Murfreesboro during those years featured him in one of his carriages (usually a surrey). His brother, Sam Paschal, was perhaps the most famous owner-trainer of walking horses in the history of the industry. Forrest Paschal passed away in January, 1990. The building which his business occupied is vacant at the time of this writing.

★ ★ ★

As we pursue our devious and ever-so-slow walk about the Square, it is now time to walk across the street to my father's meat market, the point of beginning. The next store (A-126) was the grocery store operated by Eugene Minor Woodson. Slightly less than ebony in skin color, Eugene Woodson was tall, broad-shouldered and well respected by the colored community as well as by his fellow shop owners on the Slide and on the Square. His son, Genie, and I were about the same age. We played together both on and off the Square. Genie died several years ago. His sister, Minnie Howland, is retired now and has many vivid recollections of the people and events of those times.

A man of color, H. Preston Scales was a giant amongst men, not only in stature but in versatility of talents, humility, amiability, and initiative. He was a prodigious worker with the uncommon ability to become skilled at whatever trade was necessary for him to accomplish his next goal. If asked, he would say that he was a carpenter. But then he was a plasterer, mason, plumber, funeral director, and talented trombonist. His son Robert ("Tee-Niny") Scales states that his father was never exuberant about his mortuary business. However, he did attend Gupton-Jones Embalming College and established himself on Mink Slide in a two-story building that he purchased in 1920. With his wife, Willie, attending to and taking care of the smaller details of their

Preston and Willie Scales, founders of Scales Funeral Home.

Robert "Tee-Niny" and Mary Scales. Second generation operators of Scales Funeral Home. Both have distinguished careers in city administration. Mary continues to serve as councilwoman.

The Murfreesboro Cornet Band which competed in Nashville in 1910. Preston Scales on extreme left.

Murfreesboro Marching Band before embarking on Booster Trip in 1925. Band members left to right were: Preston Scales, King George Gannaway, Willie Lee Alexander, John Savage, Virgil Officer, Aaron Wade, Ken Adams and Ed Turner.

UNCLE DAVE MACON

"The Dixie Dew Drop"

October
7
1870

March
22
1952

This Fan is in Memory of Jessie J. Messick

"Founder of the Uncle Dave Macon Days Festival."

"Dixie Dew-Drop" Uncle Dave Macon.

business, Preston remodeled the building and arranged several offices above the mortuary.

Up the steps between my father's meat market and Scales Mortuary were four office suites all occupied by colored doctors. They were Dr. James Patterson, a dentist; Dr. E.A. Davis; and Dr. James Edward Jones, both general practitioners; and Dr. Stennette, another dentist. The buildings then occupied by my father's meat market and by H. Preston Scales and his doctors' offices are no longer standing. That portion of the Slide is now a vacant lot.

Dr. Patterson was a most colorful character. He had a well-modulated voice that spoke with authority, mixed with a certain humility that never failed to persuade his listeners. He was often the exponent, declaimer, and petitioner for his people, the colored community, until he died in 1969. He and Robert "Tee-Niny" Scales accounted for most of the excellent and amiable race relations that have existed in Murfreesboro since the early days of integration.

President Warren G. Harding was serving his last, inauspicious year in the White House in 1924. The Teapot Dome Scandal had blemished many people in high places. Calvin Coolidge won the presidential election in the fall of that year and chose not to run in 1928. The economy was to continue climbing for five more years. Henry Ford was reputed by many people to be the richest man in the world with a net worth of over $150 million. He had already shocked labor and industry by paying the unheard of minimum wage of $5.00 per day. A new Ford T-Model could be purchased for as little as $300.00 f.o.b. Detroit.

The tempo of everyday life for the average American had been relatively the same for over two hundred years. The songs that America sang were for the most part in three-quarter time. "Silver Threads Among the Gold" had been composed in 1878 and was still reigning as a best seller. "When You and I Were Young, Maggie," "Down by the Old Mill Stream," and "My Wild Irish Rose" were still old favorites. "Silver-Haired Daddy," "Red River Valley," and "When It's Lamp Lighting Time in the Valley" were fast becoming popular. "When It's Spring Time in the Rockies" appeared in 1924. A noticeable departure from the norm came about that year in the song "Yes, Sir, That's My Baby." Many Americans wanted a faster beat.

A freckle-faced Hollywood starlet with bobbed hair by the name of Clara Bow answered the call for a quicker tempo. She introduced a new dance craze called the "Charleston," which was a notable and abrupt departure from "The Waltz You Saved for Me," and "Minuet in G." The pert-faced Clara Bow made her debut in motion pictures with the radical bobbed-hair style which, for most American women, ended the long-flowing tresses of the past.

The faster pace and the "Roaring Twenties" seemed to have little effect on the Murfreesboro Public Square and Mink Slide. Al D. McKnight was the popular mayor of 1924. Traffic was allowed to go in both clockwise and counter-clockwise directions around the Square. There were now more automobiles than horse-drawn vehicles. The city employed one street cleaner whose name was Todd. He pushed a two-wheeled cart about the Square. Someone suggested that Murfreesboro was a one-horse town. The street cleaner disputed this. He said that one horse could not make such a mess.

Uncle Dave Macon, the Dixie Dew-Drop and grandfather of country music, was to make his first appearance at the Grand Old Opry the following year, in 1925. He was already well known about the Square and on the Slide, with his goatee and long side burns. It was about that period that he came out with this piece of pure country music, Tennessee style:

Going down the street,
Going to buy me a ham of meat,
Going to keep my skillet good and greasy
All the time, time, time
Going to keep my skillet good and greasy
all the time.

If you say so,
I'll never work no mo,
Going to lay 'round old shanty
All the time, time, time,
Going to lay 'round old shanty all the time.

Murfreesboro had a population of slightly more than 8,000 in 1924. Its main claim to fame was that it was the home of the largest and possibly the only red cedar bucket factory in the world. It boasted the Middle Tennessee State Normal School and mentioned the accolade of occupying the geographical center of Tennessee.

Carnation Milk Company announced two years later that it was going to build a milk receiving and processing plant in Murfreesboro. That precipitated the largest celebration and parade in the annals of the town, either before or since. It even surpassed the Armistice Day celebration of November 11, 1918, and the welcoming ceremonies bestowed on Gen. Douglas McArthur in 1952.

The main industry in Murfreesboro in 1924 was the Sunshine Hosiery Mill, which employed the most people and paid the best wages. The second largest employer was the Welwood Silk Mill, located across the railroad tracks and Lytle's Creek on the Salem Road.

Not all of the small businesses were located on the Square and adjacent streets in 1924. There were fifty-two meat or grocery stores within the city limits, many of which were neighborhood shops. All of them extended credit to their customers and most made home deliveries. It was not until the advent of the chain stores in the late 1920s and early 1930s that the new term "cash and carry" came into practice.

The economy was relatively good in Murfreesboro in 1924. Every building on and off the Square was occupied. Even those buildings with upstairs offices had tenants which were mostly in the legal or insurance professions. Salaries ranged from $3.00 for a six-day week for colored delivery boys to $12.00 per six-day week for clerks and skilled personnel. The Sunshine Hosiery Mill was paying $1.00 per day for an eight-hour day, six-day work week. An average family was spending $3.00 to $4.00 per week for meat and groceries. Rents ranged from $1.00 per week in the Bottoms to $5.00 per week in blue-collar neighborhoods. Most families sheltered and fed their elderly without seeking help from other improbable sources.

The T-Model Ford was still the most popular car in Murfreesboro. It was still necessary to crank the car manually. That was a hazardous operation. Oftentimes, the spark from the magneto would cause the crank to kick backwards, and this could and often did break the cranker's arm. A man with a bandaged and splinted arm was a familiar sight on the Square. Henry Ford finally relented and installed a self-starter on the pesky critter in 1925. Also, he decided that there were other desirable colors besides black.

The young General Motors Corporation had introduced its Chevrolet, and it was rapidly gaining in popularity. It would finally run even with the Ford in 1927. Other popular cars seen around a Square without marked parking spaces, were Dodge, Buick, Essex, Hudson, and Star. Sterling Wall of Hall's Hill, who was Middle Tennessee's largest mule trader, drove to town in a Stutz Bearcat touring car. A well-known bootlegger sported a boat tailed Marman around the Square.

There were two concrete watering troughs for horses, mounted on the northwest and southeast corners of the courthouse Square. One of them still remains.

In 1900, the average life expectancy for a man was forty-five years and a woman could expect to live two and one-half years longer than her spouse. In 1924, those statistics had changed but very little. The most common diseases were pneumonia, influenza, tuberculosis, scarlet fever, typhoid fever, measles, and mumps. A noticeable factor that lowered the life expectancy rate was the significant loss of life of babies and mothers during childbirth. A giant step forward in the overall health improvement of children in Murfreesboro was the creation of the Rutherford County Health Department in 1931 and the Rutherford County Hospital in 1927.

The Health Department instituted a blue-ribbon campaign in the grammar schools in 1924. Each child was required to be vaccinated for smallpox and to have his or her teeth, eyes, and ears examined. Each child was to fill out a daily report as to whether or not he or she slept with the windows up, drank eight glasses of water, a glass of milk, and a glass of orange juice, plus several other requirements. The program was a huge success and remained in practice until World War II. Every child who successfully passed all of the requirements (99% did) would be given a blue ribbon badge and would participate in a large parade which would begin at the school and would wind around the Square, accompanied by bands and fire engines. The parents who had joined and enforced the new discipline proudly applauded as their children paraded past.

That is the way it was from Mink Slide to Main Street in those days. Those were halcyon days—a period of transformation, transience, and emergence from almost seven centuries of recorded history of the wheel, the telescope, the steam engine, the cotton gin, the telephone, the radio, and the automobile. Those living for the next seven decades would witness and experience the emergence from the horse and buggy age to an age of incalculable new inventions and standards in travel, space exploration, medicine, communication, and thence to the present age of the computer. Almost miraculously, mankind has made far greater strides during this period of seventy years than was accomplished from the beginning of civilization.

Up the Slide past Scales Funeral Home was a small men's ready-to-wear store which catered mostly to the blue-collar trade. Mr. Newt Shelton was the owner of the store. He had a son whose name I do not recall but whose age was about the same as mine, and, who, like me, was on the Square much of the time. We rambled together and climbed on top of all the buildings which had accessible roofs. Mr. Newt was a large, genial man who seemed always to be in a good humor. He was one of the several men around the Square who had a certain rapport with young people. He must have closed his business in the early 1930s, for my memory does not recall him on the scene after that period of time. The abrupt slope in the sidewalk that caused so many falls was in front of his business.

★ ★ ★

Walking up the Slide past Newt Shelton's small men's store, one came to the popular pool room and barber shop operated by "Possum" Woods, John and Erskine Lytle. "Possum" Woods was in charge of the pool room. Like the other colored businesses on and about the Square, their business catered mostly to colored clientele. My memory of "Possum" Woods is practically nil. I do remember John and Erskine Lytle as men of dignity, slender, and light-complexioned in color.

During the late 1930s, Clyde Rushing began the operation of a grocery in that location. Clyde had had much experience in the grocery business. He had managed a new concept in grocery marketing on the east side of the Square for Clarence Saunders of Memphis. More about that enterprise later. The new concept did not go over well in Murfreesboro and soon closed. Clyde Rushing's new venture in the grocery business was successful. He sold the business to his son Elvis after World War II. The store continued to be so successful that Elvis added the location on the Slide formerly held by my father twenty-five years earlier. Elvis eventually moved from the Slide and built two stores on the corner of Vine and Walnut.

Chapter III

Next to the pool room and barbershop operated by "Possum" Woods, John and Erskine Lytle was a restaurant operated by Henry Vaughn. The next store northward was Joe Alexander's ice cream parlor, soda fountain and pool room. Joe's place was more properly out of the Mink Slide area and on the west side of the Public Square. Joe Alexander was a tall, heavily built colored man. He had a kind of quiet dignity that commanded the respect of all who knew him, both white and colored.

Joe's son was William Lee Alexander. William Lee was the trumpet player in the only marching band in Murfreesboro during the early 1920s. The all-colored band was in great demand during the 1920s and into the 1930s. There were parades, fairs, booster trips, patriotic holidays, and political functions which kept those musicians fairly busy. The band was actually functioning as early as 1910, as evidenced by a picture furnished by Robert "Tee-Niny" Scales and reproduced in this book.

The band members in 1925 were Preston Scales, trombonist; King George Gannaway, drummer; William Lee Alexander, trumpeter; John Savage, player of the base horn; Virgil Officer; Aaron Wade; Ken Adams; and Ed Turner.

★ ★ ★

The next store would be identified today as Holden's Hardware Company.

This store stands near the top of the list in terms of longevity of the same business in the same location. Rollie and Katherine "Kacky" Butler Holden began their hardware business in January 1947. From relatively small beginnings, the store now carries a huge inventory of hardware goods.

After serving in the armed forces, Rollie worked as a salesman for Wilson Sporting Goods for about one year before the hardware store was opened. He and "Kacky" are now enjoying their forty-fourth year of business service on the Square.

Rollie served one year in the 1957 State Legislature and served eight years as a City Councilman. He was elected president of the Rutherford County Chamber of Commerce in 1953. In 1954, the town began to experience a business and economic growth occasioned by several out-of-town firms electing to locate in Murfreesboro. In 1953, there were only four major employers in the area. They were Carnation Milk Company, Sunshine Hosiery Mills, Sally Ann Bakery, and Rutherford County Cooperative Creamery.

With the concerted efforts of the Chamber of Commerce, the City Council, and civic leaders, out-of-town business people began to realize that Murfreesboro really wanted new businesses to locate here. The Swartzbaugh Manufacturing Company was the first to come from these efforts. Then followed State Farm Insurance Company, General Electric, Samsonite, Chromalox, Park-Sherman and others, all within a time frame of five years.

This account would be seriously amiss if Jack McFarland, the publisher of the *News Journal* during those years, was not mentioned as the major force and influence in arousing the interest of State Farm Insurance Company in locating in Murfreesboro. Jack was prominent in civic affairs and a fine newspaperman. The town lost a great citizen when he died April 8, 1982.

Fleming's Clothing Store was at the Holden Hardware location sixty-five years ago. The Flemings were Russian Jews who had emigrated to the United States only a short while before arriving in the town. They had not mastered English as yet and it was difficult for them to understand and be understood. Still, most everyone understands the language of money, so they managed to get along. They were in that location only a short while before they were succeeded by their compatriots, a family whose surname was Katz. They, too, had language difficulties. Mr. and Mrs. Katz found that they could overcome this problem by displaying a big smile as they offered their goods at a slightly lower price. Like the Flemings, they, too, soon moved away from Murfreesboro.

The next arrival at that location caused speculative brows of people over the entire county of Rutherford to raise. The new arrival on the Square was Charlie Jetton. From the standpoint of competition, he was an unpredictable force with which all the merchants had to reckon. On Friday nights, or on early Saturday mornings, the other merchants would slip by or send emissaries past Charlie's store to see what impossible prices he had painted on his windows with a Bon Ami bar and his devilish price-slashing brush.

The leading staples in Murfreesboro in 1924 were lard, flour, tobacco, and sugar. Charlie Jetton flaunted on his windows such unbelievable prices as a 50-lb. stand of lard for $2.25; a 24-lb. bag of flour for 45¢; a 1-lb. bag of sugar for 5¢; and 2 packs of cigarettes for 25¢. I recall buying from him 2 boxes (100 rounds) of .22 short ammunition for 25¢. People predicted that Charlie would soon price himself out of business, but to their consternation, he stayed and stayed. He even moved to a larger store with more and larger windows on which to wield that awful paint brush.

Charlie Jetton was an exceptionally quiet and unassuming man. Of medium height and slender waist, his head was sparsely covered with hair. His eyes were his only betrayal that he saw a bit of wit in every circumstance and that he looked at the world through rose-colored glasses. In a trade that normally did not call for any semblance of formal dress, Charlie always wore a tie. I had a special admiration for the man, since he never failed to greet me with the name "Junior," followed by some question. In a crowd, Charlie Jetton would be judged the most nondescript person there, but amongst the merchant princes around the Square, he would rate among the top ten.

Cash registers had not been on the scene very long in the early 1920s. Evidently, Charlie looked upon these contraptions with disdain, for he and his clerks handled all of their legal tender from aprons with three pockets, one for pennies, one for silver, and the third for the less used currency. Charlie—I use the given name with timidity, since he was always Mr. Jetton to me—was the nephew of James Jetton who was manager of the two-year-old Commerce Union Bank in Murfreesboro.

★ ★ ★

From there, the erstwhile Fleming-Katz-Jetton-Holden store is left behind as we walk to the Todd-Huddleston Furniture Store next door. The two partners, Herman Todd and Caesar Huddleston were operating at a time when most furniture was rather plain and usually of oak. Electrical appliances were just being introduced in Murfreesboro and would not be handled by furniture stores until the 1950s. Only a few families in the town owned an ammonia compressor refrigerator at that time. It was to be several years before the advent of TVA and its persuasive campaign to install electric refrigerators and stoves in every home. Meanwhile, the furniture stores sold ice boxes. They were usually about five feet in height, insulated, oak with brass hardware and had two doors. The door on top was where the ice was placed. The bottom door allowed the perishable items to be placed in the bottom compartment. The ice man in his horse-drawn wagon came daily. The customer would hang a four-cornered plaque on the porch which had the money denominations of 5¢, 10¢, 15¢, and 20¢. The amount under the nail denoted the amount of ice that the customer desired. Everyone knew Willie O'Keefe in those days, especially the kids. He was the ice man. With a gruffness that failed to disguise his love for kids, he let them hop on the back step of his ice wagon to pick up the shavings and small pieces of ice that were left on the floor. In 1924, Christy and Huggins operated the only ice factory in town. Consumers Supply Company, across the tracks on West Main, began the manufacture of ice in the early 1930s.

The partnership of Todd and Huddleston later dissolved. Herman's son, Charles Todd, continued the furniture business in a newly constructed building on East Main next to the Episcopalian Church. He retired from business in 1985, selling out the entire furniture inventory and real estate.

The next two buildings complete the tour from West Vine Street and up Mink Slide to West Main Street. Those two buildings were formerly occupied successively by Sam Licker, the Cohen Brothers, Abe Fisher, and now Court Square Building.

Sam Licker was born in Vilna, Lithuania, in 1869. He was twelve years of age when he first saw the Statue of Liberty. He heard later from William Goldstein, who also emigrated from the same city in Lithuania. William invited Sam to join him in Murfreesboro. Evidently, Goldstein liked what he saw in this town of fewer than 6,000 population. He liked the people, the economy, the land, and the climate. William Goldstein will be mentioned again in a later chapter.

Sam married in 1898. He arrived with his wife in Murfreesboro in 1899. Toward the end of that year, he purchased the large building on the corner of West Main and South Maple streets. His very first act of ownership was to have his name "Sam Licker" painted in bold letters at the very top of his new building. Sam opened his new men's ready-to-wear store in 1900. The business thrived and Sam Licker prospered. Later, he sold his building to the Cohen brothers, Harry and Dave. Sam moved his men's store to the south side of the Square. His story will continue when that store is reached on this slow walk around the Square.

Dave Cohen was twenty-five when he arrived in the United States in 1912. He, too, had emigrated from Lithuania. Shortly after his arrival, he began peddling from a wagon in Cannon County. His brother, Harry, emigrated soon after Dave. Harry followed Dave to middle Tennessee and began operating a peddling wagon in Van Buren County. Apparently the two brothers had arranged a pact between themselves to form a partnership when they had accumulated enough capital and credit to open a business together.

Their plans finally materialized. They purchased the two-story, two-section brick building, with two separate front entrances, complete with show windows, from Sam Licker at the beginning of the 1920s. Soon ladies' and men's ready-to-wear, dry goods, and shoes were on stationary racks, shelves, and tables. The two brothers no longer operated with mobile inventories. Dave and Harry Cohen soon became familiar household names throughout the county. They had arrived, and proved again that America was the land of opportunity.

The two brothers decided to retire during the 1950s and sold the section next to West Main Street to Abe Fisher, who operated a men's store there until the late 1970s. The other section was occupied by McAdoo Hardware Company for several years. Jim and Judy Dickson became the new owners of the hardware store. In the early 1970s, they moved to the corner of West Vine and Front streets where they began handling boats, motors, marine supplies, and fishing equipment.

In the late 1950s, Dave Cohen's sons, Mortimer and Gerald, began the operation of a large furniture and appliance business. They occupied the two locations immediately to the south of what is now Holden Hardware Company. The name of their store was Home Furniture Company, and they continued the business for about twenty years.

As we leave that section of the Square, it should be noted that there was one characteristic that each of those entrepreneurs, who were in business in 1924, held in common. Each had a relatively small amount of capital or credit available when he began his business. My father opened his meat market in 1923 on Mink Slide with borrowed money. E.P. Leach, who operated a buggy shop and loaned money on the corner of Vine and South Church streets, advanced him the capital of $300.

Regrettably, the opportunities that existed until twenty years ago for a young man to begin a private enterprise without a huge amount of capital have dwindled more than considerably. It comes down now to the question of whether the large amount of necessary capital might produce more in interest earned than the anticipated profits.

This short commentary on dwindling opportunities in America is to present the question, "Are we witnessing the slow but certain demise of small businesses in America?" This same question may be asked in regard to the field of agriculture. A young man has graduated from the University of Tennessee with a degree in Agriculture. His ambition is to own a farm and utilize the knowledge he has gained. He concludes that it would require at least one hundred acres to employ his skills and produce a decent living wage for himself and his family. After adding the cost of the land, cost of building a small home, a barn, livestock, fencing, and start-up money, he realizes that even the down payment on such an undertaking is more than he can afford. For the entrepreneurs on the Slide and the Square in the 1920s, the questions were whether they wanted to risk what little cash they had, and whether they would mind devoting the long hours that the business would require.

Word was coming up the Slide and onto the Square that Warren Myers would soon arrive. Warren lived over on Depot Hill with his wife, Lily, a part-Collie dog, and a scrawny horse. They were coming for their weekly shopping trip. As the word went around, the shop owners, their customers, and the pedestrians paused and watched for the pass-by.

It was told around the pot-bellied stoves that Warren Myers had belonged to a prominent family in Murfreesboro but nobody seemed to know the specific connection. Warren was probably about fifty to fifty-five years of age in 1924, but he appeared to be older. He managed to keep a gray beard that was about two-weeks long. He was a small man who walked with the aid of crutches. He had a fierce independence that gave the impression that he viewed everyone with disdain. People knew, when he and his entourage passed, that Warren Myers was in charge.

As they rounded the corner and came up Mink Slide toward the Square, Lily would be walking, closely followed by the scrawny horse slowly pulling the buggy that carried Warren and the part-Collie dog that sat beside him. No one knew why Lily always walked and the part-Collie dog always rode. Since Lily and the horse were quite along in years, they walked at about the same pace. She wore a turned-up man's felt hat, a dress sewn from flower-printed flour sacks, and well-worn tennis shoes.

Lily looked as if she bore the weight of all unliberated womankind as she led the procession. Observers dismissed the spectacle with the thought that the woman was content with the role to which she was relegated. Lily seldom spoke. Her husband spoke only when aroused, and that was when his condescending vocabulary came into use. Kids followed the slow-moving buggy whip that the man carried in his right hand.

Warren became impatient if his wife lingered overlong in a store. Leaning back in his buggy, he would yell, "Lil-lee." Woe be unto those who stared overlong at him or Lily. His tongue could descend like the tip-end of a bull whip.

Talk around the pot-bellied stoves was that Warren's family and friends thought he had married beneath him. He had such a resentment toward them for their feelings that he began drinking. The two began and continued a solitary existence together. Lily was cross-eyed, an opthalmic defect that was not uncommon in those days.

Chapter IV

South Side of Square (a)

Crossing over from the top of Mink Slide at Carpets by Ozborn (Sec. A-114) to the southwest corner of the Square, we come to a group of stores which belonged to the Spence heirs. They owned nineteen parcels on and immediately off the Square, which holdings made them by far the largest family ownership in the area of the Square. Their properties included more than one-half of the block on the south side of the Square (Section B) and almost the entire southwest quadrant of that block bounded by East Main, South Spring, East Vine, and South Church streets (Section C).

Having been intimately acquainted with the Square for more than sixty-seven years, I had naturally heard of the Spence estate ownership many times and was generally aware of the location of the estate's holdings. I knew that the Spence heirs were absentee owners and that former Murfreesboro Mayor Collier Crichlow managed their real estate interests for many years. I had been curious as to who those people were and particularly how those properties could have remained intact and in the same family for more than one hundred and fifty years. Normally, the vicissitudes of absentee ownership—vacancies, depressions, family differences in goals and administrations, and large offers for property—would tend to dissolve the partnership. Admirably, those heirs elected to retain their stewardship those many years.

Tommy Hord has managed the Spence estate interests in Murfreesboro for several years. He informed Margaret Greene of Long Island, New York, of my interest in the ancestor who had first owned and built on those properties. Through her correspondence and telephone conversations, the following information is presented.

Her great-great grandfather, Marman Spence, was born in 1798. He arrived in Murfreesboro in 1809, accompanying his brother John and John's son, John Cedric Spence. In 1826, Marman married Sarah Wasson, who was born in Ireland. The minister who performed the wedding was Alexander Campbell who had himself recently arrived from Scotland by way of Ireland. Campbell was a noted theologian and minister of the Church of Christ whose members were already meeting here in homes and public buildings. On January 1, 1833, they began worshipping in their own church building at the end of West Vine Street at about where Captain D's is now located.

Margaret Greene writes, "They (Marman and Sarah) lived on the south side of the Square next to a hotel and had three daughters and a son, David. At one time the hotel next door caught fire. The slaves formed a bucket brigade from Stones River (probably Lytle's Creek), the householders soaked their rugs and placed them on the roof tops. Marman was apparently a prosperous merchant. He served as mayor in 1834-35, and had many property holdings. His and Sarah's gravestone is located in the old cemetery."

The hotel reference in the foregoing account was probably the old City Hotel as mentioned in the time frame of 1909 in C.C. Henderson's *The Story of Murfreesboro.* A May, 1866, issue of the *Gospel Advocate* announces a Church of Christ Consultation Meeting to be held in Murfreesboro June 6th of that year. Members from distant places were to meet at the Spence House where they were to be assigned room and dining accommodations within the town. The Spence House later became the City Hotel. Margaret Greene tells of slaves forming a bucket brigade. Since slavery was abolished before 1865, then the fire must have occurred sometime before that year. Another fire almost destroyed the City Hotel sometime during the second decade of the 1900s. In 1923, the Spence heirs decided to build a new building on the site which would extend from the corner of South Church and South Public Square to what is now Mullins Jewelers. It was named the Spence Building and would house three separate stores under one roof (Section B-27, 25, 23). That new structure was quite an enhancement to the Square in 1923.

Mrs. Greene was asked how so many property holdings had remained intact within the same family for over one hundred fifty years. She replied that the heirs of Marman Spence had been family conscious, and had kept a deep respect for the stewardship that had been entrusted to them by their illustrious and astute ancestor. They formed a corporation during the Depression to further insure that the properties remained within the family. Margaret Greene is the president; her cousin, John Everett, is the treasurer; and his two sons are additional members of the corporation.

★ ★ ★

We pause now to peer into the building (C-27) which occupies a portion of the Spence property where part of the old City Hotel stood. The building then contained a bowling alley operated by Paty Jarman. Bowling was quite different in those days. Whereas ten pins are used today, the game used five pins then, and for several years later. Automatic pinsetters are used today, but black boys were employed for that purpose then.

The next tenant there was L.H. Wherle, who operated a paint store for a while near the end of the 1920s. On March 9, 1929, a new business with the name of Aultman's Cheerful Credit came into existence. The business was owned by the Goldsteins and the manager was Aultman Sanders. More will be written about him and his assistant manager, Lacye Welchance, when we arrive at C-111. A succession of tenants came after Aultman's moved in 1931. A later tenant was Rovin Dee Craddock who operated a furniture store there for several years. He was the father of Clyde and Richard Craddock. Milady, a ladies' apparel store, was there until recently. Appleton's now operates an elegantly decorated store there which specializes in gift items.

★ ★ ★

The building next door (B-25) is presently occupied by Martin Shoes and Shoe Repair. This business has been here since 1964. It was originated by James Martin, who opened first in a small space on Mink Slide. He later moved to the store's present location. In 1972, his nephew, Joe Martin, arrived on the scene and eventually purchased the business. A look inside the store today reveals a lot of bustling activity, both in the shoe and shoe repair departments.

Before Martin Shoes appeared on the scene in 1964, the store was inhabited by the firm of Becton and Westbrooks. Those people operated a busy cash-and-carry grocery business that was noted for its competitive prices. Albert Becton was the manager of the store. He was the nephew of Allie Clark Becton Westbrooks, who was former Mayor Hollis Westbrooks' wife. The Mayor will be recognized in greater depth as we progress up the street to another location.

An interesting rivalry was carried on by this store and Charlie Jetton when he was at the top of Mink Slide. As already mentioned, Charlie was most prolific with his Bon Ami-dipped paint brush. If the market price in town on a fifty-pound stand of lard was ten cents a pound, Charlie would paint on his store window seven and one-half cents a pound and then leave town for a day or two. Of course, this stunt was agonizing to his competitors, who habitually drove past Charlie's store each morning before they opened.

John Butler operated a feed, seed, and staple grocery store here for several years before 1943. He had moved from a west side location during the 1930s. Mr. Butler served as president of the First National Bank for several years until 1932, when the bank was closed. First National followed the trend of many other banks throughout the country in those mid-depression years. Actually, the bank could have been saved had there not been a two- or three-day run by depositors demanding their deposits. The bank eventually paid eighty-six percent of the amount owed to depositors.

John Butler, along with the other directors, suffered the loss of practically all of his assets because of the bank failure. Mr. Butler's daughter, Katherine Butler Holden, recalls the dismal days of that period which was a difficult time for everyone. The newly elected President, Franklin Delano Roosevelt, declared a Bank Holiday period of one week, which allowed the nation's banks to catch up on their bookkeeping and to stabilize their positions. The President initiated the circulation of a new temporary currency which was called "script." The new legal tender was to provide an immediate addition to the money supply. I had a paper route at the time and recall collecting the gold-colored currency from my subscribers. The new money was out of circulation in about thirty days. The National Recovery Administration (NRA) was instituted, and the country began its slow climb from the depths of the Depression. Roosevelt appointed Hugh Johnson as head of the NRA.

That was the time in which several important reforms were initiated. The Federal Deposit Insurance Corporation (FDIC) and the Securities and Exchange Commission (SEC) were to insure depositors, and monitor the stock markets. Other initial-bearing entities which figured prominently in the nation's recovery were Public Works Administration (PWA), Works Progress Administration (WPA), Civilian Conservation Corps (CCC), and, most importantly to the South, the Tennessee Valley Authority (TVA).

By the Fall of 1933, things were looking better about the Square. The post-harvest Saturdays filled the Square with people who had been absent for a long time. Every story and office building on and off the Square was occupied. Although jobs were scarce and money was in short supply, people were adjusting and were optimistic that things would get better. Those were the times that brought about the still popular Democratic theme song "Happy Days Are Here Again."

★ ★ ★

The Pastime Pool Room and Barber Shop occupied the next building (B-23) in the walk east on the south side. The four front windows and glass door were painted green to a height of six feet above the sidewalk. This shielded the patrons on the inside from what may have been the disapproving eyes of passers-by. The business was operated by Almer "Buck" Norris and Lark Stanton. Fortunately, pool rooms and bowling alleys soon acquired the favor of Murfreesboroans and the windows were cleaned up. Norris Lovvorn is the nephew of one of the partners, the late "Buck" Norris.

Heidi Lee's Submarine Sandwich Shop was a recent tenant there. The present occupants are Betty Ledbetter and Betty Plemmons, who operate the P & L Shop. They are a mother-and-daughter team who hospitably welcome customers to their store of ladies' dress fashions.

★ ★ ★

The next space eastward on the south side of the Public Square belongs to the heirs of James Maney (B-19A). In 1924, there were two stores there and the owner was Mrs. Loveman. My first memory of the occupant of one of the buildings (B-19A) dates back to about 1932, when it was occupied by an ice cream shop. It had three or four tables with metal Coca-Cola chairs, a counter, and a freezer holding several ten-gallon containers of ice cream. It was called the Blue Bird Ice Cream Shop. The place was managed by Lois McNabb, who had moved to Murfreesboro from Cannon County. Lois later married Arthur McKnight. They operated the well-known McKnight's Restaurant on East Main for many years. The Champion Shoe Shop came to that location in 1936, and remained for several years. The owner's name was Ewing Woodward. Later, Herschel Mullins annexed the space (B-19A) to his present store (B-19B).

J. Herschel Mullins* has the present distinction of having operated a store on the Square longer than any other living person, with the exception of Lacye Welchance, of whom more will be written later. Herschel arrived on the Square in 1938 at the age of twenty-two. He rented the store two doors east, which now houses the Tip-Top Barber Shop (B-15). With little cash, but with a clock and watchmaker's certificate, a huge propensity for work, and a sincere desire to be of service to his customers, he opened the doors of his business fifty-two years ago. In 1961, he bought the present location (B-19B) and later expanded with the addition of (B-19A) as mentioned earlier. Mullins Jewelers is a bustling beehive of activity. It is a family-operated business which is staffed by Herschel, his wife Mildred, their son Charles, their two daughters-in-law, Charlene and Ann plus Charles' sons, Jeff and Tim. Herschel was probably more recognizable by people around the Square when he wore his Homberg hat and his jeweler's loupe on his forehead. Now, Charles Mullins wears the loupe. He is also a master clock and watch maker and jeweler.

J. Herschel Mullins epitomizes the true spirit of entrepreneurial private enterprise. With nothing to offer but a trade, hard work, business acumen, and a desire to be of service, he has built a successful business. His story compares with countless other men and women who extoll the merits of private enterprise. In a sense, they, too, are artists who have painted skillfully on their canvasses works of art that are to be admired. Herschel is a living example of the kind of people that this story is about.

Curiously, the jewelry business seems to have enjoyed the greatest longevity of any other profession on the Square. There are Bell Jewelers, since 1879; Aultman's Jewelers, since 1931; and Mullins Jewelers, since 1938.

Before Herschel Mullins came to his location, there were Joe Rich Parsley and Norris Lovvorn, who, as partners, began the operation of a pool room in 1947. Before them, there was Charlie Sam's Grocery, which was located there for several years.

★ ★ ★

My father, C.B. Arnette, moved his meat market to (B-19B) in 1926 from (A-128) on Mink Slide. His business had done well for the times. He was then on the Square with the stately court house and lawn across the street. In the early 1950s, the lawn was diminished considerably in order to provide needed parking spaces. Automotive traffic in 1926

*See note at end of chapter.

was surpassing horse and buggy vehicles. Seldom then did a horse shy or rear at the sound of a motor car.

The greatest improvement at my father's meat market was the installation of a ten-foot refrigerated meat display case. That was a revolutionary fixture in 1926, which would greatly enhance the preservation and display of meat products. The daily chore of handling and hoisting the heavy blocks of ice would now be in the past. I remember quite well the great anticipation with which my mother and father awaited this wonderful equipment.

At that time, my father's chief competitor in the meat business in Murfreesboro was R.E. Bragg, who was located on the east side of the Square in the present location of Mid-South Sewing Center and next to Aultman's Jewelers. C.B. Arnette's Meat Market employed two colored delivery boys. They delivered the meat orders on two heavy duty Blue Grass bicycles. It was about that time that I began working each afternoon after school and on Saturdays as another delivery boy. We remained in that location until 1930, when my father moved to the R.E. Bragg store mentioned above.

Charles Augustus Lindbergh had won the applause and the hearts of the nation in April, 1927, when he crossed the Atlantic alone from New York to Paris in his Spirit of St. Louis. Calvin Coolidge was President and, as mentioned earlier, would not choose to run in 1928. The main contenders would be Herbert Hoover and the "happy warrior," Al Smith. Herbert Hoover acceded to the Presidency in the beginning of the climactic year of 1929.

That was the year of the beginning of the "Great Depression." A dark economic pall would hang over the country for the greater part of the next decade. There were plant closings, soup lines, bread lines, and suicides among the financial moguls. Amid all of those catastrophes, the merchants around the Square in Murfreesboro stood fast, continuing their accustomed daily habit of opening early and closing late. The inhabitants of Murfreesboro, which then numbered almost eight thousand, knew in the beginning that there was a depression only through reading the newspapers. Rutherford County, during that period, was geared mainly to an agricultural economy with smaller emphasis on industry. The Sunshine Hosiery Mills continued to operate at full speed and even began an expansion. Other mills and smaller businesses kept at their normal pace with seldom any lay-offs of personnel. This is not to say that the reverberations of the depression were not felt in Murfreesboro. Some people, both in high and low places, did suffer. Professors at Middle Tennessee State Normal in one period waited for several months for a pay check to be cashed. One of the four banks in town closed. However, relatively speaking, the financial crisis in 1929 and its effects were not suffered to the degree that was felt over the majority of the country.

There was a great concern amongst the small shop owners around the Square about the potential threat of chain stores arriving on the scene. An H.G. Hill store had already opened shop on the east side of the Square, and there was talk of other arrivals. That was a nationwide trend, and a real threat to all small businesses, especially to food merchants.

The independent businesses of America came up with a champion who would fight that octopus which would soon embrace within its tentacles all of the small shops in America. The champion's name was W.K. Henderson of Baton Rouge, Louisiana. His radio call letters were KWKH, a high frequency station, on which he could be heard three times a week. Mr. Henderson was a real gladiator. His listeners and supporters viewed him as a David fighting Goliath. The man formed an association which would financially support his single-handed efforts to vanquish the giant evil which the chain store represented. He promised a fight to the death. The contributions poured into the coffers of W.K. Henderson. He did make a valiant effort, staying on the air for almost two years. To his credit, he did delay the onslaught of the chain store. The majority of his listeners who were not engaged in business, supported the small store owners and for a while boycotted the chain stores. Eventually, however, it was the housewife who could not resist those low prices painted on the windows with an artist's brush and a bar of Bon Ami. The dam held for awhile, but soon the floodwaters of free trade and enterprise overflowed and finally burst the dam.

*In the most central location on the Square is the concession stand owned and operated by Aubrey Weatherly. Aubrey has been there since 1937—a span of fifty-four years. Herschel Mullins and Aubrey agree that Aubrey arrived on the scene six months prior to the arrival of Herschel.

This writer, while concentrating on the businesses around the Square, overlooked the one in the center-piece and also one of the most outstanding examples of private enterprise in the area.

Therefore, these two business men, Aubrey Weatherly the concession stand operator and Herschel Mullins the jeweler, have agreed to share the superlative of having owned and operated their businesses longer than any other living persons around the Square. Herschel concedes a slight edge to Aubrey.

Chapter V

South Side Square (b)

The next four stores (B-17, B-15, B-13, and B-11) are part of the Spence heirs' estate on the south side. B-17 was occupied by Forrest Spence in 1924. He operated a beverage shop and bowling alley there until the late 1930s. Mr. Spence was a quiet, genial man who was never too busy to speak to a kid. His daughter, Alberta, relates that her family and the present Spence heirs are not closely related. She has a brother, Forrest ("Buddy") Spence, Jr., who resides in California. Alberta Spence was assistant librarian at Linebaugh Library from 1950 through 1970.

Charles ("Chaps") Cantrell came to that location (B-17) in 1954. He operated a shoe store until 1958. "Chaps" then moved to what may be better known as the old Sam Licker Store (B-13), which had just been vacated by Cary Knight. Eventually, in 1970, he became manager of the shoe department of J.C. Penney.

Mr. Mitchell operated an electrical and lamp repair shop there for several years following Cantrell's move. Presently, the store is occupied by Medical Claims Service, a nationally recognized corporation which assists people and private corporations in filing for hospital and medical benefits. Their office is one of sixty network offices in the United States. The business is managed by Joe Todd, who also teaches at LaVergne High School.

★ ★ ★

Returning to the year of 1924, the stroller would come next to a bicycle repair shop (B-13). This writer believes that the owner there was Mr. Hunter P. Morton, who shortly thereafter moved to the south side of East Vine Street, where the First City Bank building is now located. Mr. Morton will be mentioned later, as this account continues. In 1929, "Jew" Barnett brought a fruit and vegetable business to that place. "Jew" was of medium height, had large eyes, and always wore a wool cap. The cap looked a bit unusual, since men's caps had been out of style for several years. But "Jew" Barnett drove a long, green, 1924 Lincoln touring car. Since the top of the car was usually down, the cap may have been appropriate. Mrs. Barnett assisted her husband in the store. They had a six-year-old son who was called Junior. Everybody noticed Junior when he walked up and down the street. Junior smoked cigarettes. His favorite brand was Lucky Strike.

Bell Shoe Shop was there for awhile until 1937. Then came Herschel Mullins, as already mentioned. Eventually, the Tip-Top Barber Shop came to the location in 1971 and is very much in business under the ownership of Eural Sauls.

This barber shop was first located in the old Jordan Hotel building (C-118) in 1929. Two years later it moved two doors up the street to C-114, where it was operated by W.A. ("Bill") Rushing. Mr. Rushing sold his ownership to Joe Davidson, who is still following his vocation with Tip-Top. Joe states that, from the standpoint of longevity, the Ideal and Tip-Top Barber Shops would be running neck and neck in their tenure on the Square. Both were organized in the late 1920s.

Among some of the well-known barbers who have been connected with Tip-Top are Hall Todd, W.A. Rushing, Godfrey Marable, Will Ed Blair, Elgin Lowe, and T.B. Gilley, as well as Joe Davidson and Eural Sauls, already mentioned.

★ ★ ★

In the middle of the block on the south side of the Public Square was Sam Licker's Store (B-13). Sam has been mentioned earlier as the owner, at the turn of the century, of the large building on the southwest corner of West Main and South Maple streets (A-102). Sam first saw the Statue of Liberty at the age of twelve. He arrived in Murfreesboro in 1898 and shortly thereafter met Sarah Cohen, who was visiting her sister Dora, the wife of William Goldstein. Sam and Sarah married the following year. From that union came three daughters, Bertha, Ethel, and Esther. Those three lovely girls have had distinguished business and social careers in California, New York, Florida, and finally in Murfreesboro, where they operated the highly acclaimed and successful Cotton Patch for several years. The sisters live on Cherry Lane, remaining as vivacious as ever and immensely entertaining as they display their sincere hospitality.

As related earlier, Sam sold his original store to Harry and Dave Cohen. He moved to the two-story building (B-13) which was next to the City Cafe. Soon the two floors were filled with merchandise consisting mostly of men's ready-to-wear, hats, shoes, and accessories. Sam did not present a great deal of competition to his brother-in-law, William Goldstein, who catered principally to the carriage trade. Sam had men's shoes for $3.59, wash pants for $5.95, and suits for less than $20.00. As was the custom of the Goldsteins, he stood in front of his store, his arms folded, greeting the passers-by with an unspoken invitation to visit his store.

Sam Licker was a quiet man of less than average height with steel gray hair and slender girth. His eyes, demeanor, and reserve projected that he was a man of wisdom and wide experience. There was a receptable made into the concrete curb in front of his store. Sam kept a large

American flag hanging on a staff which on every occasion he diligently fitted into this receptacle. Mr. Sam Licker died in 1950. The immigrant boy from Lithuania had found that America, and particularly Murfreesboro, Tennessee, was the land of opportunity.

William Cary Knight became the new owner of the business in 1951. He was the father of Drs. Joe and Robert Knight. After several years, Mr. Knight moved his business two doors eastward to B-9. Charles ("Chaps") Cantrell then moved his shoe business to B-13. When "Chaps" moved, Jewell's Clothes Machine became the new tenant. In 1979, Hudson's Flower and Gift Shop moved there from the north side of the Square where it had been located since 1969. George Hudson, who is deceased, assisted his wife in the business for several years after his retirement as manager of the meat department at Kroger's.

★ ★ ★

The origin of the original City Cafe (B-11), a Murfreesboro institution for over fifty years, is not entirely clear. Former Mayor Hollis Westbrooks remembers he was told that the restaurant had been owned by a camera buff who lived on Salem Road. The restaurateur and part-time camera buff sold the City Cafe in 1910 to Dorsey J. Cantrell. The seller promised, as a condition of the sale, to help manage the place for four years. However, after receiving the cash sale money from Cantrell, the man left town permanently. Legend held that the place was first opened in 1900 with the front and back door keys thrown away. Its doors were never closed for over half a century of operation.

The City Cafe was a large restaurant even by today's local standards. The serving area contained a long square U-shaped counter with marble tops and revolving enameled stools. The east and west walls were lined with beige marble-top tables and bent wood chairs. There was a huge kitchen staff with colored cooks and helpers. Midway between the front and kitchen sections was another serving area with a tall cabinet and wood top counter. The bakeries were not furnishing pre-sliced bread before 1937, so each waiter sliced the bread for his customers.

The most outstanding and charismatic element of the City Cafe was its owner, Uncle Dorsey Cantrell. The uncle appellation came from the fact that he had a lot of nephews, and most of these nephews worked for him. Since his nephews were naturally good waiters, the fact that they worked for him was no evidence of nepotism.

Uncle Dorsey was more than six feet tall, and had a huge neck to support his large head. He had large, pendulous arms and a slightly protruding stomach under his big torso. He had the physique to back up his temper which often prompted him to manhandle a person who was disorderly in his restaurant. In any military unit, Dorsey Cantrell would have been the top sergeant of all the sergeants. His formidable appearance, his words, and his demeanor exuded authority. This blustery facade was emphasized all the more by the truly gentle nature of the man. Whenever a baby was in the restaurant, Uncle Dorsey had to pick it up and carry it around. Politicians observed how he handled this affection, but most could never match his sincere love for babies and children.

Uncle Dorsey was an easy mark for anyone who was hungry or in need of lodging. In those days, there were plenty of opportunities for one to demonstrate his charitable instincts. But Uncle Dorsey had no patience with anyone who was panhandling or looking for a handout so that he might purchase a drink of liquor. I have seen him grasp a man by his collar and the seat of his pants, propel him out the door, across the sidewalk, and deposit him on the street.

Such was Uncle Dorsey Cantrell, who was perhaps the most widely known and respected man in the county. Among the many nephews who served as waiters for him were Doc, Cary, and Buford Cantrell, Dorsey, and Homer Gray. Other waiters were Ben Tarpley, assistant manager, Ben Brown of Lofton's Ben Brown Store fame, and me. The City Cafe had never employed waitresses before 1936. That year and during my three-month tenure, Peggy Brown (wife of Ben), and Audie and Sara Overall came aboard.

The wage scale at the City Cafe in 1936 for a new waiter was $7.00 for a 69-hour work week, plus all the food that the new waiter wanted to eat. Whether or not this was a good salary for those times depended on how hungry the new waiter was and how much he ate.

My greatest compliment from Uncle Dorsey came on the day that I timorously walked up to the great man to inform him that I would be quitting in another week. I wanted a two-week vacation before heading back to school. He put his arm about my neck and said in dripping words, "Hon, I can't let you quit so soon. One week's vacation is all you need." It turned out that the one week was all I needed.

The menu at the City Cafe included hamburgers, 10¢, ham and weiner sandwiches, 10¢, double header (ham and egg), 15¢, triple-decker club sandwich, 25¢, and plate lunches (meat, three vegetables, dessert), 35¢. Beverages were 5¢ with the exception of ice cream sodas and milk shakes for 15¢, and malted milks, 20¢. Soon after Pres. Franklin D. Roosevelt came into office in 1933, prohibition was lifted, and the sale of beer was permitted in Murfreesboro. For several years, the City Cafe was one of the few establishments in town that served beer. Its alcoholic content in the early days of its reintroduction was 3.2%.

The rear door and porch of the restaurant was about fifty or sixty feet from Vine Street. During the mid-twenties, a hidden well was uncovered between the porch and the street. That old hand-dug well was similar to the well recently discovered on the north side of the Square. It was left uncovered the first night after discovery. A citizen well-known for his thirst for white corn liquor ambled into the well, but luckily did not physically injure himself during the fall. The next morning, a passer-by heard his cries for help. Several people joined in the rescue, and quite a crowd gathered. Some women of the local W.C.T.U. were watching and heard the man say as he emerged from the well that he would never do it again. One of the W.C.T.U. ladies said, "Congratulations for resolving never to drink again." The man replied, "I didn't say I wasn't going to drink any more. I meant I wasn't going to fall into any more wells."

Hollis Westbrooks recalls that Uncle Dave Macon came into the City Cafe one day. Uncle Dorsey, wanting to show off Uncle Dave to his customers, asked him "to tell us a big lie." Uncle Dave promptly stated that this is a good place to eat.

When circuit court or the grant jury was in session, the witnesses and other persons likely to be called would assemble at the City Cafe to await their summons. Grundy Kerr from Halls Hill had a deep, stentorian voice. It was his duty to step out on the south balcony of the court house and summon the next party to appear in court. Cupping his hands around his mouth and slowly emphasizing each syllable of the man's name, he would issue a call that could be heard around the Square and inside the doors of the City Cafe. Grundy Kerr was a tall, imposing man, with silvery hair and a wide mustache. He was the father of Mary Warfield, the uncle of Rutherford County surveyor John D. Kerr (deceased in 1960), and the great uncle of Sam Kerr, who recently retired as Murfreesboro's assistant recreation director.

After the restaurant closed its doors in the 1950s, Stroud's Appliances became the new occupants. Later there came Singer Sewing Machine Company, which operated there until 1984. On its departure came Marti and Liz Shoes, which is a franchise shoe store. Sandra Doty has been the store's manager since its occupancy began in 1984.

★ ★ ★

The partnership of Spain and Hudson both owned and operated a hardware store at the next two addresses (B-7 and B-9) in 1924. Liz Spain, prominent interior designer and niece of one of the partners, Foster Spain, states that the hardware store began operations before the turn of this century. An accompanying picture, reported to have been made around 1900, shows the firm's signs which advertise Studebaker and Mitchell wagons. Liz further states that their store was different from most hardware stores in that it stocked sterling silver and fine chinaware. One of the store's clerks was Johnnie Brown, who later was employed by Rollie Holden when he opened Holden's Hardware.

The firm had for several years occupied two sections (B-7 and B-9). B-9 was used primarily for the storage of wagons and agricultural implements. In about 1928, C.B. Leatherman and Company occupied B-9. An advertisement dated October 14, 1929, states that Leatherman carried dry goods, ladies' ready-to-wear, druggets, rugs, and window shades. Mr. Leatherman was Foster Spain's wife's brother. Mr. Leatherman will be encountered again in two later locations.

After C.B. Leatherman and Company, there came the firm of Becton and Westbrooks to that location (B-9) on the south side of the Public Square. The year was 1935 and not a very good year for starting the large grocery store that the two partners, W.H. Becton and W.H. Westbrooks, envisioned, but they were intrepid men. Willie Hall Becton was the brother-in-law of William Hollis Westbrooks.

At 87 years of age, Hollis has the distinction of being the oldest surviving former business man on the Square. Former Mayor Hollis Westbrooks is a man of many honors and distinctions. He served eighteen years as Mayor of Murfreesboro, the longest tenure at the mayor's office in the city's history. He served as chairman of Rutherford County School Board for about fifteen years. He served as state representative of Rutherford County six years. These are just a few examples of the accomplishments of this dedicated and conscientious public servant and businessman. Largely through his efforts, Cannonsburgh Village came into being in 1976. That early nineteenth-century restoration and replica of the village which preceded Murfreesboro has proven to be a popular Middle Tennessee tourist attraction which also involves the participation of many local citizens.

Hollis Westbrooks was born March 11, 1903, in the little community of Link. When he was pressing his candidacy for state representative back in the 1960s, his highly educated opponent asked during a public debate in Smyrna, "Where were you educated, Mr. Westbrooks?" Hollis glibly replied, "At Link University."

The former mayor is noted for his bone-dry wit. He has an uncommon knack of discerning a bit of humor in every question or problem. Abraham Lincoln and Mark Twain were masters of this trait. He has remarkable and acute memories of the Square, its stores, and its people.

Hollis first began his association on the Square in 1924 as a clerk in the employ of Charlie Jetton, who at that time operated a store on the east side of the Square (C-113). Otis Lamb, who appears later, was a fellow clerk. There was no cash register in the store. The clerks and Mr. Jetton wore long aprons with divided pockets in which to hold the change and small amounts of currency. That method allowed faster transactions, since it was not necessary to walk to and from the register. That was long before the time of central check-out counters.

Examples of prevailing prices of popular items in those days are as follows: 24-lb. bag of flour, 45¢; sugar, per pound, 5¢; cigarettes, 2 packs for 25¢; steak, per pound, 15¢; hog lard, 4½¢ per pound, or $2.25 for a 50-lb. stand.

Customers entering grocery or clothing stores then would find many of the counters covered with cheesecloth or muslin. That was to shield the contents of the counters from the dust that seeped in from the often dusty streets. The city used a large water tank wagon pulled by a team of horses to sprinkle the streets, but that settled the dust only temporarily.

Eleven years later, in 1935, W.H. Westbrooks and his brother-in-law, W.H. Becton, began a grocery business in the store recently vacated by C.B. Leatherman and Company (B-9). It became a successful enterprise—successful enough for the partners to open another store at B-27, as already noted. In 1947, Becton and Westbrooks organized a new company, the B and W Cigar and Tobacco Company. They became engaged as wholesale distributors of tobacco products in Rutherford and most surrounding counties. Upon the death of Becton, Hollis became the sole proprietor of the company. Well past retirement age, he finally did retire in 1986, after selling the business.

Former Mayor Hollis Westbrooks presently resides at Murfreesboro Health Care Center. He has slowed down a bit, but seems to have pleasantly adjusted to his new environment. This writer never tires of visiting with the man who enjoys company and who always provides interesting conversation.

The next business at the location (B-9) was W.E. Knox Grocery and Meat Market. W.E. was the son of W.E. Knox, Sr., who was a partner in the Knox and Freeman Furniture Company only two doors eastward (B-5). James Rushing, the son of Clyde Rushing, who has already been mentioned, operated the meat market at that place.

In 1951, W.E. Knox accepted a position as manager of a photographic studio in Hopkinsville, Kentucky. James Rushing built some chicken houses in the area behind the present location of Jackson Chevrolet Company and began an egg production operation.

In 1951, Cary Knight moved his clothing business from the old Licker store (B-13). Mr. Knight remained there until his death in 1968. The building was then sold to Joe Harrison.

Joe is a very enterprising practitioner of private enterprise. He had already leased the next door eastward building (B-7) from the Crescent Amusement Company in 1957. Now the two buildings housed his business of Martinizing Cleaners, a name which was changed in recent years to Big B Cleaners. Joe opened the front and rear walls (of B-9) so his customers could drive through the building as they deposited their clothes to be cleaned. Joe Harrison has been involved in extensive real estate purchases and developments since he first opened on the Square in 1957.

★ ★ ★

As previously noted, the next door (B-7) was occupied in 1924 by Spain and Hudson Hardware Company. This was the main section of their operation. Hoyt Smith, who is 90 years of age this year (1990), was a clerk in the store in 1927 and 1928. Hoyt is very active physically, puts in a garden each year, has an agile mind, and speaks almost as fast as the rapid-fire radio broadcaster, Walter Winchell. In about 1929, Mike Brown became the new owner of the hardware business which was then occupying only one section of the former two stores.

The next occupant of B-7 was the Roxy Theatre, which was owned by the Crescent Amusement Company of Nashville. The theatre came in the early 1940s. Murfreesboro had grown somewhat during the 1940s, and it was believed that the town could support two theatres. The Princess Theatre on College Street was also owned by Crescent. Extensive renovations were undertaken on the old hardware store; the floor was slanted, air conditioning was installed, and a spectacular marquee was mounted on the front of the building.

With the advent of television in the early 1950s, it was found that the Roxy Theatre was not economically viable and it consequently was closed. In 1956, the aforementioned Joe Harrison leased the building from Crescent. The floor was again leveled and Joe moved in with his soon-to-be-successful One Hour Martinizing Cleaners. It should be remembered here that he was to buy the B-9 building from the estate of Cary Knight in 1968. Joe combined the two buildings into one operation. In 1979, he bought the B-7 building from W.B. Hamaker and Tom Lane, who had received the building from Crescent as partial payment for two drive-in theatres which the patrons had sold to Crescent.

★ ★ ★

James Byron ("Bide") Freeman was born in 1875. His son, Lawrence, states that at the age of twenty-five, his father opened a "racket" store on the Square in location B-5. It was a kind of store that specialized in no particular line of goods. It might handle shoes, boots, grocery staples, clothes, novelties, and various and sundry items. Elsewhere on these pages, one may note the sign J.B. Freeman on his store in a picture made about the turn of the century. Later, Mr. Freeman entered into a partnership with W.E. ("Uncle Bud") Knox. They were to handle fine furniture and soon became one of the most successful furniture stores in town.

"Bide" Freeman was a tall, handsome man with steel gray hair which he parted in the center. He had an outgoing personality, and always seemed to have a few words to say to me in my frequent wanderings on the Square.

I recall "Uncle Bud" Knox as ancient in appearance during those days in the late 1920s. Tall and lanky, he walked with a perceptible limp. His accustomed mode of dress included a derby hat, a starched, white, detachable collar, a black string tie, and striped moleskin pants. "Uncle Bud" did not drive a car, because he owned a tall, black, Ivey Johnson bicycle. This he rode to and from the store each day. He had a black metal clip which fitted above his ankle and over the moleskin pants on his right leg to keep his cuffs from becoming engaged in the sprocket chain. The story was told about town that the courageous Mr. Knox one day mounted one of the first motorcycles that came to Murfreesboro. He started the machine and rode around the Square twice before he realized that no directions on how to stop the noisy contraption had been given him. On the second round, he headed out East Main. Several onlookers realized that "Uncle Bud" was in a real predicament. They called ahead to the two tollgate houses between Murfreesboro and Woodbury, warning them to raise their gates. Fortunately, the story had a happy ending. The machine ran out of gasoline a few miles short of Woodbury in the Pilot Knob area.

Mr. W.E. Knox was a gentleman of the old school. With his formal attire, a constant twinkle in his eyes, he was a credit to the dignity and professionalism of his fellow merchants around the Square. The business continued until 1958. "Uncle Bud" died in 1939.

Rollins and Levan Furniture Company was the next business in B-5. Later, Dixie Furniture Company operated there until it moved to South Church Street. Tom Brown had owned that property for many years, and upon his death in the early 1930s, the building passed to his daughter, Louise Brown Byck. Mrs. Byck sold the property to Ferrell Holloway in 1986. He operated Holloway Fashions there until the latter part of 1989, at which time the property was sold to Rutherford County. The building, which has provided space for a "racket" store, furniture stores, and a clothing store, now provides office space for the county.

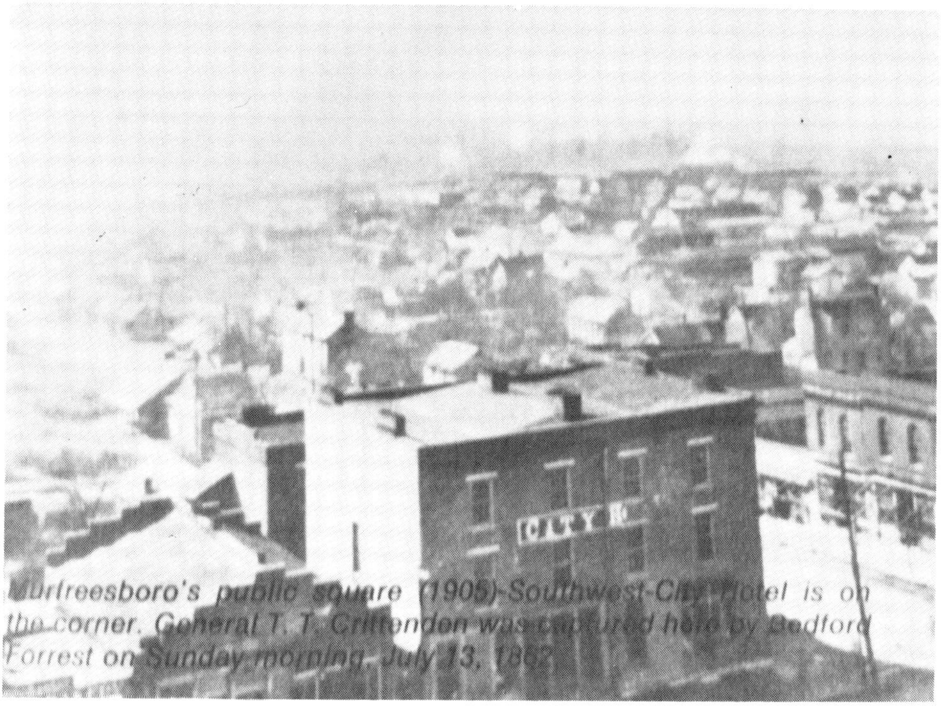
Murfreesboro's public square (1905)-Southwest-City Hotel is on the corner. General T. T. Crittenden was captured here by Bedford Forrest on Sunday morning, July 13, 1862.
CITY H

Old City Hotel on southeast corner of Public Square. Portion of Mink Slide at right, circa 1900.

SPAIN & HUDSON
MITCHELL WAGONS
SPAIN & HUDSON
LUNCH ROOM

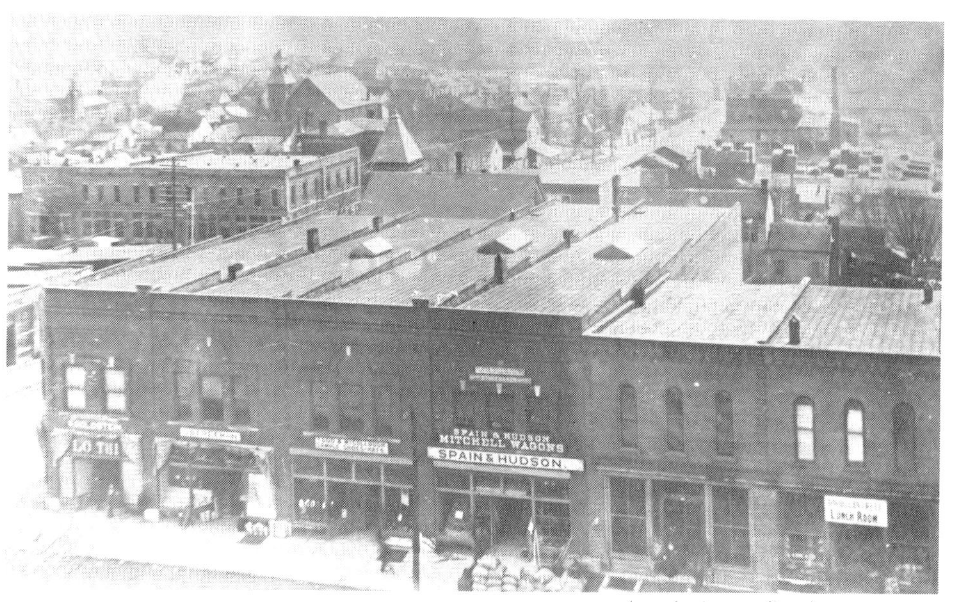

Spain & Hudson

Herschel Mullins of Mullins Jewelers. Has operated his own business on the Square since 1938. (Longer than any living person.)

Hollis Westbrooks, long time merchant on the Square, public servant, founder of Cannonsburgh and Mayor who served in this office longer than any man in the history of Murfreesboro.

Goldsteins, circa 1910-1915. Note Frank Burgdorf at extreme right.

Night view of Goldsteins, circa 1960.

Southside Square, circa 1923.

Chapter VI

Goldsteins—West Vine—South Church

For more than three quarters of a century, the name Goldstein was synonymous with top quality and high fashion in ladies' and men's ready-to-wear. As Marshall-Field, R.H. Macy, and Sachs-Fifth Avenue were at the national pinnacle in this merchandise category, Goldstein's held a similar ranking in middle Tennessee.

The founder of the firm was William Goldstein, who arrived in Murfreesboro in 1885. He had recently disembarked in New York City from a ship that had transported him from his home town of Vilna, Lithuania. He arrived in Murfreesboro with his personal luggage and a backpack which contained his entire merchandise inventory. Evidently, the contents of his backpack were versatile and desirable enough to whet the buying appetites of many people around Murfreesboro and surrounding counties.

He soon married a new arrival in Murfreesboro whose name was Dora Cohen. From that union, there were three sons, David, Maurice, and Bernard, and one daughter, Leah.

From a mixture of plodding perseverance, good business acumen, and frugal living, William was able in 1900 to negotiate the purchase of the brick store building on the southeast corner of the Public Square (B-1). The building was on the same parcel of land which William Lytle had reserved for himself before the auction of the Public Square lots in 1812. William Goldstein, the immigrant from Lithuania who still had difficulty with the English language, could now discard his pack and display a much larger inventory on counters and tables.

As his business grew, his children grew, and his inventory grew. David and Bernard followed aptly in their father's steps. They purchased the adjoining building (B-3) on the west side to accommodate the expanding inventory of ladies' and men's ready-to-wear and cloth materials. The corner building (B-1) became the ladies' department, and the adjoining newly-acquired store housed the men's suits, hats, shoes, and accessories. From the early years, the Goldsteins insisted on the best quality name goods and the latest styles that were on the market in New York. Flo, David's wife, and later Sis, Bernard's wife, augmented the search and procurement of those goods that would soon make the name Goldstein's a household word in middle Tennessee. The family possessed a flair for salesmanship and instinctive appreciation for quality and taste—characteristics which seem to be inherent in the Hebrew race.

There is another trait which this writer believes to be unique among Jewish store owners. William, who died in 1929, had a certain chair by the front door which he occupied every day. David and Bernard stood outside the front door each day that the weather was suitable. Sam Licker, already mentioned in this story, was to be found in front of his store as well as was Sol Arbit, who is to be mentioned later. I have noticed, in dealing with Jewish antique shop owners in Scotland, England, and Holland, that they observed this same custom. Frank Burgdorf, the tall, handsome manager of the men's store at Goldstein's, was not of the Hebrew race, but he also engaged in this high visibility custom when he was not busy in the store.

Goldstein's, in more than seventy-five years on the Public Square, employed many local men and women. My mother, Sarah, and my Aunt Annie, who later became Mrs. Tom Dill, both worked as salesladies there prior to 1912. The store generated more media advertising than any other business in Murfreesboro for several decades. There was full-page advertising toward the end of every week, and preceding special observances such as Christmas, Valentine's Day, and Mother's Day.

It was about 1935 when Goldstein's purchased the old firehall (B-122), which stood at the rear of their store. The firehall was demolished, and the store was expanded all the distance to Vine Street. That involved a huge innovation, since the upper floors and basement were extensively rebuilt and remodeled.

Goldstein's continued to flourish during and after World War II. In the 1970s, Bernard, the surviving son of William, the founder, leased the store and their name to Alden's, the catalog store in Chicago. Alden's operated there into 1983, when the lease expired and the business was closed. In February 1984, the building was sold at auction to Dr. Charles Smith, Bill Webb, and this writer. In 1987, the owners sold the property to Joe Swanson, who subsequently sold it to the City of Murfreesboro.

Thus ended one of the most important and most famous business enterprises in the history of the Square. The Goldsteins would have to rank high on the roster of merchant princes of Murfreesboro. Theirs was a story of humble beginnings with high aspirations and success probably beyond their aspirations.

The Goldstein building (B-1-3) completes our tour of the south side of the Square. We turn right on South Church Street and walk toward the corner of South Church Street and Vine, where the Murfreesboro Fire Hall (C-122) was once located. Passing along the side of the former Goldstein building, we note that the old rock foundation and the entire original brick wall are still visible. The concrete walkway was formerly an uneven, brick sidewalk.

★ ★ ★

The next building was the Fire Hall. That edifice of splendid Italianate architecture with its stone quoins and galleried tower was also the City Hall prior to the time the City Hall was located in the old Cumberland Presbyterian Church building (D-127) in the late 1920s. The Fire Hall had housed the old steam fire engine and horses before the department became motorized during the late teens of the twentieth century.

At twenty-three years of age, Buck Qualls was probably the youngest Fire Chief in the State of Tennessee. Buck had been a member of the Fire Department and was made Chief in 1924. That was a position he was to hold for forty-eight years. Buck seemed to possess natural leadership abilities. Reticent and aloof, he commanded the respect and cooperation of the men who served under him. He was about 5'10" in height and looked well in his Chief's uniform, which always seemed to be freshly cleaned and pressed. Chief Buck Qualls retired in 1972 and died in 1988.

When a fire was reported at the Fire Hall, an alarm was signaled in the boiler and engine room of the Christy and Huggins Ice and Bottling Works on what was then the Manchester Pike. The engineer on duty would promptly blow the large brass steam whistle which could be heard over the entire town. There was no more eerie and ominous sound when it released its low throaty notes at midnight and gradually eased into a treble clef and then receded back to the deep sound again. The whistle would summon all of the members of the Fire Department who were not on duty at the Fire Hall. It would also awaken even the deep sleepers in Murfreesboro. Lights could be seen coming on in the houses up and down the streets and people would look about to see if there was a red glow in the sky.

In the early 1930s, a new Fire Hall was built on the corner of East Vine and South Spring streets. Ed Morris and a Mr. Sneed established a new automotive concern in the old Fire Hall. They held the dealership of the Willys-Knight and Whippet automobiles for Rutherford County. The Whippet car was the forerunner of the Willys Jeep of World War II fame. Ed Morris later held the Plymouth dealership and was located on West College Street during the 1930s. His wife was the late Mary Nelle Morris, who was a well-known feature writer for the *News Journal.*

The partnership of Sneed and Morris was short-lived. The Willys-Knight and Whippet cars were not to enjoy a wide acceptance. John Valley White ("Po Boy") promptly leased the newly vacated building for use as a restaurant on the spacious lower floor. "Po Boy" was now able to fold up his tent and leave the sawdust floor location on Mink Slide. He carried his "nothing over a nickel" reputation with him and soon was doing a landslide business. White people would enter the front door, and colored people would enter from the left side or Vine Street entrance. The business flourished for awhile, even though some said that "Po Boy" was still adding sawdust to his large hamburger and sausage sandwiches.

"Po Boy" recognized the value of publicity and had a flair for new innovations. He decided that a flagpole sitter would do the trick. In those days, people were trying to set records in almost any endeavor. There were dance, rocking chair, staying awake, kissing, walking, bicycling, flying, and all sorts of other marathons going on over the nation. "Po Boy's" flagpole sitter would set a new record for flagpole sitting and Murfreesboro would become famous as the place where it had happened. As is so often the case, the best-laid plans of mice, men, and flagpole sitters oft go awry. For some unremembered reason, the sitter chose to go or was ordered down from his perch on top of the flagpole after three or four days.

However, the tenacious "Po Boy" was not to be deterred. Loud-speaking public address systems were not very common in those days, especially a system whereby the voice or music could be clearly audible in a radius of four city blocks. "Po Boy" procured four large horn-type speakers and mounted them in his galleried belfry high above the street. The system was an immediate success. From the moment "Po Boy" turned the switch and increased the volume, he knew that everyone off, on, and approaching the Square would know about his business. However, his restaurant did not become inundated with customers as expected. In fact, there was a rumbling about town that was not coming from his loud speakers. Instead of soft, mellow, pleasing-to-the-ear music, his speakers were blaring forth harsh, strident music and songs that were often punctuated with piercing, static noises. The climactic event occurred about two weeks after the system was installed. It was Sunday morning, and church services had commenced. Suddenly, the four horns that pointed in four directions atop "Po Boy's" belfry burst forth in raucous songs that carried through the roofs and ceilings of the Baptist, Church of Christ, Methodist, Presbyterian, and Episcopalian churches. "Po Boy's" publicity campaign was an eminent success. For some unaccountable reason, the horns came down from the belfry the following day.

"Po Boy" soon left the erstwhile City Hall, Fire Hall, auto dealership, and restaurant building. Little Tommie Wrather and his family were to be the new tenants. He would continue the nickel hamburger tradition. Little Tommie was not much over four feet tall, but his head and chest were quite normal in size. His wife, daughter Mattie Hall, and son-in-law assisted in the business. After a few years of successful operation, they moved across the street to another location (C-115). The Goldsteins purchased the old City and Fire Hall building from the city in the early 1940s. The building was demolished, allowing Goldstein's to expand all the way to Vine Street. A passer-by can distinguish today the demarcation line between the new expansion and the old brick building that was erected at the turn of the century.

★ ★ ★

Our walk down South Church Street continues across Vine Street. On the corner (B-101) was the firm of E.P. Leach Buggy Company. Mr. Leach kept a few buggies in stock during the late 1920s but seldom made any sales. He augmented his business by making personal loans. Mr. Leach was occasionally in his office, but left most of the management of his business to Mr. Dallas Cook.

★ ★ ★

Next door and westward of the Leach building on Vine was a grocery store that was operated by a Mr. Willard (B-107). Later that building was occupied by Lamb and Watkins Coffee Company. The latter partner was Norman Watkins, who at the time of this writing is residing at a Shelbyville nursing home. The company imported the raw coffee beans from Central and South American countries and processed its own blends in roasting ovens. The pleasing aroma of coffee emanated on the Square five days a week.

★ ★ ★

It is time now to turn around and walk back to the corner of Vine and South Church streets. We turn right and walk about seventy-five feet to a blacksmith shop. My memory goes back to a time frame when there were some horses and a pony tied to a rail in front of the shop. A tall, muscular man was hammering on a horseshoe which was held by a pair of tongs on the anvil. The blacksmith's name was Mr. Fann. His face and arms were an unnatural tan which resulted from long hours spent above his flaming forge. Mr. Fann had two helpers who were busy working on buggy and wagon wheels. The spotted pony at the rail was mine. Her name was Lady, and she was missing one shoe. The other three shoes were well worn. Mr. Fann would charge $1.00 for putting four shoes on the pony. The shoes would last three to four months.

★ ★ ★

The next building southward was a small restaurant and ice cream shop operated by Tom Brown and his brother Dan. The two brothers were Seven Day Adventists and they celebrated the sabbath on Saturday. In those days, all ordinary businesses were prohibited from opening on Sunday. However, because of their religious beliefs, they were allowed to open on Sunday.

The Browns were very popular men among the kids in Murfreesboro. They froze their own ice cream, and, furthermore, they peddled their ice cream up and down the streets of the town from a horse-drawn wagon. For a nickel, one could buy a heaping cone of vanilla, peach, strawberry, or chocolate ice cream. It should be mentioned here that most kids seldom handled any coin of a larger denomination than a nickel.

In about 1930, Frealin Qualls occupied that building with a restaurant. Frealin was Buck Qualls' brother. The location was considered most strategic, since it was directly across South Church Street from the hosiery mill. The mill's employees had only a half-hour break for lunch, so they had to dash in, eat, and dash out. Frealin, his wife, and helpers would anticipate the needs of their customers and could usually have the food in place when the whistle across the street blew. The Qualls enjoyed a successful business there for several years. When the Veterans Administration Hospital opened in the late 1930s, Frealin was chosen to be the head chef of the kitchen at the facility.

★ ★ ★

For three decades, the Sunshine Hosiery Mill was considered the number-one industry in Rutherford County. It far surpassed other local industries in dollar value of production, number of employees, scarcity of seasonal lay-offs, working conditions, and employee relations. It was considered a real privilege to obtain a job at that place. If a person could claim that he or she worked at the hosiery mill, that person could obtain credit at most any store in town.

Francis Garant and his father, who lived in Nashville, founded the mill directly after World War I. They originally were to manufacture hosiery from long staple cotton. They had wholesale jobbers throughout the United States and Canada who sold their product nationwide. In 1924, the Sunshine Hosiery Mill had a daily production of 12,000 pairs of hosiery of fine gauge and quality. The mill was equipped to do its own dyeing and bleaching. It employed more than two hundred people, and its operating expenses were $2,500.00. Those were post-war boom years, but even during the Depression years the mill continued to prosper, and soon its work force numbered almost five hundred employees. An observer could easily imagine how much of a boon the mill was to a town that boasted a population of slightly more than eight thousand people in 1930.

A new employee at the mill in 1924 could expect to earn the much-appreciated sum of $7.00 for a 70-hour work week. Later, the working hours of each employee were reduced and a three-shift eight-hour working day was initiated. In those years, there were two familiar sounds heard all over town: the arrival and departure of steam locomotives at the depot, and the punctual steam whistle at the Sunshine Hosiery Mill when it blew at 7:00 a.m., 12:00 noon, and 5:00 p.m. Lest the reader be shocked at the low wage of $7.00 per week, it should be explained that a husband and wife could live quite well on a budget of $2.50 to $3.00 per week for groceries.

By the close of the 1920s, the mill began the manufacture of the newly-developed rayon hosiery and anklets. That was followed shortly thereafter by the mill's expansion to a full-fashion department, which involved the manufacture of silk hosiery. The silk was obtained from Japan. The change from rayon to silk proved to be immensely successful and resulted in a large increase in the work force and a huge increase in the salaries of those who worked in the new full-fashion department. I recall that, in 1936, Leon Bowles, who worked in that department, purchased a new Air-Flow Chrysler, which was almost at the top of the line for luxury automobiles in that time.

The Sunshine Hosiery Mill made another great transition at the beginning of the 1940s when it began the manufacture of the newly-developed nylon hosiery. Mr. Francis Garant, in 1930, had obtained the services of a German whose name was Max Waller. It was he who set up the full-fashion department that year and maintained it into the 1940s.

It was indeed a far cry from the cotton hosiery in the 1920s to nylon in the 1940s. Only a woman could appreciate the vast difference between the two kinds of hosiery. Lucky was she who could find a pair of nylon hose during World War II.

The mill continued to prosper for a short while after the second World War. It began to decline in 1948 and began a succession of layoffs which continued until the Sunshine Hosiery Mill was closed in approximately 1952.

Thus fell the curtain upon what was Murfreesboro's most important industry for one-third of a century. Thousands of employees had been financially rewarded during an economic period in which there were seldom, if any, options as to where a job could be found. Perhaps more importantly, those people had gained a level of self-respect that could not be measured in dollars and cents. Then, of course, there were the great financial benefits that filtered down to the cash registers, banks, professions, trades, rooming and boarding houses, and the general population of the town.

Jess Jernigan, who was a long-time employee at the mill, related that reunions of past employees of the Sunshine Hosiery Mill were held for several years. He states that they have not held a reunion for four years but that there remains about two hundred former employees. Jess is eighty-seven years of age and appears to be in good health. He claims that the days are not long enough for him to do all the things that need to be done. His memories about the mill are sharp and nostalgic.

The mill was sold at public auction around 1954 by auctioneer Clyde White. Whitney Steagall and Richard LaRoche were the attorneys who had closed out the affairs of the mill. When the hammer fell on the sale of the property, the law partnership was the new owner. Whitney Steagall has been the Chancellor of Rutherford County since 1974. He retired today, August 31, 1990, the date of the writing of this page. Richard LaRoche is still quite actively engaged in his law practice.

The mill was leased to a shirt manufacturing firm which operated about three years. That was an unsuccessful operation, and the mill was closed again. Shortly thereafter, the property was sold to Rutherford

Properties, which was headed by Dr. Carl Adams. The last vestiges of the old mill's building were destroyed when the construction of First City Center was begun in 1987.

City Hall and the Fire Department in 1925. Young fireman second from left was "Buck" Qualls who was soon to become Fire Chief, probably the youngest Fire Chief in the state.

City Hall and Fire Department on corner of South Church and West Vine Streets in 1934. From left to right: Orman Benson, Arlie Prater, Winfrey Vaughn, Assistant Chief Johnnie Gray, City Manager Sam Cox, City Recorder and Judge William M. Draper, Fire Chief "Buck" Qualls, Hollis Qualls, James "Snooks" Baxter and Homer Gray.

Sunshine Hosiery Mill, circa 1923.

E. MAIN
JORDAN HOTEL
PRINT OFF. I.O.O.F. HALL
OFFICE
PAINT SHOP
DRUGS
MEAT
TIN SMITH
COBBLER
PLUMBLER
EPIS. CHURCH
S. CHURCH
S. SPRING
E. VINE

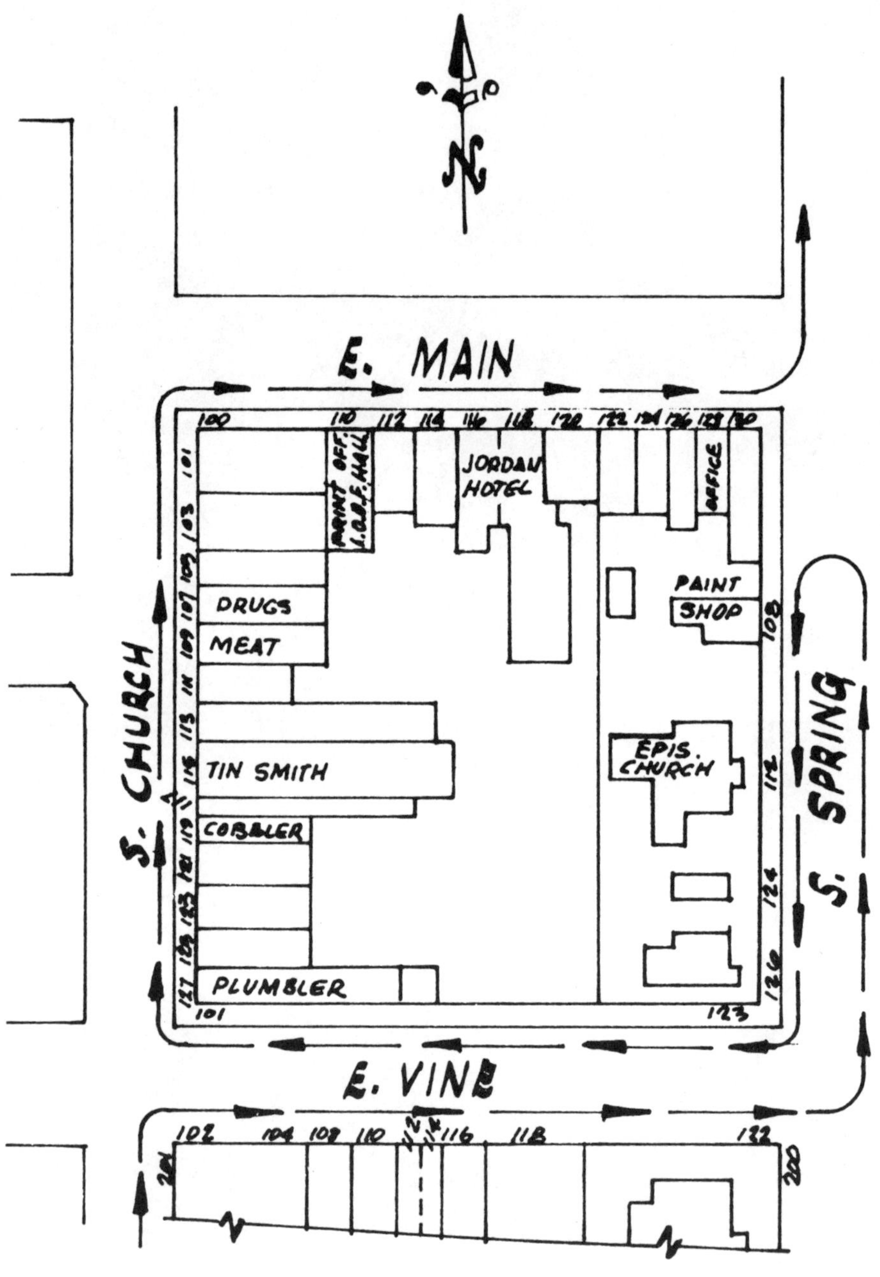

SECTION - C

Chapter VII

East Vine—South Spring

The two-story brick building on the corner of East Vine and South Church streets (C-102-104) was quite old in 1924. It had recently been bought by the Sunshine Hosiery Mill from the heirs of Adam Bock, a German immigrant.

Goodspeed's *History of Rutherford County* reports that Bock was a manufacturer of superior carriages and buggies at the time of the history's publication, which was in the 1880s. Adam Bock was born in Hesson-Darmstadt, Germany, February 8, 1833. He learned the carriage-making trade from his father. In 1851, he arrived in New York City and shortly went to Louisville. He worked at his trade for eight years in that city and moved to Murfreesboro in the spring of 1860. He enlisted in Company I of the First Tennessee Infantry, which is reported to be the same regiment in which Sam Davis served.

Bock was discharged in the summer of 1865. In November of that year, he became engaged in the manufacture of carriages in company with others under the name of Osborn, Bock and Company. Another partner in the concern was George Walter, who had recently arrived from Germany. The partnership existed for fourteen years. In 1879, Bock purchased the interests of his partners and operated the business until his death in 1916. His son, John Adam Bock, continued the business until the building was sold to the hosiery mill in the early 1920s. John Bock and his family had a residence around the corner from Vine on Spring Street, where he operated a small shop in his back yard. I recall that he repaired a pony cart axle for me in about 1929. The axle required a new left-hand thread on one side, and he was the only craftsman in town who carried left-hand dies of the necessary size. The charge was fifty cents.

Shortly before the auction of the Sunshine Hosiery Mill, the mill owners sold the Vine and South Church Street corner (Bock buggy factory) to attorney John J. Jewell at private treaty. Mr. Jewell renovated the two-story building to produce store space on the first floor and office suites on the second level. Attorney John Rucker occupied one of the suites until he moved into a new office complex on the north size of the Square. The Tennessee Department of Employment Security occupied one section of the bottom floor of the building. Milton Tolbert recalls that they moved from here in 1962. The Music Shop, owned by Joe Van Sickle, occupied the other portion of the bottom floor. Marvin Burton purchased the business and remained for several years until they were apprised that the First City Center was going to occupy the entire block. The Music Shop moved to the old Woolworth (Fred's) building on the east side of the Square in 1988.

★ ★ ★

In 1924, the next building eastward along East Vine Street was used for auto storage (C-108), and the next location eastward was a blacksmith shop (C-110). That shop (C-110) later was the bicycle repair shop which was operated by H.P. Morton. Mr. Morton had formerly operated on the south side of the Square and had moved here in 1926. He was a tall, angular man of dignified appearance and always wore a tie. One would think that he was capable of a higher calling than the operation of a bicycle repair shop; however, there was a large number of bicycles in Murfreesboro in those days. Most of the retail shops used bicycles for deliveries, and it was still one of the favored modes of transportation for many people. My father's business used three bicycles for deliveries, and usually one of those was in the shop. His monthly bicycle repair bill amounted to $25 to $35. Mr. Morton supervised the bicycle repair, but most of the work was done by a helper.

The most prized bicycle then was an Ivey Johnson, which sold for $40 to $50. The next in popularity but not necessarily in sales was the Blue Grass, which was distributed by the Belknap Hardware Company of Louisville. It was a heavier bike, having two crossbars from the seat to the handlebar post. Both of these bicycles used the Morrow rear wheel brakes (front wheel brakes were yet to come), which seemed to be superior to the New Departure brake. The Elgin was next in popularity and probably accounted for more in sales than any of the rest. It was distributed by Sears, Roebuck and Company, and was listed in their catalogue for $26 to $30 for the 28-inch model. It was available with either single or double bar seat to steering post and carried the New Departure brake.

When H.P. Morton went out of business in the middle 1930s, an important era in personal transportation ended. C.C. Henderson in *The Story of Murfreesboro* relates that the velocipede (tricycle) was introduced here in 1870. The old fair association featured velocipede races, advertising by flaming posters that young ladies would participate in the events. The posters represented "the girls dressed in blouses and bloomers of red, their hair flowing in the breeze and a wildly cheering crowd encouraging them in their wonderful flight."

The high bicycle or "penny farthing" was introduced about 1880. It had a wheel about five feet high in front and a small wheel about twelve inches in diameter in the rear. The next type was the solid-tired low wheel, and later the pneumatic wheel. The bicycle craze was at its height in the 1890s. Mr. Morton's bicycle repair business began to fade in the early 1930s, and he vacated the building.

Cawthon's Tin Shop moved to that location from a building just south of present-day Aultman's Jewelers. More will be written about Mr. Cawthon when the shop he occupied in 1924 is reached.

★ ★ ★

Charlie Clark bought both locations (C-112 and C-114) in the early 1930s. He was a long-time merchant in Murfreesboro. He first appears in this space with the firm Farmers' Produce Company. His main thrust was chickens and eggs which involved the purchase from local growers of that kind of produce. He sold to the local retail and restaurant trade. Later, Charlie leased a portion of the vacant lot across Vine Street, where he began to trade in hides and junk metals. In 1939, he sold the building (C-112 - C-114) to Roscoe Brown, who has been mentioned earlier as a partner with R.H. Smith in the firm of Smith and Brown Tin Shop, situated one block westward on Vine. Carl Brown, Roscoe's brother, recalls that Charlie sold the building to Roscoe for $10,000. The tin shop moved to a new building on the corner of Spring and Sevier streets in 1956. The business grew and eventually began to install heating and air conditioning units. Roscoe's son Gary grew up in the business and took over the reins of operation in 1984. His successful business is now located on Commercial Court Street.

Charlie Clark moved to the southeast corner of South Church and Vine streets. During the 1940s, he built a new building and warehouses on several acres on Hilliard Street. With that move, he relinquished the produce business and changed the name of the firm to Clark's Iron and Metal Company. Charlie Clark served several terms as a City Councilman. Charles Harvey Clark, Jr., died in 1963. His son Charlie Clark III took over the firm and continued to increase the volume of business. He passed away in 1987. Again, there was a son familiar with the operation and ready to take over the helm. This was Charles Harvey ("Chuck") Clark IV. Clark Iron and Metal Company is functioning very well under the leadership of "Chuck" Clark. This young businessman has recently become the father of a son who was named Charles Harvey Clark V.

★ ★ ★

Ed Morris, who has been mentioned previously as an automobile dealer, began to occupy C-116 during the early 1930s with a Studebaker dealership. In the latter 1930s, Ed moved to West College Street, where he operated a Plymouth dealership. While on Vine with the Studebaker dealership, Ed employed Ralph Odom as shop foreman.

Ralph, who was Dr. Eugene Odom's oldest brother, attended an automotive engineering school in Kansas City as a young man. Sometime after his graduation, he opened an automotive repair shop. Immediately after World War II, he accepted the Kaiser-Frazer dealership. Mr. Kaiser, of ship building fame during the war, seemed to have all the qualifications to successfully manufacture and market automobiles, but the Big Three in the industry did not have much empathy and liking for another competitor. The post-war Tucker died aborning. The Packard Motor Car Company, which used the famous slogan "Ask the man who owns one" discontinued the operation shortly after the war. Studebaker met its demise in the early 1950s.

Kaiser manufactured several thousand of the Kaiser and Frazer cars, and the country's first compact car, the Henry J., and established a nationwide network of dealers. Those cars were widely acclaimed and accepted by the public, but there was not enough room for another auto maker. Possibly, if Kaiser had had Lee Iacocca, he may have made it.

★ ★ ★

The next two buildings (C-116 and C-118) were quite spacious and were occupied in 1924 by Dr. G.B. Giltner, a veterinarian. Giltner was mayor of Murfreesboro from 1910 through 1918, and was followed in that office by N.C. Maney, 1919-1922, and Al D. McKnight, 1922-1929.

Mary Bryant Giltner was Dr. Giltner's daughter. She had a great love and appreciation for horses. Dr. Bob Womack recalls that B. Giltner was considered the finest equestrienne in the entire South during the 1930s. Bob accompanied his father to the horse shows in those days. He remembers that she exhibited gaited Kentucky saddle horses in preference to Tennessee Walking Horses. In the late 1940s and 1950s, she began showing harness horses in the roadster-to-bike class. Possibly because of her age, she felt more confident in the seat than in the saddle.

Dr. Womack remembers that she continued actively showing horses after she had passed the age of seventy. He says that even in her post-seventy years, she was a beautiful woman. Mary Bryant Giltner passed away recently. She probably was awarded more prizes at horse shows, and promoted the industry more than any woman in history.

Dr. Giltner used the smaller building (C-116) as his office and also as a place for the treatment of small animals. The large building (C-118) next door had been used as a livery stable at an earlier time. The doctor later used the area for housing the animals which he treated.

Attorney William H. Woods was born, reared, and attended the schools in Murfreesboro. We were in the same graduating class at Central High School in 1935. When the local National Guard was called to active duty in 1940, Capt. William H. Woods was an officer of his unit. At the end of World War II, Bill began the practice of law in Nashville. After almost forty-five years of successful practice in the legal profession, Bill retired last year. He has kept well acquainted with the affairs and changes in Murfreesboro and enjoys reminiscing about people and places.

Bill remembers that his father, Dr. Sam H. Woods, occupied the two buildings on East Vine Street following the retirement of Dr. Giltner. There was another veterinarian in town during the late 1920s and 1930s.

His name was Dr. A.C. Topmiller, who was located on West Main Street. The doctor had the double distinction of being the state veterinarian and of holding the rank of Captain in the National Guard.

Dr. Woods was known throughout the county as "Mr. Democrat." He was also respected for his outspokenness. Dr. Sam was a busy man with his practice, his political affiliations, and his active participation in harness racing at local fairs. His youngest son, Sam H. Woods, followed in his father's professional footsteps. He joined his father in the practice. They eventually located on West Lytle Street between Haynes Candy Company and the old Red Rose building.

Dr. Sam Jr. enjoyed a successful practice for many years, retiring two years ago to reside in Hawaii. For several years, he was involved in a partnership with Tom Givan in the curing and marketing of Tennessee country hams.

The space (C-116) originally occupied by Giltner and later by Woods became a furniture store operated by Ed Crockett. Ed began his operation about 1940 and continued into the early 1960s. Following his occupancy, Ollie Adamson's wife operated a restaurant there.

The space (C-118) became the home of Stump's Gas and Oil Company in the early 1930s. O.M. Stump was an affable, rotund man, who always seemed to be calm and relaxed. He operated a discount gas and oil station, which involved the transportation of his gasoline in his own tank truck. There were three grades of gasoline in those days—traffic, regular, and high test. The lowest octane fuel was traffic at 12¢, regular at 14¢, and high test at 16¢. A customer then expected free services such as windshield cleaning, and tires checked as well as the oil and water. Mr. Stump augmented his income by renting a portion of his building to the James K. Polk Hotel for the storage of guest automobiles. In addition, he supplied a pick-up and delivery service for the hotel patrons.

In about 1955, Mr. Stump retired from the business. His son Thompson ("Tommy") had been raised up in the business. He subsequently began a successful operation on Broad Street, popularly known as Tommy's Esso. He is presently enjoying retirement. Upon Mr. Stump's retirement, Gene Thompson began a rug cleaning business there (C-118) which continued until the entire block became the new First City Center in 1987.

★ ★ ★

On the corner of East Vine and South Spring streets was a frame dwelling (C-122) which had a continuous porch fronting on both Vine and Spring. It was the residence of Dr. G.B. Giltner and his family for almost all of the first quarter of the present century. Fire Chief Buck Qualls and his family were the next occupants of that house.

★ ★ ★

Across the street on the northwest corner of Vine and Spring was the frame residence (C-126) in which Sam Lasseter and his older brother,

Bob, spent their earliest years with their mother. Sam Lasseter appears later when the Sovran Bank is reached on these pages. Sam was born in 1912.

"Cap" Ransom followed them at that residence. Mr. Ransom had suffered paralysis in his early years, which required him to be confined to his bed or wheel chair. During the summer months, a Negro man pushed "Cap" in his wheel chair to Buchanan-Tarpley Drug Store on the east side of the Square. With a cap on his head and a blanket over his legs, he would hold court on the sidewalk with his friends who were accustomed to congregate at that place. "Cap" had a wire frame with a loop on one end which was around the index finger of his right hand. The other end of the wire supported a cigar which "Cap" could easily insert into his mouth and remove with a slight movement of his index finger. Even with his affliction, Mr. Ransom always seemed to be in excellent spirits and had an ever-present smile. The property was purchased in the 1960s by the Commerce Union Bank, and the house was destroyed.

★ ★ ★

Next door (C-124) was a brick residence which was built about the turn of the century. Attorney Granville Ridley, Jr., bought the house during the late 1940s, converting it to a law office. Later, in 1952, his nephew Granville Sumner Ridley "Buck" Bouldin joined him there in the practice of law. Before Mr. Ridley arrived, the brick house was the home of Harry Cohen and his family. He was the Cohen brother who was a partner in the Cohen Department Store already mentioned.

The Ridley name has been prominent in the annals of Murfreesboro for more than one hundred and fifty years, especially in medical and legal professions. Granville Ridley "Buck" Bouldin occupied the building until 1987, at which time the Sovran Bank bought the site. The building was demolished and now the bank and its parking lot occupy the eastern half of the entire block. Mr. Bouldin moved his practice to a building on the east side of the Square.

★ ★ ★

The next site northward on Spring (C-112) was occupied by the St. Paul's Episcopal Church, which was consecrated in 1897. In 1926, the church building was moved to its present location in the 300-block on East Main. The move was considered quite a project in those days. After the frame structure was mounted on its new foundation, a new veneer of Sewannee stone was used to cover the exterior walls. It may be well to mention at this point that the present location of St. Paul's Episcopal Church was formerly occupied by the congregation which now meets as the First Baptist Church, just a block up the street.

Near the end of the 1930s, an imposing structure of Greek Revivalist architecture was erected on the former site of the Episcopalian Church. This was the new Medical Arts Building, which was to house the offices of a succession of doctors until 1978, when the Commerce Union Bank bought the property. Shortly thereafter, the building was

St. Paul's Episcopal Church as it appeared on North Spring Street in 1909.

St. Paul's Episcopal Church as it appears in 1991.

demolished. During its more than thirty-five years of occupancy, Drs. John Cason, W.T. Robison, J.A. Scott, Jack Yearwood, Kenneth Kaufmann, Ben Patton, Carl Young, Lois Kennedy, C.C. Harris, and Ron Wright were among the distinguished tenants of the Medical Arts Building.

Before the construction of the Medical Arts Building, there was a small brick building just north of St. Paul's Episcopal Church (C-108). It was the small electrical repair and fix-it shop that was operated by Will Coleman. He was a tall, quiet, and mechanically talented man who always seemed to feel inclined to accommodate all who entered his shop, even a kid like me who could have but little money to spend on Mr. Coleman's fix-it abilities.

Possibly the reader should be reminded here that our armchair tour of the Murfreesboro Public Square and its immediate environs is in the time frame of 1924, sixty-six years ago. In most cases, the writer attempts to project the reader forward through the time of Ed Bell's observations and occasionally up to the present. With this reminder, we do an about face in front of Will Coleman's shop and walk southward along Spring Street past the St. Paul's Episcopal Church, past the brick house that was to become Granville Ridley's and "Buck" Bouldin's offices, and turn right on Vine Street at "Cap" Ransom's house. Behind his house, there was an entrance to a large vacant lot which provided a rear service entrance for most of the businesses contained in the entire square block. The lot also served as a convenient space for people to park their buggies and wagons, especially on Saturdays when this type of space was at a premium.

On the right of the entrance, there was a large advertising billboard owned by "Otho" Cannon. Mr. Cannon owned most of the billboards in and around Murfreesboro. Later, and on the death of Mr. "Otho," the business was transferred to Robert Lasseter, who operated it until the late 1970s. Bob was a prominent newspaperman during his earlier years and was a great admirer of Ed Bell. Bob was instrumental in marketing Ed's last book, *The Lonely People,* as well as some of his earlier works such as "Fish on the Steeple" and "Tommie Lee Feathers." He was intensely interested in Linebaugh Library, serving as its chairman for a number of years. Bob was the older brother of Sam Lasseter, of whom more will be written later.

Past the billboard and near the corner building on East Vine and South Church streets, there was a large vacant lot fronting on East Vine. That area was owned by the Spence heirs. Margaret Greene, one of those heirs already mentioned, states that they leased to certain individuals who wanted to construct six stores on the property. Jess Allen, a plumbing contractor, was one of those individuals. Six small store buildings were erected in 1946. With the addition of those stores, the Spence heirs then owned twelve stores in the southwest quadrant of this block that was bounded by East Vine, South Church, East Main, and South Spring streets.

★ ★ ★

George Campbell states that the original tenants in the new stores were Hicks Neal Meter Service, Economy Auto Store, Jess Allen Plumbing Company, Rutherford County Farmers Co-op, B and W Tobacco Company, and Ruel Auberry Grocery Store. George occupied the Economy Auto Store. The well-known Luther Myers was one of his employees. In 1948, the business moved to a larger space below Aultman's Jewelers, where the Sunshine Health Store is now located. Hicks Neal later moved his business to a large building which he built on West Burton Street. In the late 1970s, the Commerce Union Bank bought the two end stores eastward (C-119 and C-121) from the Spence heirs. The two stores were demolished, permitting the bank to have an ingress and egress on Vine Street. There are now four stores in the complex. The present tenants are United Rubber Workers, Local 779 (C-117), Foster Watch Repair (C-115), Adkins Television (C-113), and Sam Weaver's Barber Shop (C-107). Foster's Watch Repair and Adkins Television have been long-time occupants of their respective stores. Bill Barrett was formerly an employee of "Pud" Adkins. Upon Mr. Adkins' death, Bill bought the business.

Among the several tenants who have been in business in the interim between the original occupants and the present are the Will Hall Grocery Store, Rutherford Hospital Thrift Shop, Murfreesboro Antique Shop (owned by Allie Clark Westbrooks and Minnie Lee Adams), J.C. Mason Furniture Company, Edith Carter Restaurant, John DeGeorge, Jr., Restaurant, and Eura Wilson Floor Service.

Chapter VIII
South Church—Southeast Side Square

East Vine Street is left behind as we mentally round the corner and begin the trek up South Church Street. All of the buildings in that block date considerably before the turn of the century. At least two were built around 1820. The first (C-127) was occupied by Edwards Plumbing Company. Plumbing was relatively a new service in 1924. The majority of the houses in town were still without indoor toilets. However, most of the houses were served with running water. There were several neighborhoods that were served by a community water faucet.

After Edwards Plumbing Company, there came a succession of grocery stores to that location. First, there was C.B. Arnold, who later operated a nursery on East Main Street. Then there was Blankenship Grocery, followed by Miller's Grocery Store, which was owned by the Becton and Westbrooks partnership. They sold the store to Ike Reed. Hollis Westbrooks recalls that Ike operated the first self-service store in town. He kept his perch on a stool behind the cash register from where he cheerfully informed his customers where his merchandise was located. If a lady customer requested a certain amount of side meat, Ike would hand her a knife and point out where the meat was stored. Then there came Harrell Grocery Company (C-127). In 1948, my father, C.B. Arnette, moved his business (C-109) to that store. He went into semi-retirement in 1949, after having been in the meat business for thirty years.

Later, a new business operated by a new partnership had its beginnings there. This was the firm of Batey's Camera and Office Supplies, which was owned by Hollis Westbrooks, Tom Batey, and Arthur Cranker, Westbrooks' son-in-law. The business prospered. Eventually, Tom Batey bought the interests of his partners and moved to a new building constructed by those partners on South Spring Street. The new building housed both Batey's and the B and W Tobacco Company. Today, Tom Batey and his son Teb own and utilize the entire building in their operation of Batey's Camera and Office Supply Company.

Next came Baldwin's Appliance Company to the C-127 location in 1972. Baldwin required more space than the one building afforded, so he rented the store next door (C-125). On October 29, 1990, Mike Baldwin moved his appliance business to the Jackson Heights Shopping Center.

The store at (C-125) was occupied by Minor Bragg's *Rutherford Courier* in the early 1930s. Mr. Bragg moved his newspaper from Woodbury, thus beginning a successful business that is still underway after sixty years. In the early days, he initiated circulation drives which offered cash prizes to those who brought in certain numbers of subscriptions. Also, the *Courier* advertised on its pages that subscriptions would be traded for turkeys, hens, and other produce. Soon the business outgrew those quarters and the presses were moved to a building behind the old Commerce Union Bank on East Main Street. The *Courier* was a folksy newspaper, a paper that was never noted for taking the middle of the road, especially in the field of politics. Minor Bragg was a civic-minded man who spearheaded many drives that greatly enhanced the town of Murfreesboro.

John Burkhalter came to that store (C-125) with a variety store which specialized in shoes and eventually surplus goods obtained from army surplus and other sources. In November, 1990, Annette's Restaurant expanded from the one building (C-123) into the two additional spaces (C-125 and C-127) just vacated by Baldwin's.

★ ★ ★

The building (C-123) has been occupied by a restaurant for sixty-seven years. My relatives, whose names were Ben, Hall, and Leslie Arnette, opened a restaurant there in 1923. In about 1931, my aunt, Mrs. W.E. (or "Miss Bessie") Shipp, opened Mrs. Shipp's Coffee Shop at that location. She remained there until about 1950, at which time she moved to a location in the 100-block of East Main Street. My aunt had two sons, Hodge and Kenneth Shipp. Hodge died prematurely of a heart attack in the early 1970s. Kenneth became coach of the New York Jets in the late 1970s. Ken recalls that, when his mother had the Coffee Shop on South Church, they depended to a large extent on the hosiery mill trade. Mrs. Shipp was a good restaurateur. With her unique personality, quality food, and quality service, she ran a successful business in each of the locations in which she operated. She will appear later in this account.

At about the time Mrs. Shipp left her place (C-123), my uncle Lytle Arnette and his wife, Marguerite, began their own restaurant there. They named it the L and M Cafe after the initials of their first names. Lytle had been an employee of the Sunshine Hosiery Mills for about twenty-eight years. They, too, operated a successful business, retiring in 1973, after twenty-two years at that location (C-123).

Now Annette Patterson is continuing the sixty-seven-year restaurant tradition that the place has acquired. It is probably a record for a restaurant to remain so long in the same location in Murfreesboro.

★ ★ ★

Until Frank Gardner with his Murfreesboro Printing Company moved to (C-121), the place had housed a grocery store at least since 1924. At that time, "Sook" Dill operated a grocery there. Hollis Westbrooks recalls that Mr. Dill had painted a large inside sign that read "In God we trust, all others cash." Mr. Dill was a man of versatile talents. He was also an auctioneer, a sign painter, and later operated a restaurant. Mr. Finley came to that place when "Sook" Dill discontinued his store there. He advertised that he carried Plain and Fancy Groceries.

In about 1930, W.A. Davis came to that building. Mr. Davis, his wife, and two sons had just moved to Murfreesboro from Lewisburg. Mr. Davis was a good grocer. His wife and sons, W.A., Jr., and Tommie, assisted in the store, thereby keeping salary expense down and within the family. He later moved up the street to where Sunshine Health Center is presently located.

After W.A. Davis, there came O.A. Lamb and his son Ewing to (C-121). Mr. Lamb had served his apprenticeship under Charlie Jetton, who had no peer as a tutor in how to make money in the grocery business. Oddly enough, none of those grocers, from "Sook" Dill through O.A. Lamb, used cash registers to contain their receipts. All of the owners and clerks made change and deposited the cash in the pockets of their aprons. There was a tall, pot-bellied stove in the center of the store around which the customers and walk-ins congregated. The stove was mounted in a square box which contained ashes. The ashes alleviated the need for cuspidors. Mr. Lamb followed the old Charlie Jetton tradition of running leader-specials each weekend such as bulk lard, cigarettes, and other staples. For many years, he was the only grocer who carried salt fish in his stock. It was a small lake herring that was headless and was kept packed in a brine solution, all contained in a fifty-gallon wood barrel. The Lambs also specialized in many kinds of garden seeds and slips for spring planting. Mr. O.A. Lamb died in the mid-1960s, and his son carried on the business until the last of the 1970s. With the closing of that store (C-121), the Square witnessed the passing of the last traditional old-style grocery in town.

The firm of Murfreesboro Printing Company has been well known in the town for many years. It was operated for many years by John Bonner, who had worked for the *News Banner, News Journal* papers during the 1920s and 1930s. When he retired, the new owner became Frank Gardner.

★ ★ ★

The next building northward (C-119) was a store of average width, but a partition was installed which allowed two businesses to be contained. In 1924, there was a paint store there (C-119A). When the paint store moved, Della Plunkett brought a millinery store to that space in the latter 1920s. Later there came Eddie Fleming and his wife, who operated a restaurant there for several years. Sula and Moody Lamb followed the Flemings at the place and remained successfully there until the 1950s, when they moved to a new restaurant out on East Main Street. Presently, that space is occupied by Latrice's Creations and Sewing by Floria Jean.

Probably the best known sportsmen in Murfreesboro were the brothers Henry Cannon "Red" and William Grayson Shearin. They operated the Electric Shoe Shop in the half-building (C-119B) beginning in 1923. They fished and hunted avidly in a day and age when few businessmen in town took time to engage in such activities. The two shoemakers were well-liked and respected by their many customers and friends. They closed the Electric Shoe Shop in 1960 after thirty-seven years. "Red" Shearin had a son whose name is Larry, who is approaching retirement age in Homosassa, Florida. William Shearin had a daughter, Mary Ann, and a son, Fred. Presently that space (C-119B) is occupied by the Christian Science Reading Room.

★ ★ ★

Charles R. Cawthon owned the next two buildings (C-115, C-117) up the street in 1924. He had a tin shop there and did a flourishing business during the 1920s. With the Depression, there came an almost abrupt halt in the construction business. Mr. Cawthon had reached retirement age and elected to vacate the two stores. Both were quickly rented, as were all of the buildings in the Square area, even during the Depression era and into the late 1950s. Charlie Cawthon served on the Murfreesboro City Council several terms.

Mrs. W.E. Shipp began her venture into the restaurant business in the narrow confines of (C-117). It was only twelve feet in width, permitting only a counter, space for stools, and a narrow aisle for the waitress. Since her expectations were not very high, she did not bother to name the place. The year was 1929 or 1930. "Miss Bessie" opened the business with a total capital of forty dollars. She permitted me to work there on Saturdays and during the summer months as both a waiter and short-order cook.

When she moved later to another location (C-123), there followed a procession of tenants to the small space. A barber shop operated by Faulkner Barnes was the tenant who perhaps stayed the longest. Kenneth Ayers, who now has a shop on the Lebanon Road, was one of the four barbers who worked with Faulkner there in the late 1950s and early 1960s. Later there came a book and card shop operated by Mrs. J.V. (Grace) Thomas, who was the mother-in-law of George Campbell. The Eddie Arnold Record Shop followed Mrs. Thomas. Nowadays, the space is occupied by the Wayne Griffith Clock Works. Wayne formerly worked as a typewriter and adding machine technician at Batey's Office Supplies. He became interested in clock collecting and repairing as a hobby. Soon the demand for his services was so great that he decided to devote full time to this interesting occupation.

When Charlie Cawthon left his two stores (C-115, C-117) in the early 1930s, there was another small partitioned section in the front portion of (C-115). That was occupied by little Tommie Wrather and his daring nickel-hamburger restaurant. We encountered Tommie earlier, as the occupant of the old Fire Hall across the street. Tommie was small, his business space was small, but his hamburger could stand up to the best hamburger in town. On Saturdays, his place was so busy that most of his customers had to stand up while being waited upon.

★ ★ ★

Morris Hoover moved his furniture store there to occupy the whole of (C-115). In the 1940s, he was joined as a partner with Roy Newsom who had heretofore operated a radio repair shop. The store was then styled as Hoover and Newsom Furniture Company. Roy Newsom was the brother of the well-known Alice Newsom Ray, who has been so closely connected with Cannonsburgh and the Rutherford County Historical Society.

George Campbell's Economy Auto Store followed Hoover and Newsom in that store (C-115). George has been mentioned earlier in his store around the corner on Vine Street. He wanted more visibility and larger quarters for his business. The highly visible and popular Luther Myers followed George to the new location.

The Sunshine Health Center has been the occupant of that store for many years. This store offers such unique services as reflexology, polarity, and therapy.

In 1924 and for several years, Charlie Jetton ran his cut-rate and popular grocery store in the building then designated as (C-113). Former Mayor Hollis Westbrooks was introduced to the Square at that place, as well as O.A. Lamb. W.A. Davis promptly moved his grocery business up the street (C-121) when Charlie vacated the building during the early 1930s. Mr. Davis retired from business soon after World War II. His son Tommie continued there in the grocery business until the mid-1950s. At that time, he chose to own a franchise for the operation of a Ben Franklin store at this same location. He later sold the store and began another business in Smyrna.

Later, Hazel Jakes Jetton, another popular restaurateur in Murfreesboro, outfitted a new restaurant at that location (C-113). She later sold the business to Hampton McClanahan and his wife, Sallie, who had operated Mac's Truck Stop on Broad Street several years earlier.

Mary Beth's Fashions occupied this space for awhile before Steve Davis brought his Steve's Antique and Pawn Shop to this location in 1984. Steve reports that about ninety per cent of his business is involved in the buying and selling of jewelry.

The next two store spaces are probably the oldest structures on the Square and possibly the oldest building in Murfreesboro. The two stores (C-109 and C-111) were believed to have been built around the year 1810. They both have a common roof and a single, thick, brick, dividing wall which would indicate that the entire structure was built at the same time by the same owner. According to John Cedric Spence, who kept a diary of Murfreesboro from 1829 to 1870, most every building around the Square burned at one time or another, especially during the 1840s. Even the courthouse fell prey to the burning propensity.

According to an article in the May 12, 1912, issue of the *Home Journal*, the building was erected in 1810 by Jonathan Currin, who, with several partners, conducted a general merchandise business therein for a number of years. Prior to 1912, the building was occupied for awhile by the Parton Meat Market. A remodeling was being done at that time so that the building could be used by a motion picture company.

Excerpts are given below from the rather long journal article printed in 1912:

> ... Currin had to go to Philadelphia to purchase nearly all the various supplies for his store, for he handled all of the "latest" things of that period. He went to the Quaker City annually and, it is said, he always made the journey on foot. The goods would be shipped by crude boats to Nashville and overland to Murfreesboro.... It cost 25¢ to convey a letter from Philadelphia to Murfreesboro.... An interesting relic found in this old building was a letter written to the elder Currin by his son just a short time before the battle of New Orleans, January 8, 1814. The younger Currin wrote of the impending conflict as if he was full of trepidation and beseeched his parent to pray for his safety. The young Volunteer (it was during this war with Great Britain that Tennessee was given the perennial sobriquet, the "Volunteer State") was with Old Hickory in the Crescent City when his troops gave General Packenham and his "redcoats" what Paddy gave the drum. Young Currin emerged from the battle safe and sound, returned to Murfreesboro, and was for a number of years associated with his father in business here.... The timbers of the old building, erected 102 years ago, are white oak, hewn by hand with broad-axes and in a perfect state of preservation, as, also, are the walls, which were made of brick, sun dried and kiln burned.... There are none living today who remember the old house, and its associations, in its infancy, but possibly there may be some of the descendants of Jonathan Currin who will read this story with more than passing interest....

Back to the present, it is interesting and gratifying to note that some of the descendants of Jonathan Currin are reading this story eighty-nine years later with more than passing interest. Some of them remain in Murfreesboro. They are: Kate Currin Mifflin, Mary Kathryn Murfree, Al C. Mifflin III, Robert Bell Mifflin, Matt B. Murfree III, and Robert Bell Murfree. Kate Currin Mifflin and Mary Kathryn Murfree are great, great, great-granddaughters of Jonathan Currin, the builder of the two stores (C-109 and C-111).

Those two addresses are now occupied by Aultman's Jewelers and Mid-South Sewing Center. Many well-preserved records and accounts with dates as early as 1818 were found in the common attic above the two stores in 1932 by this writer.

Sam Burnett operated a barber shop (C-111), where Aultman's Jewelers is now located. Sam's oldest son was one of the barbers in the shop. His next son, Bryant, became one of the mid-state's most popular magicians. He was in great demand at schools, conventions, and other public events for many years.

Aultman Sanders was to move his Aultman's Cheerful Credit from the corner of South Maple Street and the south side of the Square (B-27) in 1931. As mentioned earlier, his business was owned and sponsored by Goldstein's.

Mr. Sanders would have been an asset to any community. A veteran of World War I, he was a captain in the local National Guard. Low in stature and big in humor, he could speak with authority as the occasion demanded. He was the scout master of our local Boy Scout Troop 105. He was an accomplished bass soloist, singing in his church choir. He was the lead soloist in the local black-face minstrel show. His "Ole Man River" performance always drew much applause. His wife was the talented violinist, Ruby Taylor Sanders. He actively managed the jewelry store until he passed away in 1955.

From its beginning, March 9, 1929, and for many years, the business was called Aultman's Cheerful Credit. Lacye Welchance came aboard almost at its inception, and is still very much aboard after sixty-one years. She can rightfully claim first in longevity on the Square, first lady of the Square, or matriarch of the Square. She is actively engaged every day in the management of the business. To this writer, she is just as alert and personable as she was more than sixty years ago.

Lacye Welchance first appeared on the Square in 1928 as a clerk at F.W. Woolworth's five-and-ten-cent store. Shortly thereafter, she worked as a sales clerk for Shacklett, Staley, and Sanders. David Goldstein admired her sales abilities and hired her to accompany Aultman Sanders as the Cheerful Credit Store was launched. There she has remained.

Miss Lacye can tell many tales of young couples she helped get started on the sea of matrimony when they purchased first the engagement and then the wedding rings. She states that in those days the business never required a credit report. What was required was one-third down plus one dollar per week. Their business was the first in Murfreesboro to begin weekly installment sales. No interest was charged. The store in its early years carried jewelry and inexpensive ladies' ready-to-wear dresses and coats. The dresses sold in the range of $7.95, $12.95, and $15.00, with none over $20.00. The engagement and wedding rings ranged from $69.75 to $200.00. Seldom did a ring sell for as much as $200.00.

Miss Lacye recalled to mind an erstwhile familiar character on the Square whose nickname was "Apple John." The black man was much admired by all the people on the Square. Tall, dressed in a black overcoat even on hot days, unshaven, with a dark, felt hat perched at an angle on his head, he was often given to quoting Scripture. His favorite was the verse, "It is not what goeth into a man but what cometh out." Since "Apple John" was Miss Lacye's favorite of the many characters on the Square, it is thought appropriate to refer to him here.

Lacye Welchance's husband, Vernon "Slim" Welchance, died in 1990. He had worked as a traffic clerk at the Sunshine Hosiery Mills almost from its beginning until the day it closed. As this is being written, Miss Lacye is still running a successful business.

★ ★ ★

Before my father opened his meat market on Mink Slide in 1923, there was only one meat market in the Square area. The owner of that enterprise was R.E. Bragg. His shop (C-109) was next door to what is now Aultman's Jewelers. Hogs, cattle, sheep, and goats were slaughtered locally and were sold through those two markets. Most of the slaughtering was done about two miles out on the Franklin Road in a building located on the bank of Stones River.

In about 1928, packing houses in Nashville began selling meat in Murfreesboro. The little slaughter house west of town soon became obsolete. My father moved from his store on the south side (B-19B) in 1930 to the location on South Church Street (C-109) when Mr. Bragg closed his business. This was to be C.B. Arnette's Meat Market and Grocery until 1949.

Ennis Harris and his wife established a new business there (C-109). They called it the Fabric Center. They carried a well-stocked inventory of piece goods and dress materials. Following Mr. Harris, Art Cranker, who was Hollis Westbrooks's son-in-law, operated a stationery store there for several years. Then Billy Henson came there with his office supply business. The name of the new business was Hasco. Billy and his wife operated there for about twenty-five years. When they vacated the building, Marion Bean, who operated the New Home Sewing Machine Center next door (C-107), leased the store (C-109) in order to expand his growing operation. The larger business is now styled Mid-South Sewing Center. The names New Home, Singer, and Bernina are painted in large letters across the mid portion of the two buildings.

The City Drug Store occupied the next building (C-107) toward East Main during the early 1920s. B.B. Kerr owned the business, and the pharmacist was Stanley Thompson. The Kerr family has been prominent in the annals of Murfreesboro throughout the ninety years of this century. Mr. Kerr was active in the drugstore business from almost the beginning of this century until his death in 1949. He was chairman of the County Board of Education for twenty-four years. That was when Central High School was located on North Maple Street where Middle Tennessee Electric is now located. Colonel Kerr (he was a colonel on the governor's staff) was popularly known by every boy and girl at Central.

Whenever the school won an important football game or accomplished some spectacular feat, the Colonel would visit Central, mount the stage, and appear before the suddenly assembled and cheering student body. They knew what was about to happen. With a few preliminary remarks, he would announce a holiday for the rest of the day. Colonel Kerr would have won any election that depended on the votes of the students at Central High. During the latter part of the 1920s, he moved his drugstore two doors up the street (C-103). Mr. Kerr was the father of three sons and one daughter: Fred, Ben, B.B., Jr., and Elizabeth.

When the City Drug Store moved, H.M. Tutt established a grocery store there which was quite large for Murfreesboro in the 1920s. It was a bustling business during the time it was there, but it suffered the bug-a-boo of several Murfreesboro stores in those Depression years. It had too many non-paying credit accounts. Mr. Tutt's credit customers for the most part would have paid their charges but simply just could not make ends meet in those distressing times. It seemed that the grocery stores and gasoline service stations were the first to feel the crunch at the scarcity of money in those days. Many stores were forced to operate on a cash only basis. For H.M. Tutt, it was too late. In later years, he was to remark that he was broke a year before he knew it.

Chapter IX

Southeast Side Square—East Main (Southside)

Lewis and Estelle Brinkley came to the store (C-107) in the early 1930s and remained until about 1950, at which time they moved to a new store on the corner of Tennessee Boulevard and East Main. They did a flourishing business during their entire business career. Homer Harris was head of the meat department for many years. Lewis and Estelle Brinkley were accommodating people. They worked hard and followed good business rules.

In the 1930s, Lewis had three colored porters who delivered all of the market orders on bicycles, as did most of the other grocery stores about the Square. The chief porter was called "Beef." Actually, he was the chief of all the porters on the Square. "Beef" was ebony in color, barrel-chested, of medium height, had big eyes, and generally had his way about town. During the hot "dog days" of August, when all was still around the Square and there was no noise except the whirring of the ceiling fans in the stores, "Beef" would come pedaling on his bicycle and singing one or the other of the two popular songs, "Lazy Bones" or "Stormy Weather," at the top of his voice.

Their son, Lewis Brinkley, Jr., organized an orchestra in his later high school days. The band became popular and played throughout middle Tennessee for several years.

Murfree and Donald O'Brien followed the Brinkleys to that store in 1950. Donald was a silent partner in the grocery and meat enterprise but assisted his brother at busy times. O'Brien's Market became a popular institution on the Square and did a thriving business. They remained there until 1970, when Murfree retired from this business. He had bought some commercial property on Memorial on which he had built a large store to be leased to Frank's IGA. He has since developed that property to include other stores which are leased to individuals.

Then came Marion Bean to that place, which had for many years served as a grocery store. At first he called his business the New Home Sewing Center, but with the acquisition of the space (C-109), he changed the name as previously stated. It should be noted here that the James Maney estate owns five buildings (C-107, C-113, C-115, B-119A, and E-16) on the Square.

There were four Italian families on or about the Square during the time frame in which Ed Bell strolled from Mink Slide to Main Street, making his interesting and pertinent observations. The forerunner of those interrelated families was Sam DeGeorge. As a young man and new arrival to these shores, he recognized that America was indeed the land of opportunity and freedom. He quickly realized that by hard work and frugal living, he could support a family, live comfortably, and share the American dream. Not only did he want those advantages for himself but also for his wife-to-be and other close relatives. For almost two decades, he worked tirelessly to bring those other relations to America and particularly to Murfreesboro. Through his efforts, four families of industrious, frugal, colorful, and patriotic citizens became established in similar businesses on and just off the Square. Near the close of his days (he died in 1947 at the age of 70), he must have received a joyful satisfaction in seeing those families successfully and happily ensconced in Murfreesboro.

Sam DeGeorge was twenty-two years of age when he arrived at the port of New Orleans from Cefalu, Italy, in 1899. Cefalu was a small town near Palermo. Sam was small in stature, had very little money, and had no English-speaking ability, but he did have a wealth of initiative, ambition, and a desire to work hard. This he did. After some odd jobs around New Orleans, he obtained a manual laborer's job on the railroad. By some good fortune, he arrived in Murfreesboro in 1904.

With still only a smattering of English-speaking ability, Sam opened a small fruit stand in the building which now contains Shacklett's Studio (C-103). He did quite well in the new business, working long hours and living simply in the large quarters above the store. He wrote his younger brother, John, in Cefalu to come help him in the growing business. John DeGeorge arrived in 1907.

In 1909, Sam decided that he could afford a wife and that he could leave the business in the hands of his brother while he returned to his home town from which he had departed ten years before. There, he met and married Rosa Tamburo. He brought his bride back to Murfreesboro, where they resided above the store. Their first son, Vincent, was born in 1910, and the second son, Tony, was born in 1911.

In the meantime, John married Clara St. Charles of Nashville in 1910. They, too, joined Sam, Rosa, and their expanding family in the large area above the fruit stand. John and Clara named their first child, born in 1911, Vincent. During that year, Sam had his brother join him as a partner in the growing business. That arrangement lasted until 1913 when the partnership was dissolved. Sam moved to the location (D-122) which is now occupied by Granville S.R. Bouldin and his son, Sumner, attorneys at law.

The year 1913 was a momentous one for the Sam DeGeorge family. The immigrant from a small Italian village must have felt that he had reached the zenith of the American dream when he purchased a recently-built spacious brick house on North Spring Street. It was one of the finest houses in the north section of Murfreesboro. However, Sam and Rosa did not rest upon their laurels. They wanted more of their relatives in Italy to follow them to the small town in the heart of Tennessee. More about those aspirations later.

John and Clara DeGeorge with their two-year-old son Vincent now had the store (C-103) with the large upstairs living area to themselves. Clara was to bear two more sons, Mike and Johnnie. Vincent and Mike are presently residing in Nashville and Johnnie resides in Chattanooga. Johnnie was a distinguished and much decorated fighter pilot in World War II. As a boy in grammar school, Johnnie had a knack for beating the base and snare drums. After the war, he used this talent to become a member of some of Nashville's most noted orchestras. Later he became president of the Musician's Union in Nashville.

When Rosa DeGeorge left Cefalu, Italy, in 1909 for America, she left, among her relatives, a younger brother whose name was Andrew Tamburo. Andrew came to Detroit in 1915. After working there a short while, he joined the Army and served until the Armistice in 1918. Sam and Rosa DeGeorge invited him to visit them in Murfreesboro. True to form, Sam could always find a place in the store for a relative, so Andrew was soon working for his brother-in-law.

In 1919, Andrew met Grace Meshotto of Nashville, who was Sam's niece. They were married shortly thereafter and began living with the DeGeorges in their spacious brick home on Spring Street. In 1920, Andrew found a restaurant that was for sale in Tullahoma. Sam loaned him $1,000.00 to close the deal, so Andrew and Grace Tamburo then owned their own business. In 1924, they decided to rejoin their relatives in Murfreesboro. The Tamburos purchased a building (D-121) on East Main Street, two doors west of the old Cumberland Presbyterian Church (D-127, D-129), which later became the City Hall. Andrew and Grace had two children whose names were Tony and Stifanina.

In later years, Andrew was to buy three other buildings in the same block on East Main. Those are now occupied by the City Cafe (D-107), the Pipe Shop (D-109), and the Palace Barber Shop (D-111).

Sam DeGeorge still had other relatives in the hometown of Cefalu, Italy. His sister, Concetta, had married Joseph Meshotto. To that union, the following children were born: Dominick, Grace, Clara, Mary, Vance, and Sam. Sam's sister, Concetta, and those six children arrived in Murfreesboro in 1926. In 1927, they began the operation of a restaurant on the corner of College and Maple Streets (F-125).

Sam DeGeorge was a small man in physical stature, but the bigness of his heart, made him a towering figure in his love and concern for his family and relatives. Through his efforts, the Italian element on and about the Square now comprised four families or twenty individuals.

The next building (C-105) is owned by the John DeGeorge estate. It has a longevity period of ownership by the same family of seventy-eight years. The reader may recall a previous page on which it was stated that Sam DeGeorge originally owned that building, took John as a partner in 1911, and sold his interest to John in 1913. Johnny and Clara DeGeorge retired in the early 1960s, moved from their balconied apartment on the Square to a house on Spring Street, and have since passed from the scene.

Shacklett's Photography now occupies that building. Dick and Ginny Shacklett have passed the business to their daughter, Gloria Wilson, and their son, William H. Shacklett. Dick and his wife are now in the background but still wander in. Their studio has been one of the foremost photography shops in Murfreesboro. Dick became famous in the photographic world back in the early 1950s when he snapped a once-in-a-lifetime picture of a speckled trout leaping through beaded drops of water for a fly lure. He has brought imagination, skill, and vision into a profession at which he has excelled. Gloria and Bill are carrying on the business with real artistry and with their own charisma. Gloria was Festival Coordinator of Uncle Dave Macon Days, Inc., from 1984 through 1991. She is now president of the corporation that manages the most popular annual celebration in Rutherford County. Bill began assisting his father in the photography business in the early 1970s.

★ ★ ★

James K. "Cap" Clayton owned the next building toward East Main (C-103) in 1924. His estate still owns that property in 1990. It housed the well-known firm of Kerr and Martin Drugs for many years.

As mentioned earlier, Col. B.B. Kerr moved his drugstore business (C-107) to the location (C-103) in the late 1920s. His pharmacist, Stanley Thompson, accompanied the move. Also, Frank Martin, a pharmacist, entered into a partnership with the Colonel. The firm was then called Kerr and Martin Drug Company. The partnership was to last until 1949, when Col. B.B. Kerr died.

Attorney John Rucker recalls that he tended the soda fountain there during the summer of 1933. The drugstore had a stationary canopy above the sidewalk. Every year on election night, there would be an election party in front of the store. Traffic was cut off from this portion of the Square, allowing hundreds of people to gather on the street to observe the election returns. Above the sidewalk canopy was a large blackboard about 12 feet by 12 feet on which votes were posted as they arrived from the precincts, counties, or states, depending on which election was being held. After Col. B.B. Kerr died, Frank Martin continued the business under the new name of Martin Drug Company.

During the late 1960s, the Commerce Union Bank leased the former drugstore building from the James K. Clayton estate. The building underwent extensive renovation to comply with the expanding bank needs. During the late 1970s, the bank demolished that building, the bank building, and all of the other buildings fronting on East Main Street in the 100-block on the south side. The James K. Clayton estate still owns the site on which stood the drugstore. The empty lot is still leased to the Sovran Bank.

★ ★ ★

The Commerce Union Bank came to Murfreesboro in 1924. It located on the corner of East Main and South Church streets (C-101). In 1924, there were four banks in Murfreesboro. Eight years later, there were only two: the Murfreesboro Bank and Trust Company and the Commerce Union Bank. Jim Jetton was the bank's first manager and remained in that position until 1928. Harry Carter succeeded Jetton that year and remained manager until 1949. In that year, Sam Lasseter became chief executive officer of the local Commerce Union Bank. He retired from his position in 1978 to become chairman of the bank's board of directors. Sam was born in 1912, was president of his senior class at Central High, and was quarterback of Central's football team. For awhile, he ran the soda fountain at Jack's Cafe, which will appear later. Sam began his sojourn with the Commerce Union in 1935. He went into the armed forces in 1942 and returned home in 1944. At that time, he was appointed assistant cashier of the bank.

Sam was asked the amount of total deposits when he assumed the reins at the bank. He stated less than one million dollars. What were the total deposits when he retired as CEO? About $100 million. What was the amount of interest that the bank paid on savings? Two percent. What amount of interest did borrowers pay? Six percent. On secured loans, the rate of interest was four percent. Sam explained that the Commerce Union raised the amount of interest paid on savings in 1962 to four percent. During the recession years around 1978, the bank paid fluctuating rates of fourteen to sixteen percent on savings. The rate charged to borrowers varied almost from day to day from sixteen to nineteen percent. Those were hectic times in the banking industry.

Among those who were so prominent in the operation of the bank were Miss Sue Thompson and Oswald Edmondson. Miss Sue was assistant to Sam Lasseter and Oswald was head of bookkeeping. Those two individuals made important contributions to the popularity and success of the bank.

John Pierpont Morgan appeared before a Senate Investigating Committee on December 18, 1912. He was asked what did he look for most in a prospective borrower from his banking firm. Expecting him to respond with the obvious answer, security or the applicant's ability to pay back the loan, committee members were surprised to hear him say the one word "character."

In my conversation with Sam on this matter, I knew that he had been confronted with this question thousands of times. I asked what was his rule of thumb when a person applied for a loan. Although expressed in different words, Sam responded with almost the same identical answer that J.P. Morgan had given seventy-nine years ago. He said that he asked himself whether the person would "run under a rock" when the going got tough or was the person of the "right stock." Sam knew almost everyone in town and was acquainted with their backgrounds. Apparently his often snap judgements must have worked, as is evidenced by the successful operation of the bank under his leadership. Sam Lasseter is now seventy-eight years of age and shows no signs of retiring from his active ownership of Wayside Inn and other properties.

The Commerce Union Bank housed several attorneys' offices on its second floor. Among those over the years who occupied those offices were Eugene Holloway and his three lawyer sons, Eugene, Jr., John, and Wiley. Gene died prematurely in the 1940s as the result of an automobile accident. John Holloway served as Mayor of Murfreesboro during the late 1940s and early 1950s. Wiley served as Circuit Judge for several years.

Winston Price was an associate of John Holloway in the late 1940s. He moved to Florida about 1950. Alvin Collins occupied his office above the bank probably longer than any other attorney. When the building was demolished in the late 1970s, he moved to the Clark House in the 300-block on East Main Street. This venerable lawyer has always been a courteous man. He dressed immaculately, wore a Homberg hat, and drove a 1948 model Packard into the 1980s.

Even the basement of the bank was income-producing property. A set of steps on the north side of the building descended to the Tip-Top Barber Shop. There, P.W. Carter was the chief barber. There were three other chairs in that tonsorial parlor manned by Ed Price, Howard Bridges, and Roy Wilson.

Nothing now remains of that building which once housed an institution that was so intimately involved in the economic lives of so many people on the Square and in Rutherford County. The empty remaining lot with its artistic landscaping is the only vacant space around a Square that has been uninterrupted with buildings this century.

Around the corner and down East Main Street, the first building (C-110) was occupied in 1924 by three entities: the Tennessee Power Company; a printing company; and the I.O.O.F. Lodge, which was located on the second floor. The Tennessee Power Company remained there with an expansion (C-112) until the late 1930s when the Tennessee Valley Authority supplanted the local Tennessee Power Company. Hicks Neal, Bob Waller, and Raymond Dunn were some of the chief executives in the electric office. Minor Bragg moved his *Rutherford Courier* paper into the location (C-110) which was vacated by the power company.

★ ★ ★

The space (C-112) was later leased by the power company as a place to display electric stoves and refrigerators. People in town were then switching from ice boxes to refrigerators. Most of the first ones on the market had a condenser mounted on top with ammonia gas as the refrigerant. Freon gas was to appear several years later.

"Put's" Place occupied that space (C-112) for several years. "Put" was a short rendition of his full name, Putnam. For some of those years, the owner called the business Put's Bar-B-Que Place. "Put" moved to Chattanooga during the 1950s. He was the father of the well-known Margaret Putnam, who was associated with the Home Economics Department at MTSU for several years.

★ ★ ★

The next space (C-114) housed the Tip-Top Barber Shop, which was headed by W.A. Rushing. Mr. Rushing was an enterprising man who became involved in a subdivision development while continuing his profession. The development was Rushwood in the present post office area. He built several houses there during the early 1950s. Among some of the barbers who worked there were Hall Todd, Elgin Lowe, and Joe Davidson. The latter barber bought the shop from Mr. Rushing, remained there for about one year, and then moved to a building on College Street near the Murfreesboro Federal Savings and Loan Company. The Commerce Union Bank had purchased the intervening buildings, thus causing Joe and his fellow barbers to move.

Eastside Square 1923.

Lacye Welchance of Aultman's Jewelers. Has been actively engaged on the Square since 1929. (Longer than any other living person.)

"Apple John" Summars. Well known personage on the Square for one half century, 1920-1970.

Sam DeGeorge in front of his business in 1906. Present site of Shacklett's Photography. Man at left was Dan Brown.

To the Central High School student body, he was the most popular man in town. Col. B.B. Kerr, President of the Rutherford County Board of Education and long-time prominent druggist.

Sam Lasseter

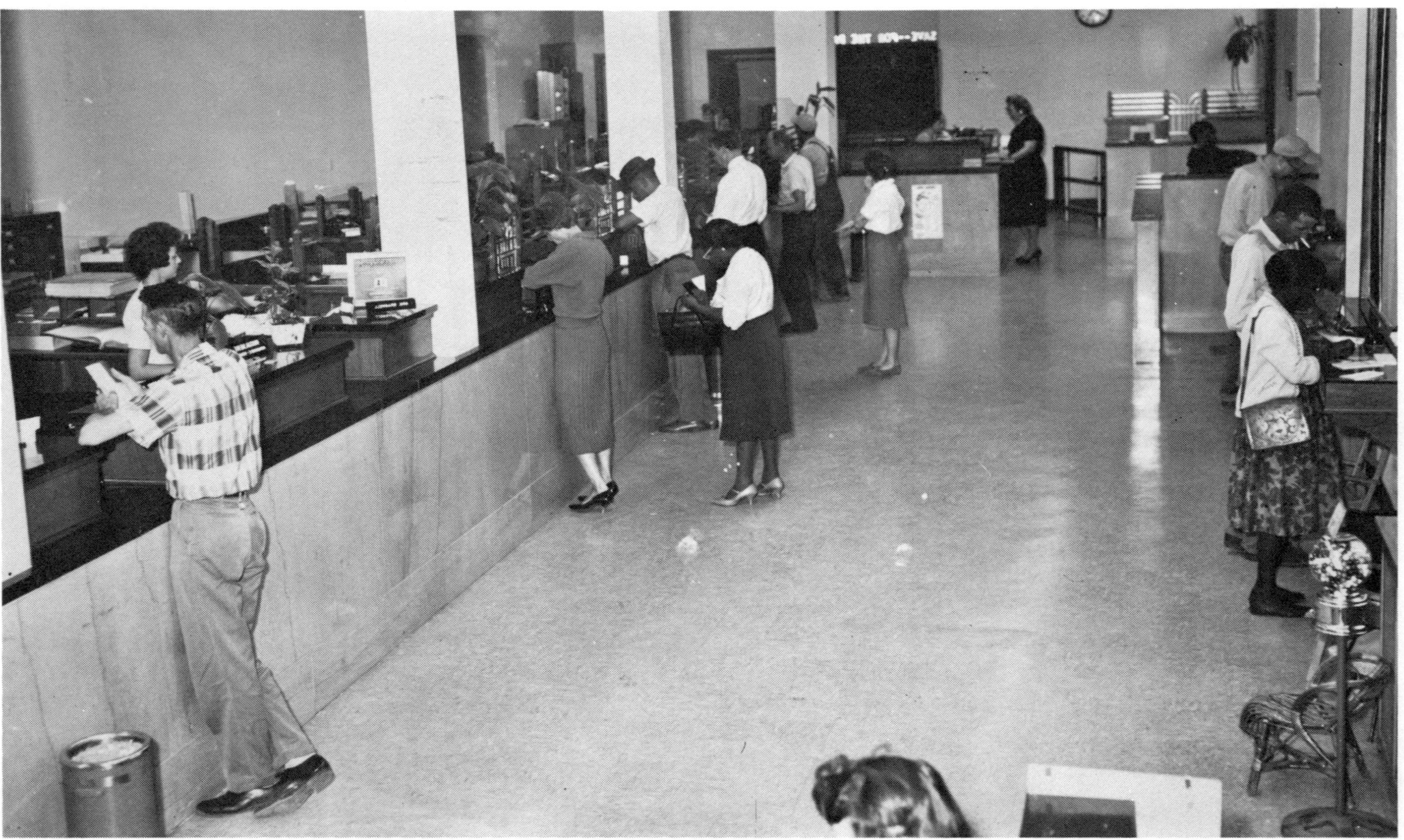

Interior of Commerce Union Bank, circa 1955.

Chapter X

East Main (Southside)

It was a notable social event that occurred on the evening of December 14, 1862, at the mansion of Col. Charles Ready. The Ready mansion came later to be known as the Ready House and finally as the Jordan Hotel in the 100-block on East Main Street.

Under the date line of August 31, 1912, Gen. Basil W. Duke of Louisville recalled to a *News-Banner* reporter his memories of what was probably the most widely attended and celebrated wedding that had ever been held in Murfreesboro. The participants were Miss Mattie Ready and the dashing cavalry commander of the Confederate Army, Gen. John H. Morgan.

The following excerpts from the interview with Gen. Basil Duke about this merry and joyous evening are presented below. In seventeen days, one of the bloodiest battles of the Civil War would commence only two or three miles from the scene of the wedding.

> ...General Morgan met Miss Martha Ready while his command was on duty around Murfreesboro, after Johnston's army had gone to Shiloh. Later he participated in Bragg's Kentucky campaign, then returned to Tennessee and laid siege to the heart of the beautiful Tennessee girl with all the dash and brilliancy that marked his career as a total capitulation was announced and the marriage was announced for December 14.

The bride received one of the most novel wedding presents in history. Just a week before the wedding, her soldier lover fought the battle of Hartsville, and captured 2,100 Federal prisoners. That army of discomfited "boys in blue" came to be known as "Gen. Morgan's wedding present to his bride."

> ...All the officers of high rank who could reach Murfreesboro had assembled for the wedding—General Bragg among them. Distinguished civilians were present in great numbers...the house was packed with people to its full capacity.

> ...The house was decorated with holly and winter berries—the lights from lamps and candles flashed on the uniforms and the trappings of the officers, and were reflected in the bright eyes of the pretty Tennessee girls who had gathered.

...The raven-haired, black-mustached Morgan, in his general's uniform, looking like a hero of chivalry, the bride, a girl of rare beauty, tall, dark-haired, and blue eyes, with a creamy complexion and perfect features, and standing before them, to perform the ceremony, in his full military uniform, Bishop Polk, himself a general of the Confederate Army, and Bishop of the Episcopal Church.

...Miss Ready's bridal dress was one of her best ante-bellum frocks, for it was not possible at that time to purchase material for a trousseau.... General Duke was certain that the bride could not have worn anything more becoming. He remembers that she wore a bridal veil.... There were some pretty maids also who rivalled the bride in beauty, almost.... General Morgan's attendants were as dashing a set of young soldiers as any bride could wish at her wedding.

...Two or three regimental bands had been provided for the occasion. They were stationed in the house and on the porch, and there was plenty of music. Outside in the streets thousands of soldiers were assembled, who by the lighted bonfires, celebrated the wedding in proper style, cheering Morgan and his bride.

After the wedding there was a great supper served in the Ready mansion where the wedding party and invited guests were feasted beautifully.... Turkeys, hams, chickens, ducks, game, and all the delicacies and good dishes a Southern kitchen could produce were on the board, while Colonel Ready's cellars still had a sufficient stock of wine to provide for the many toasts.

After the wedding supper, the bands were called in and the gallant soldiers and the Tennessee belles danced to their hearts' content....

Thus ends this night of rejoicing and merrymaking, an unimaginable contrast to the scenes of bloodshed and carnage that many of those guests would witness in just a few days.

General Morgan was killed at Greenville, Tennessee, September 4, 1864. Three or four months after the death of General Morgan, a posthumous child was born to him, a daughter who was known as "Johnnie" Morgan. Mrs. Morgan afterward married Judge Williamson of Lebanon, who had been a colonel in the Confederate Army. She lived about twenty years after the death of General Morgan.

The headline of an article in the *News-Banner* one day in September 1912 read: "THE JORDAN HOTEL CHANGES HANDS." These are some excerpts from that article:

...whose fame as one of the best "country" hostelries in the land has spread to the four corners of the map was sold at public auction.... The sale was made for division among the owners,

Messrs. J.C. and Lee McDearman and Clay Reeves.... The first bid was made by "Ferd" Miles who started the property at $7,500 ... the two gentlemen continued to raise each other $500 a clip until $12,000, the bid of Mr. Love was reached and to whom the property was finally sold... Mr. Miles, the present proprietor, will continue in charge for sixty days.... Mr. Miles has had much to do with bringing the old Jordan up to its present high standard of excellence and popularity and his retirement will be regretted.

...The building which was originally a two-story brick was built in the early '50s by Col. Charles Ready, who occupied it as a residence.... The east room on the ground floor was used by Col. Ready as a law office and was the frequent rendezvous of some of the most eminent disciples of Blackstone that ever pled a case.

...Col. Ready died on June 4, 1878. The property was left to his heirs, from whom it was soon purchased by the late Edward L. Jordan, who gave it to his two sons, M.F. Jordan, who died in 1909, and Leland Jordan, now cashier of the Murfreesboro Bank and Trust Company. M.F. Jordan bought his brother's half interest and added another story to the building, remodeled and converted it to what is now the Jordan Hotel. The property was subsequently sold to David Gemmel, who in turn traded it to Jesse C. Beesley, by whom it was transferred to its late owners, J.C. and Lee McDearman and Clay Reeves.

Mr. Love, the new owner in 1912, soon sold the hotel to Ferdinand Washington Miles, the unsuccessful bidder on the day of the auction. Dr. Robert Miles, retired chief of surgery at the Baptist Hospital in Memphis, states that his grandfather, F.W. Miles, bought the hotel in about 1917 and sold it in the latter 1920s to A.V. Jordan. The doctor's father, Harry Miles, began operating the hostelry upon his return from World War I and continued in that capacity until the property was sold in the late 1920s to A.W. Jordan of the same family, who had owned the hotel in the late 1800s. Arch W. Jordan died in 1934, having willed the property to his eight children. Ernest Jordan and Minnie Huddleston were amongst these eight children, along with Ben Batey's mother. The Jordans also bought the Mason Court office building. They then owned more than one-half of the block from the Commerce Union to Spring Street.

The Murfreesboro Building and Loan Association was founded by Arch W. Jordan and his son Ernest in 1929. It was headquartered on the ground floor of the old hotel. Other offices began to move to the hotel and apartments were created on the upper floors.

Among those who had offices there over the years were Huddleston and Jones Insurance Agency, Kitty's Beauty Parlor (Sara Bell's mother), Murfreesboro Antique Shop (Mrs. Gusta Maney), the Kiddie Shop

(Annie Mary Snell Haynes), Herman Jackson Appliance Company, Knight and Shipp Appliance Company, Richard Smith's Book Store, the Production Credit Company (Deery Riggs, manager), and the Federal Land Bank (John Jarrett, manager). Cannon Maney had an insurance company there for several years. His brother, James Maney, succeeded Cannon in the agency but at another location.

After Mr. Arch W. Jordan died in 1934, his son Ernest assumed the reins of the five-year-old Murfreesboro Building and Loan Company. In 1941, the name of the institution was changed to the Murfreesboro Federal Savings and Loan Company. It moved to the ground floor of the old Putnam Overall building in about 1941; soon it occupied the whole building. More will be added later about that successful financial institution.

★ ★ ★

Past the Jordan Hotel was the large two-story office structure called the Mason Court Building. It ended at the corner of South Spring and East Main streets. It was built in 1891. For its time, that building was probably the most architecturally advanced in town. The owner was a young attorney and entrepreneur whose name was Pleasant P. Mason. Even by today's standards, one would be hard pressed to find his equal in Murfreesboro in the field of diversified ventures.

P.P. Mason was born in 1860 in Rutherford County. He graduated from Cumberland University in Lebanon at the age of twenty-one. Shortly after his admission to the bar in 1882, he began taking an active interest in local and state politics, being appointed states attorney in 1885, and at the same time was chosen attorney for Rutherford County.

One of Mason's earliest ventures in building was an opera house which was built on the west side of the Square. In 1891, he built the Mason Court Building (C-120, 122, 124, 126, 128, 130). In 1892, he was a stockholder in the incorporation of the Murfreesboro Street Railway. His fellow participants were Bromfield L. Ridley and Thomas B. Fowler. Their equipment consisted of eight cars, twenty-four mules, and about two miles of trackage. Evidently the people along the route preferred walking. The enterprise was abandoned January 1, 1894, with a total loss of $65,000 to the stockholders.

At about the same time, and seemingly without discouragement on the failure of the railway system, Mason, Ridley, and Dr. J.E. Thompson started the Murfreesboro Waterworks. This was the beginning of the present system.

In 1895, P.P. Mason started a soap factory. He made one batch of ten thousand pounds which was offered to the local merchants. At the same time, the Enterprise Soap Factory of Nashville sent their salesmen to town with soap prices of less than one-half of the amount it cost Mason to manufacture his product. The local merchants could not resist the discount price and stocked up with enough soap to last several years.

Mr. Mason laid the first sewer line in Murfreesboro. The line ran from Tennessee College under College Street and emptied into Lytle's Creek. This occurred during the 1890s.

Pleasant P. Mason would occupy a prominent place in a list of those men who have exercised the greatest influence in shaping the destiny of the town. Mary Mason, who now resides at Stones River Manor, recalls Pleas P. Mason as a handsome, debonair man of impeccable manners. Her husband, William A. "Bill" Mason, was the nephew of P.P. Mason. She recalls Pleas coming to visit them shortly after they were married in 1922. The elder Mason had a son whose first name was Richard. He served as Lieutenant Governor of Arkansas during the teens or the 1920s.

Mason Court was a popular office building from its inception, especially for the legal profession. Among the prominent lawyers who occupied offices there were Capt. Richard Beard (father of Jean Faircloth MacArthur's mother), Clarence Cummings, Alf Huddleston, Attorney General "Red" Knott, and William Wright.

Doctors who held offices here were W.T. Henderson, C.C. Harris, W.J. Sanders, J.R. Gott, B.W. Rawlins, and Dr. Norton. Sanford Cox, Horace Welchance, and Gilbert McClanahan operated the Men's Shop there for awhile. Horace Welchance was the manager of the shop.

The Cupboard Tea Room operated a restaurant there for several years. Mrs. Shipp followed the Tea Room with her Wagon Wheel restaurant. She came there in 1955 and remained there until about 1968.

The Square has been the parade ground for many celebrations during its one hundred and eighty years of history. Perhaps the most notable of these events were: (1) the dedication of the Confederate Soldier monument on November 7, 1901, (2) the Armistice Day parade November 11, 1918, (3) the celebration of the Carnation Milk plant opening in 1927 and (4) the welcome of General Douglas MacArthur to Murfreesboro April 30, 1950.

Fortunately, there is an eyewitness account of the Confederate Soldier dedication as written by William Moffitt, Jr. and contained in Bromfield L. Ridley's *Battles and Sketches, Army of Tennessee.*

The statue upon its limestone base was first erected on the east side of the court house yard with the bronze Confederate soldier facing the entrance of East Main Street to the Square. In only a few years, it was moved to its present site.

At this point in our tour about the Square, the reader is invited to reflect upon some excerpts from the poignantly interesting account of that day:

Nov. 7, 1901 — This, perhaps, was the proudest day in the history of this beautiful little Tennessee city—when a handsome monument erected by this loyal people in commemoration of the valor of the Confederate dead, whose dust now mingles in the fields of this section, was unveiled with elaborate and dignified ceremonies. Fully 3,000 persons gathered at the Court Square this morning to witness the dedication of the memorial.

Intermingled in the vast assemblage were hundreds of veterans of the lost cause, many of whom had traveled miles to be present and pay tribute to their fallen comrades.

Here and there over the big audience which surrounded the stately structure were men and women, many of them bent with age, with tears trickling down their cheeks. These tears spoke forcibly the sentiment of the people, or at least their interest in the solemn, but at the same time happy occasion. Some of the old-time Southern melodies, as rendered by a bevy of pretty young ladies from Lebanon, were very striking, and as the sweet strains wafted out over the crowd, heads were bowed in remembrance of the fallen heroes.

By far the audience was the most distinguished that has gathered in Murfreesboro in years, likely in the history of the city. In the assemblage were many prominent sons of Tennessee, including the remnants of the Army of Tennessee. They were there from Major Generals down to the Johnny Reb who carried the musket. One happy feature of the dedication was that all of the comrades stood upon an equal footing; they were all comrades in the strongest sense of the word, engaged in a love feast. Among the more prominent men who were present were: Senator William B. Bate, Governor Benton McMillin, Hon. James B. Frazier, of Chattanooga; Hon. James D. Richardson, Hon. John C. Ferriss, of Nashville; Hon. E.D. Wilson, of Nashville; Judge Frank S. Wilson, Comptroller Theo. King, Hon. N.W. Baptist, Hon. J.N. McKenzie and Dr. J.B. Cowan, of Tullahoma.

Nature smiled upon Murfreesboro for the day. The sun was shining brightly, a slight breeze afloat, just enough to rustle the Confederate flags and bunting, which were displayed in profusion over the business portion of the town. It was an ideal autumnal day.

In front of the monument Captain Richard Beard, master of ceremonies, had a large speaker's stand erected. Just over this improvised stand in a neat frame resting upon the massive testimonial of love and esteem, was the original Eighteenth Tennessee battle flag, which passed through some of the most terrific battles of the civil strife. With this flag, five color sergeants fell.

Before the ceremonies commenced the young ladies of the Lebanon Orchestra took seats upon the stand. There were Mrs. Lillard Thompson, chaperone; Misses Emma and Edna Beard, Mary Barbee, Annie Hearne, Irene Neal, Sammie Carter, Annie May Thompson, Mrs. Harry Freeland, Mrs. A.S. McDowell, and Misses Gertie Fakes, Mary Prewett and Olive Mace. Then came the invited guests, as follows: Governor Benton McMillin, Hon. James D. Richardson, Dr. J.B. Cowan, H.E. Palmer, Hon. James B. Frazier, John C. Ferriss, Gen. William B. Bate, Judge F.S. Wilson, Dr. T.A. Kerley, Mrs. J.B. Murfree, D.P. Perkins, Gen. H.H. Norman, in charge of the unveiling, Miss Julia Ransom and others.

Those to occupy places upon the stand had been seated, when Company B and Troop A, of Nashville, came marching up the wide road leading from the station. They carried their large flags, and as they fluttered in the little breeze the old "Johnny Rebs" were cheered lustily. Approaching the stand, they circled around the structure and during the ceremonies stood "at rest." They were received at the monument with a pretty demonstration, which the old comrades apparently enjoyed.

The master of ceremonies, Captain Beard, stepped to the front of the stand and presented Rev. T.A. Kerley, who delivered the invocation. He paid honor to the Confederate wives and sisters who had sacrificed their all in the vicissitudes of war and the dark days following the fall of the Confederacy. He dwelt at length upon the bravery in standing face to face with adversity and poverty during the long years of the struggle. He asked that the hand of God ever be with the noble women and guide them in their future laudable undertakings. "May they be shining lights to the whole land," he concluded.

Here the young ladies of the Lebanon Glee Club struck up a combination of stirring Southern melodies, ending with that soul-inspiring song, "Dixie." The enthusiasm of the assemblage knew no bounds. Their cheers rent the air.

Here the unveiling committee, composed of Captain Beard, Judge Richard Ransom and Captain Daniel Perkins, took charge of the exercises, assisted by General H.H. Norman. Miss Julia Ransom, one of Murfreesboro's fair daughters, arose from the center of the stand and pulled a small cord which unveiled one of the prettiest little monuments erected on a Southern battlefield. A thousand hands clapped their approval. Engraved upon the east face was this inscription:

"In commemoration of the valor of Confederate soldiers, who fell in the great battle of Murfreesboro, Dec. 31, 1862, and Jan. 2, 1863, and in minor engagements in this vicinity, this monument is erected."

On the north face is:

"Lest we forget—1861-1865."

On the west face is:

"A monument for our soldiers,
Built of a people's love."

On the south face the inscription reads:

"Honor decks the turf that wraps their clay."

Following the unveiling, the boys of the Tennessee Industrial School band played. Their work was very creditable and well received.

Captain Beard then introduced Colonel Bennett H. Young, a brilliant Kentuckian, the orator of the day. In presenting the speaker Captain Beard made a few remarks, in which he referred to the trials and tribulations of those who raised the monument fund. He said that the monument should have been erected thirty years ago, telling of the work of the old Monumental Association in the years gone by; how they raised $800 for the purpose, which was spent in the base. The work was taken up by the Daughters of the Confederacy, who, after years of constant and persistent effort, raised an additional $800, which was supplemented by $1,200 raised by the Palmer Bivouac. He said:

"There have been other monuments erected on the battlefields more gorgeous in design, but none on the face of the earth was ever erected for a higher or more noble purpose."

The master of ceremonies introduced Colonel Young, the orator, as a noble son of the Bluegrass State, which sent thousands of courageous and gallant men to aid the South, which fact, he said, was attested by the presence of their dead upon every battlefield in the West. These soldiers kept the lamps of chivalry in the hearts of many.

Colonel Young, the polished orator that he is, was at his best, and though he was at a disadvantage on account of the breeze carrying his voice toward the back of the stand, his delivery was excellent and his effort a masterpiece. He was eloquent and his frequent reference to the hallowed dead aroused the old-time enthusiasm of the Southern people gathered about him. Often his remarks were punctuated with violent outbursts of applause. He said in part:

"It is a great distinction to have been a Confederate soldier; it is a greater thing to have been a Confederate woman; it is a noble thing to have been a Tennessee Confederate, a representative of the great "Volunteer State" of the South that did so much to make the contest of the Southern people for liberty illustrious and immortal.

"Nearly forty years have passed since the great conflict was fought near to where we stand, and which today you are commemorating by this monument. It takes rank as one of the great battles of the American war. Nine thousand killed or wounded on the Confederate side—one-fourth of the entire force engaged; 8,780 killed and wounded on the Federal side, and 3,500 prisoners, speak in unmistakable tones of the fierceness of the conflict."

Here the speaker unrolled the battle-scarred jacket he wore during the war, and as he exhibited the garment, with the remark that he would rather have it known that he had worn the gray than to be the greatest king on earth, the assemblage again became demonstrative.

"Bragg's army at Murfreesboro was composed in a large measure of Tennesseans, who receded from Tennessee with a sullen and grim courage which boded no good to the foes who sought to dispossess these men of their State and their homes. Of the forty regiments of Tennesseans with him—all were ready, if need be, to die in defense of Tennessee.

"This superb monument to our dead would not have been possible had it not been for the patience and zeal, the interest and usefulness of the women, who labored so long to erect this memorial. We call it 'ours' because it belongs justly to the Confederates. I doubt not that many who helped at the inception of the undertaking have been denied the happiness of witnessing its fulfillment, but we can feel their sweet presence though they passed over the river before success crowned their work. If they are not here we shall at least in gratitude remember them and their devotion to the cause and their absence alone mars the completeness of this occasion.

"The Army of Tennessee, never the best equipped of Confederate forces, met more defeats without destruction, endured more hardships without complaint, made longer marches with less straggling, followed more unfortunate leaders with fewer desertions, showed more cheerfulness in distress and exhibited greater fortitude in disaster than any military organization known in history. It was always hopeful in misfortune, brave in action, patient in privation, valiant in conflict, constant in trials, unmurmuring in difficulties and unconquerable in spirit, and no more brilliant display of extraordinary qualities was ever shown by this wonderful army than in the battle to whose slain you this day dedicate this shaft."

Again the Lebanon Orchestra discoursed sweet music, this time "Old Kentucky Home." As this followed the speaker from Kentucky, the scene was dramatic.

The exercises were closed with the reading of a poem by E.D. Hancock, entitled, "The Southern Soldier." The poem was one of some length, and in arranging it Mr. Hancock utilized the entire inscription upon the memorial monument.

The benediction was said by Rev. W.L. Logan.

After the exercises the visitors were invited to luncheon at the homes of Murfreesboro's hospitable people. Almost every citizen of the little city was a host during the day. Some of them had three and four visitors at their homes.

The afternoon was spent by many of those from distant cities in riding through the town and visiting the various points of interest upon the surrounding battle fields. Many of the old veterans tramped the fields over the entire afternoon in effort to locate a spot they might recognize. Several of those who had not been on the field in almost forty years were successful in locating old landmarks and in all they spent a most enjoyable day. The young ladies of the Lebanon Glee Club gave a concert at the armory during the afternoon, while the Tennessee Industrial School band held forth at the public square, rendering several selections.

Tonight the Vendome Stock Company, of Nashville, played to a crowded house, this being a part of the day's festivities.

Every road in the country led to Murfreesboro this morning. Hundreds came in from the surrounding country, but the largest crowd arrived on the Nashville special. Upon this train came the Confederate cavalry troop under command of Lieutenant W.T. Hardison and the infantry company commanded by Captain Mark S. Cockrill, and the Gaines Rifles, Captain Kramer. On this train were many State officials and citizens of Nashville.

Scene at base of Confederate Soldier statue on eve of unveiling November 7, 1901. The status was first placed on east side of courthouse facing East Main Street. Note spire of Cumberland Presbyterian Church which later became City Hall.

View of East Main Street from courthouse, 1923.

Pleasant P. Mason. Foremost Murfreesboro entrepreneur at turn of century.

Men's Shop in Mason Building on corner of East Main and South Church Streets. Left to right: Neil Lancaster and store operator Horace Welchance.

Whittler's Club in the Mason Building. Left to right: Dr. Warren Garrett, Dr. W.T. Henderson, Alvis Huddleston, Dr. C.C. Harris, and Dr. Paul Lynn.

N
101
103
104
123
COLLEGE
200
100
112
POOL HALL
MILLY
UNDERT'KG
ELECT. PICTURE THEATRE
NEW ELKS HOME
TAILOR
MASONIC BUILDING
UNDERTAKING
N. CHURCH
N. SPRING
MOSBY HOUSE LATER JAMES POLK HOTEL
BAKERY
AMER. RAILWAY EXPRESS CO.
OFFICE
OFFICE
OFFICE
CUMBERLAND PRESBT'N CHURCH
DRUGS
E. MAIN
125
115
110
108
103
101
107
109
111
113
115
117
119
121
123
125
127
129

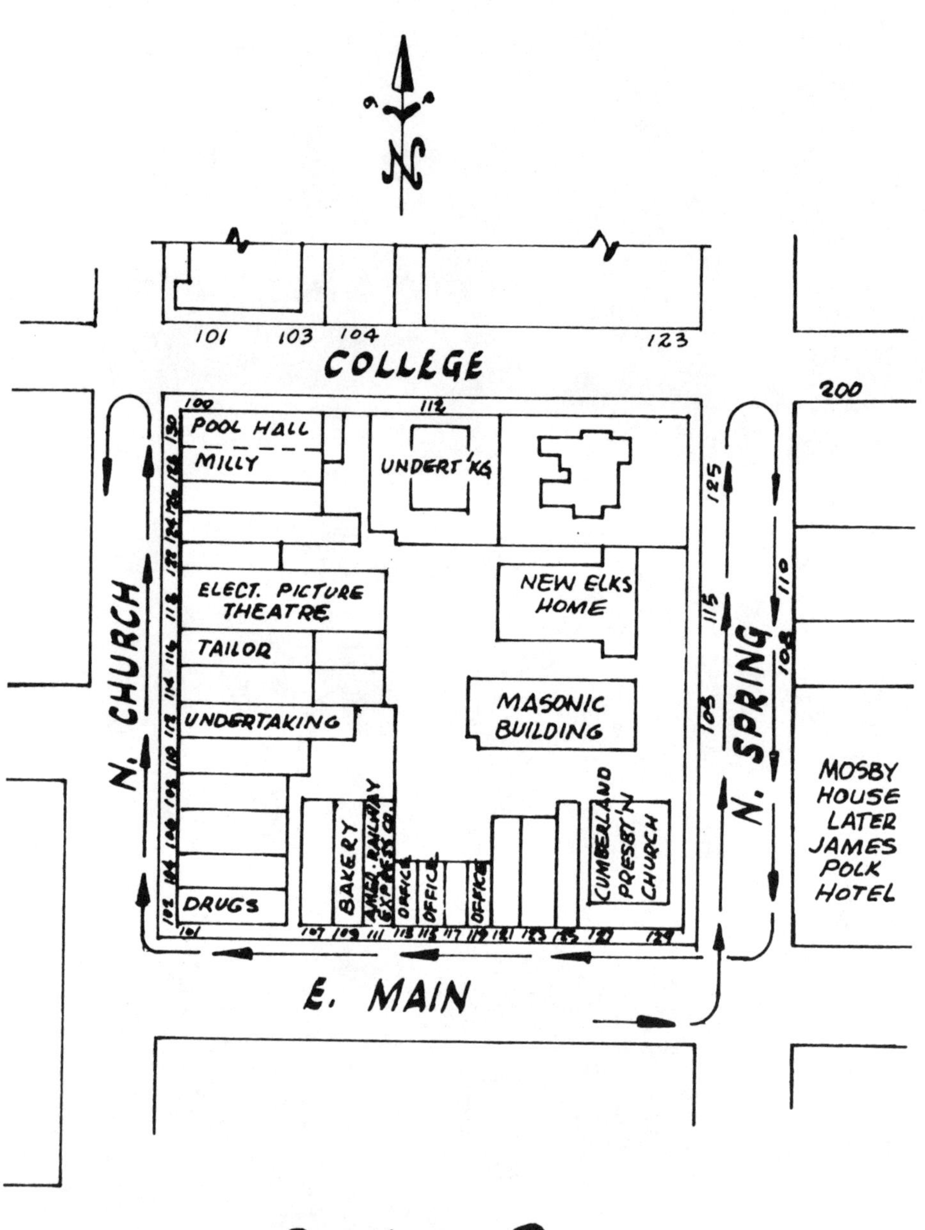

SECTION - D

Chapter XI

North Spring—East Main (Northside)

Leaving what was the old Mason building on the southwest corner of East Main and South Spring streets, we cross East Main to the first location behind what was recently the First Tennessee Bank (D-103). In 1924, that space was a vacant lot. Robert Bell Murfree, the great grandson of the esteemed doctor, states that the lot extends westward to the property on which the former City Cafe is located. Robert states that his father, Dr. Matt Murfree, Jr., built that building in the late 1940s. It was arranged for the building (D-103) on Spring Street to connect with the Murfree property around the corner on East Main (D-123, 125).

The building is presently occupied by Larry Brandon, attorney. The brokerage firm of Edward D. Jones managed locally by Earl Hull was the tenant there from 1977 to 1989. The ownership of the property has continued within the Murfree family from Dr. J.B. Murfree to the present owners, Matt Murfree, Jr., and Robert Bell Murfree.

★ ★ ★

The next building (D-105, 107), was relatively new in 1924. The three-story building was called the Masonic building. That was the meeting place of the York Rite Bodies of Masons. Dr. J.R. Gott, for many years (through the 1920s, 1930s, and 1940s) occupied a suite of offices on the second floor of that building. A Mr. Neal, who conducted the Central High School Band during the early 1930s, kept a room there for teaching his music students. Dr. W.K. Tilley had a suite of offices on the first floor during the late 1930s.

That property was a vacant lot in 1914 and was owned by the Wendels, who lived on the corner of East College and Spring streets. Wendel sold the property that year to the Union Trust Company, which erected the three-story building and sold the third floor to the Masonic Order. Dr. W.C. Bilbro bought the first and second floors. The Wright brothers are the current owners.

★ ★ ★

The next building (D-109) in 1924 was a handsome structure built in 1914 by the Murfreesboro Lodge No. 1029, B.P.O. Elks. The fraternal order had grown to a membership of two hundred twenty-five men who were of the leading businessmen of Rutherford County. With its convenient, almost center of town location, it was a favored afternoon meeting place for businessmen. Because of its ballroom, and other arrangements, it was often used for entertainment purposes by various town social organizations. Men sitting on the front porch in rocking chairs were familiar sights during the summer months.

Unfortunately, that existence was rather precarious. It was sold to the Stones River Club in 1938, then to the City of Murfreesboro in 1948, then to Ellis Gray in 1952, then to Linebaugh Library in 1953, then to the City of Murfreesboro in 1967, and finally to the children of William T. Wright, a prominent local attorney during the 1950s and 1960s, and until he died in February 1975. Their names are William T., Wayne C., James C., Randall A., Richard S., David K., and Wilma A. Wright. This imposing array of the children of attorney William Wright own several properties in this immediate area and elsewhere in Murfreesboro. The building was demolished in October 1986.

★ ★ ★

The next property northward (D-125) was on the corner of North Spring and East College streets. It was occupied by a single-story frame house with a gingerbread decorated front porch. In the 1930s and early 1940s, it was used as a funeral home by the partnership of McKnight and Harrison. Originally, in 1929, the partnership was McKnight and Sutton. Then it became McKnight, Sutton, and Holly. In 1930, the partnership was composed of Al D. McKnight (former mayor) and Price Harrison. Mr. Harrison was the father of the well-known, versatile Price Harrison, Jr., who publishes the successful *Angus News*. The partnership was dissolved in 1945 and the building was demolished to make room for a new service station on that corner. The important U.S. 41 highway entered West College Street until the early 1950s to continue down that street to North Maney, where it turned right to finally meet the Manchester Pike. It is now difficult to imagine how those narrow streets could accommodate the large trailer trucks and heavy automobile traffic that passed through town in those days.

There was a Pure Oil station that was built on the empty lot. It was manned by Aubrey Cook, who was probably the most prominent service station operator in town. He was one of the few men who could manage a busy station in a white shirt, tie, and dress suit. The property was owned by Hubert Elrod in 1946.

James V. Braswell later owned the property and sold it to Milton Beckman in 1978. Milton renovated the service station, converting it to a small office building. Johnson and Bailey, architects, established themselves in the building in 1979. In 1989, the space became occupied by Edward D. Jones and Company. Earl Hull had brought his brokerage firm from down the street (D-103). While renovating the service station, Mr. Beckman also erected a small building on the front section of the lot. It was to be called The Prescription Shop. That was a new concept in the dispensing of pharmaceuticals in that the store limited its inventory to drugs only and offered drive-up window service.

★ ★ ★

Walking across North Spring Street at that point, the pedestrian would come to the Delbridge Building. Ed Delbridge has an office suite on the second floor. Ed has been one of Murfreesboro's most successful entrepreneurs. He operated a successful photography shop for several years, after which he sold his business to Paul Vaughn. In the early 1960s, he built the deluxe Mercury Apartments. Other apartment ventures followed, which included the huge Sanbyrn Hall and Chelsea complexes. He continues as a director at Mid-South Bank and Trust Company and at the Christy-Houston Foundation. Ed and his wife, Clara, have been particularly noted for their philanthropic activities.

The Delbridge Building also houses the Christy-Houston Foundation, the International Travel Agency, the Exchange Club, and the Colonial Dress Shop. The shop was founded by Katie Delbridge, the mother of Ed, in 1959. She was there until 1979. Joyce Keith is the present owner of the business. The travel agency was founded by Brownie Burkett in the early 1970s. She had the first travel bureau in town. Bernie Krohn of Nashville is the present owner of the business. Brownie Rogers is still at her desk as manager.

The Delbridge Building at 200 West College Street was built in a smaller fashion by Lizzie Williams in 1941. She established her popular Cupboard Tea Room in the downstairs area. Carl Hickerson's wife, Louise, operated the tea room for a short while. Ed bought the building in 1956, and moved his photography shop from the Jackson Building. He remodeled the entire building, adding two wings. Dr. McCord Pope occupied a large portion of the ground floor.

The home of Grantland Rice, the famous sportswriter, was there on that corner of North Spring and College streets. He was the man who coined the phrase, "It's not whether you won or lost, but how you played the game." An iron plaque mounted near the street points out that that was his birthplace.

★ ★ ★

The next building southward in 1924, 118 North Spring Street, was the home of Dr. J.F. Blankenship and his family. He also maintained his office and treatment rooms there. Nowadays, that address is occupied by the Wright Group; John Landsden, attorney; Mutual of New York, represented by Larry McFarlin; William Davis, C.P.A.; and the National Spotted Horse Association.

The sons and one daughter of William Wright, deceased, own that building (118) as well as the next connecting building (108 North Spring). Their father, attorney Wright, bought the property (118) in the early 1970s. Willie already owned the next door building (108 North Spring

Street) and then combined the two. The latter building was once the birthplace of the Rutherford County Health Department. The Health Unit was initiated in 1924 through a New York grant. Dr. Harry S. Mustard became the first head of that most fortunate philanthropy for Rutherford County. It was under the auspices of that institution that the famous Blue Ribbon campaign was initiated in all of the schools in the county. The pilot program was closely watched by many communities throughout the United States.

★ ★ ★

On the corner of North Spring and East Main streets there once stood a large handsome brick house which was the home of the Mosby family. To the east of that property was the great Italianate house that belonged to Dr. J.H. Nelson. The Mid-South Bank now occupies both of those properties and more.

In 1929, the Murfreesboro Hotel Corporation was formed. It was headed by James Jetton, who had recently managed the Commerce Union Bank. Enough stockholders subscribed to the hotel prospectus and the hotel was built. It was indeed a credit to Murfreesboro. It was a showplace, a hotel that any town would be proud to own. Corinthian pillars, Greek architecture, stone quoins on the corner, an immense handsome lobby, a ballroom, restaurant, elevators, adjunct offices—all of those assets contributed to the beauty and quality of the hotel. Mr. J.F. Stiles was imported to be its first manager. Mr. Bridges became the first chef. The Grand Opening seemed to be a harbinger of many future years of successful operation. The hotel did operate many years—until about 1975—but lo! the stockholders were never to receive any dividends or any portion of their investments.

John O'Brien bought the hotel in the 1970s as an investment and sold it shortly thereafter to the Mid-South Bank and Trust Company. The John H. Nelson home had already been demolished several years earlier and now the hotel suffered the same demise. It had played its part in the multi-framed composite of Murfreesboro.

★ ★ ★

The northwest corner of East Main and North Spring streets (D-127) contains a yellow brick building which was recently occupied by the First Tennessee Bank, headquartered in Memphis. That corner once contained the historical Cumberland Presbyterian Church. In the early 1930s, the City Hall moved from the old fire hall on South Church and Vine streets to the old red brick single-story building from which the church had moved. That was to be the administrative office of the City of Murfreesboro until the early 1950s. In 1924 and onward for several years, the mayors were Al D. McKnight, Collier Crichlow, and W.T. Gerhardt. The City Manager during that period was Sam Cox, the City Judge was W.C. Draper, and Cecil Smotherman was Office Manager. Joe Lovell was with the Water Department and was to soon head that department until his retirement in the 1970s.

Even the basement of the building was utilized. The paper boys were permitted to use that space while folding the *Nashville Banner* papers before delivery. A beginner with ninety to one hundred subscribers could expect to earn about two dollars per week if all of his subscribers paid on time. A more experienced carrier might earn three and one-half dollars with a larger route. In about 1934, as the depression deepened and penniless transients began arriving in town, cots and bedding were installed in the basement for the use of those people. It was then called Cox's Hotel after the name of the city manager. Holland Parker handled those accommodations until the early 1940s, when they were no longer needed. When the City Hall moved to its present location, the old building was demolished.

Carl Walling was an oil distributor who had recently moved to Murfreesboro from Walling, Tennessee, located between McMinnville and Sparta. A good business man and of an enterprising nature, he spearheaded the organization of a bank that was to be called the National Bank of Murfreesboro. A new yellow brick building was erected on the former church and City Hall site. Hulon Spicer was appointed chief executive officer in 1955. That institution became an integral part of the banking community of Murfreesboro. In 1971, it was supplanted by the First Tennessee Bank which remained there until 1990.

★ ★ ★

In 1924, the next building toward the Square (D-123, 125) was occupied by the medical offices of Dr. M.B. Murfree and Dr. V.S. Campbell. Over the intervening years, up until the present, that two-story building with its stair steps in the center of the structure has been occupied by many well-known tenants. Dr. Matt B. Murfree, Jr., became the successor to his father's extensive practice. He practiced there until his death in the late 1970s. The well-known gun collector and photographer, H.O. "Hot" Todd had his studio on the second floor for many years. Dr. H.J. Jamison occupied the suite on the left of the building's entrance during the 1940s. Dr. Jamison was the medical examiner for the Murfreesboro Draft Board after World War II began. The National Life Insurance Company occupied several rooms upstairs for many years.

That office building is owned by the second generation descendants of Dr. Matt B. Murfree, Sr. They are his grandsons, Matt B. III, and Robert Bell Murfree.

The Murfrees were among the earliest settlers to arrive in this area from North Carolina during the first decade of the nineteenth century. Each succeeding generation has seemed to have produced leaders who were prominent in the professional, civic, and social fields of the town. There was Dr. J.B. Murfree, who was one of the foremost physicians of Rutherford County during the major part of the nineteenth century. He served two terms as mayor of Murfreesboro during 1874-75. There was J. Mary Noailles Murfree, who wrote under the pseudonym of

Charles Egbert Craddock. She was the author of Victorian classics such as *The Prophet of the Great Smoky Mountains, In the Tennessee Mountains, Where the Battle was Fought*, and others. Now representing the fifth generation of Murfrees in Murfreesboro are Matt B. III and Robert Bell Murfree. Matt is a prominent attorney in the firm of Murfree and Cope. Robert is president of the First City Bank.

★ ★ ★

It was mentioned earlier that Sam DeGeorge had been instrumental in bringing Andrew Tamburo to Murfreesboro. When Andrew returned to the town after World War I, he managed to buy the next building (D-121). He and his wife were frugal, good managers of their restaurant, and did not mind the long hours that a successful business required. Later, they became able to buy the three-building complex up the street (D-107, 109, 111). When Andrew's restaurant moved to where the second City Cafe (D-107) was located many years, James Maney became the new owner of the location at (D-121). The James Maney estate is the present owner of that location in 1990. Ray's Steak House was there for several years during the 1950s. Dick Shacklett brought his photography studio there to remain until its removal to the east side of the Square.

★ ★ ★

The next address (D-119) comprised the Dr. Edmund B. Allen Infirmary in 1924. in the early 1920s, the doctor's infirmary was the nearest semblance to a hospital that the town possessed. Dr. Allen had served in the U.S. Navy before World War I, and later attended medical school in Nashville. His wife, attired in a nurse's uniform, assisted in the operation of the infirmary which also occupied the upper floor. Their son, Dr. Edmund B. Allen, Jr., became a dentist and conducted his dentistry in the upper portion of the building for many years after his father passed away in the mid-1960s.

The present owners of the former infirmary building are J.M. Rogers and Larry Trail. They run a busy law firm at that place.

The photography studio (D-117) of Leo Ferrell continued for many years. His estate leased the building to Guaranty Federal for some years. Bill Cunningham bought the property in 1972 and conducted his realty business there for almost one year. Tom Reed bought the building in 1973 and continued his law practice there until he was appointed City Attorney in 1990. One of his partners, Lynn Watson, was appointed Assistant City Attorney at the same time. Tom Reed remains the owner of the building.

★ ★ ★

The next two buildings (D-113 and D-115) were known as the Ridley Building from at least 1923 until 1991, when Gary Simpson bought and renovated the property to house his City Cafe. Bromfield L. Ridley had owned the building during the first part of the century. Upon his death, his widow continued leasing of the property. When she died, her son, Leon, and subsequently his daughter and granddaughter kept the property within the family until it was sold a few years ago to Ed Netherland, who sold it to Gary and Pat Simpson.

The Elizabeth Micheaux Shop was at the location (D-115) for several years. It was operated by Lena Petrie. Ruth Wood was there for several years with her Buttercup Shop. When the Georgetown Shopping Center opened, she moved to that area. A piano sales and repair followed the Buttercup there.

For the fourth time, Mrs. W.E. Shipp appears here (D-113) in this story about the Square. In this instance, her business is called Ken's Snack Shop. Her son, Kenneth Allen Shipp, later became the coach of the New York Jets football team. Mrs. Shipp came here in about 1940. The Snack Shop became a popular and successful business, and it continued until 1954. The Murfreesboro Beauty School, operated by Elizabeth Floyd, was the next occupant of the building.

Attorney John Rucker began his law practice in the upper portion of the Ridley Building. Graduating from Central High School in 1933, he attended Cumberland University for one year, passed his bar exam in 1934, and hung out his shingle the same year in the west side of the upstairs section (D-113). Shortly thereafter, John entered the Middle Tennessee State College for a four-year term to receive his Bachelor of Science degree. He was connected with his grandfather, Judge John E. Richardson, in the practice of law. Judge Richardson had served as circuit court judge for several years. John's father, Ellis Rucker, also occupied the upstairs section. He was in the real estate business. John recalls that there was only a pot-bellied stove to heat their three offices. The east section of the upper floor was tenanted by the law partnership of John and Darwin Hancock. The Rucker triumvirate occupied the upstairs section from 1934 until 1940, at which time John moved to the Mid-State Building on Vine Street as already stated.

★ ★ ★

The complex of three addresses (D-107, 109, 111) was owned by John M. Butler in 1924. He has been mentioned earlier, and will appear again in connection with Howse and Butler and the First National Bank. It was also related earlier that Andrew Tamburo bought these buildings, moving his restaurant to one (D-107) and renting the other two stores to other businesses. One of the locations (D-111) was occupied by the American Railway Express in 1924. G.B. Sawyer represented the Railway Express in Murfreesboro during the 1920s and 1930s. He later moved his operation to a building close to the passenger depot. Mr. Sawyer was a city councilman during the 1930s.

The Tennessee Gas Company occupied the building (D-111) until 1953. The company was managed locally by Mr. McCarty. In 1953, the Palace Barber Shop, owned by P.W. Carter, moved from the basement of the Commerce Union Bank Building to that location. After thirty-eight years, the Palace is still very much in operation under the leadership of Randall Hall and Irene Walker. Some of the barbers who have worked here over the years are: Robert Drake, W.C. Batey, Kenneth Ayers, Charlie Pitts, and Clayton Willard. Jim Taylor is in charge of the shoe shine department. He is seventy-seven years of age and has been shining his customers' shoes at the same place for these thirty-eight years.

A bakery was operating in (D-109) in 1924. It was operated by Dan and Tom Brown who have been mentioned earlier. The Browns also made delicious ice cream and pedaled it from a horse-drawn wagon which advertised its approach by a tinkling bell—two cones for a nickel!

John Jenkins ran a five-pin bowling alley there for several years. It cost five cents to bowl a game. Other tenants there were: Knox Business College, Carl Lawson Business School, A.N. Miller Insurance Company, Neil Lancaster Novelty Shop, Edsel Ford James' Tobacco Shop. This last is now operated by Dawson Wimsett. Barton Dement practiced law on the upper floor of that building for several years.

D-107 was occupied by J. Pascal Elrod in the early 1920s. He moved there from the partnership that he had held with his brother on the north side of the Square.

When Andrew Tamburo retired in the 1950s, the City Cafe on the south side of the Square, which was operated by Uncle Dorsey Cantrell, was closed. The name "City Cafe" was adopted by the new owner of the restaurant in (D-107). That was Morris McKnight. He later sold to Ethel and Ernest Watson, who had had much experience in the restaurant business. They did a very successful business for several years. Because of the failing health and subsequent death of Ernest Watson, the business was sold to Frank Cooper in the late 1970s. The business continued to thrive with the Coopers retaining most of the cooks and waitresses who had worked for the Watsons. In the mid-1980s, Frank Cooper sold the City Cafe to Gary and Pat Simpson.

Mr. and Mrs. Simpson have a full house at almost every meal period. Even the morning coffee frequenters fill almost all the chairs each day. Gary and Pat Simpson are congenial restaurateurs. This is evidenced by the waiting line at each noonday meal.

Recognizing that they could not efficiently continue to take care of their growing number of customers, they have recently moved to renovated and expanded quarters in the old Bromfield L. Ridley double building (D-113, D-115). The old restaurant building that has been serving meals for fifty-five years is now empty.

Stifanina Tamburo Hayden is the owner of the three-building complex that was bought by her father in 1936. She talks of the 100-block on East Main with fond recollections. That was where she was reared. She remembers just about every occupant of those buildings these many years.

For a young boy during the late nineteen twenties and early thirties, the court house yard could be counted upon to provide an interesting Saturday menu of attractions. There would usually be a white or colored preacher who would preach awhile and then pass around a hat. They must have collected enough for their services for often the same preachers would return on successive Saturdays. Occasionally, there would be a soap box orator who would speak for or against some political question. These impromptu and unannounced appearances were usually held on the north side of the court house yard.

The east side of the court house was where the major action was held. A large platform against the court house and under the ancient sycamore tree would be built a day or two in advance of the well publicized event. Since ninety-nine per cent of the voters in the county were democrats, those events were mostly on behalf of candidates vying against one another within the same party. The principal offices sought from the shady platform on the east side of the court house were the legislative seats, the United States congressional and senatorial seats and the governorship. Each candidate seemed to fill the chairs on the platform with local and visiting dignitaries along with a sprinkling of ladies to adorn the select assembly. Most candidates either brought or hired a local band to serenade the huge crowds with patriotic music.

Possibly the most endearing and sentimental participant in those court house yard attractions was a little girl of about ten years of age. Her father was a tenant farmer whose family lived on the west side of the Lascassas Pike just before Bushman's Creek. Occasionally, the father would bring the child to town on Saturdays. The girl had almost an angelic face. Her father would hold her in his arms while she sang some of the popular sentimental songs of the period with a talent that seemed to be beyond her years. The appreciative audience would contribute liberally as long as the father chose for the child to sing.

In September of 1930, Lady Delores arrived in town. She was an attractive endurance driver and aviatrix who had just arrived from Nashville where she had finished a successful one hundred hour endurance drive. She approached several of the store owners around the Square with a promise to escape from a straight jacket while hanging upside down from the court house. She would accomplish this daring act for a nominal sum of money. The merchants accepted her offer and the well publicized act was set for four-thirty P.M. on Wednesday of the following week.

Lady Delores wasted no time in making herself well known about town and in the county. She arranged to be the main attraction in a window tableaux at McCord's Drug Store on the north side of the Square. She sat at a table sipping tea all day long while conversing with on-lookers. On Sunday she tossed the first ball in a game between Manchester and the Y.M.C.A.

The lady did hang up-side down in a strait-jacket from a beam placed near the east entrance to the court house. As promised, she accomplished what appeared to be an impossible feat.

These were some of the sights and sounds around the Square in those years. The Square was indeed an interesting place to be on Saturdays.

The Elks Club on North Spring Street in 1923.

Gen. Rosecran's Headquarters, January, 1863.

The palatial James K. Polk Hotel. Presently the location of the Mid-South Bank & Trust Company.

View of one hundred block on East Main Street. Note Ridley Building on left, part of which houses present City Cafe. Note also the large Cumberland Presbyterian Church which later became City Hall.

View of courthouse from East Main Street, circa 1908.

Mary Noailles Murfree, whose pen name was Charles Egbert Craddock.

Home Bakery on East Main Street operated by brothers Tom and Dan Brown, circa 1921. Later became Tamburo's Restaurant and later the City Cafe.

Interior view of A.L. Smith Drug Store, circa 1923.

Chapter XII

Northeast Side Square

The *Home Journal* headline and sub-headlines for Friday, March 28, 1913, read in this manner:

A CYCLONE STRIKES MURFREESBORO
HALF MILLION DOLLARS IN DAMAGE DONE TO BUSINESS HOUSES AND OTHER VALUABLE PROPERTY. MOST DESTRUCTIVE STORM THAT EVER VISITED THIS COUNTY. PEOPLE AWESTRICKEN AND BUSINESS ALMOST PARALYZED.

The story was one week late. The cyclone came at 2:00 Friday morning, March 21, 1913. A full page was devoted to the story. A few excerpts follow:

> Historic Murfreesboro ... fell like wheat before a reaper ... traveling at the rate of sixty-five miles an hour ... looking similar to the ancient city of Pompeii after its fall ... the dark and lowering clouds began to roll up from the southwest ... blinding flashes of lightning and terrifying peals of thunder ... our noble firemen and their trusty chief braving elements such as they had never done before ... the young lady night operators at the telephone exchange, Misses Mabel Hill and Minnie Yearwood ... much credit is due ... pieces of flying timber were breaking the glass in the building they occupied, these young ladies, still in their teens, proved themselves heroines by remaining at their post, with the lightning playing hide and seek all over and about them and the thundering roar of the storm ... it approached the city from the southwest ... from a point between the freight and passage stations ... its track was about 100 yards wide ... across the Public Square, taking in the entire north side ... those from the center of the block east were totally wrecked ... the first to sustain great injury was the firm of Woodfin and Moore ... no one was killed and but one person hurt, Mr. Hall Jones, a prominent stockman of this city, was fearfully crushed ... with that "bull-dog grit" so characteristic of Murfreesboroans, our merchants and property holders, though disfigured and still in the ring, will soon have Murfreesboro like Phoenix of old.

With this introduction, we begin a trek from what is now Henry's Florist Shop on the corner of East Main and the Public Square (D-102) toward the Methodist Church. The roof of the A.L. Smith Drug Store was lifted from its brick walls during the catastrophe described above. "Dock" Lytle Ledbetter owned the property in those days and until 1924 when he sold it to A.L. Smith. Mr. Ledbetter had inherited the property from his father, Civil War Capt. William Ledbetter.

A.L. Smith's Drug Company was the picture of antiquity on the Square. Mr. Smith bought the store from William Wendel, who started a pharmacy there in 1903. Mose Hirsch had operated a dry goods store there. Then at the end of the century, the Guggenheim Saloon stood there.

A drug store in those days had rows of glass-stoppered display bottles which lined the front of the store. Buckets of garden seeds and barrels of turpentine and linseed oil sat in front of the wooden display cases in the old brick building. An early pharmacist made his own tinctures and fluid extracts from crude drugs displayed in glass bottles.

For several years and until his death in 1968, Mr. A.L. Smith was considered to have maintained a business on the Square longer than any other person. The address in 1924 was 102 East Side Public Square (Section D-102). The tenure of Mr. Smith and his drug store on the corner of the Square and East Main was fifty-nine years—from 1909 into 1968. This appears to be a record, even into this year of 1991. His son, Herbert, managed the business during his father's final years. Herbert became well known about town as the writer and producer of the popular Lion's Club minstrels held during the late 1950s and 1960s. When his father died, Herbert decided to retire. He sold the store and business to Richard Douglas in 1968. Herbert Smith passed away in 1988.

Richard Douglas was also a noted gun fancier and collector. He has helped this writer on numerous occasions in the purchase and sale of guns. Richard sold the store in 1982 to Henry Phillips, who began the operation of a florist shop at that location. Richard Douglas moved his business to Highland Terrace and named it Terrace Drugs.

Henry Phillips is the son of the former Murfreesboro resident, Bomar Phillips, who was connected with the Charles L. Briley Company and also a member of a popular gospel singing quartet. Bomar moved to Winchester in the early 1950s to head the Farm Bureau in that city.

The florist business that Henry Phillips established in 1982 has grown considerably. On any given day, a visitor will note much activity by the busy staff both in the basement and on the ground floor. About three years ago, Henry decided to take a closer look at the building he now possessed. It was his intention to accomplish an extensive renovation to the building. Not wanting to lose any of the building's character, he decided to accent and expose the true architectural qualities that the structure already possessed. This involved removing the ceiling to expose the original embossed metal ceiling and the stripping of the walls to expose the old handmade bricks. Henry discussed the matter with Dawn Eaton, executive director of the Main Street program. Dawn offered free designer assistance to the property owner that would enable him to select the proper course he would prefer to take. In this case, Jeff Holmes and Mike Picklesimer, both architects in Nashville and living in Murfreesboro, volunteered their expertise. After much consultation and pondering on his options, Henry embarked on the project with the results that are so wonderfully evident to the viewer. A notable departure from the original design of the building was the installation of an outside stairwell from the basement to the southside sidewalk. Henry Phillips received the 1990 Main Street Governor's Award for excellency in design and renovation of the former A.L. Smith Drug Store.

★ ★ ★

Donald Knight and Martha Ann Haynes Knight own the next two stores (D-104 and D-106). Donald believes that Tillman Haynes, Sr., bought the property in the mid-1940s. James R. Jetton was the trustee representing the owners in 1924. It is interesting to note that the first five stores in this block (102, 104, 106, 108, and 110) were originally of the same architecture and design. They were all built in the same time period, about 1880, and were known as the Barton-Ridley Buildings. The removal of stucco, signs, and facades have shown identical windows and masonry decorations in each structure.

Jack's Cafe was located next to A.L. Smith's Drug Store (D-104). Jack Haney opened the cafe in about 1922 and remained until about 1929. Jack was an officer in the U.S. Army during World War I. He was the husband of Ethel Licker Haney, who is probably better known nowadays as one of the Licker sisters. Jack's Cafe was a popular hang-out place for the young people of Murfreesboro.

There was the Knowles Conservatory of Music on East College Street in the 1920s. The brothers Jessie and Tommie Knowles often conducted their orchestra in the rear section of Jack's Cafe. "Tiny" Smith and his band also played there. Sam Lasseter's first job was to tend the soda fountain at the place. I recall that during the 1920s, Jack's was the only place in town where an Eskimo Pie could be bought.

Mrs. Potter followed Jack's at that place. Milt and Cass Stockard came next to continue the short-order restaurant that catered especially to the teens of Murfreesboro.

Rone's Jewelers came (to D-104) in about 1950. Ed Alsup was the manager of the store for practically its whole existence there. Heritage Jewelers followed Rone's, and they are the present tenants.

There is a set of steps between D-104 and D-106. They lead to offices on the second floor. Judge James Elliot Stockard had a large office there during the 1930s. He was formerly City Judge and was then trying petty cases brought before him in his capacity as a squire or magistrate. The judge had a son whose given name was Ambrose ("Brose").

"Brose" was a very good wrestler. When a carnival came to town, there would be a wrestling ring attraction in one of the side shows. A wrestler would stand on a platform in front of the tent and issue a fierce challenge to the crowd. He would fight anybody. "Brose" would always accept the challenge and would usually defeat the challenger. He was a little less than medium height, muscular in build, had a yellowish blond crew cut and somehow had acquired wrestler's cauliflower ears. "Brose" became a naval officer in World War II.

Other tenants in the upstairs offices at that place were Joe Netherland's Insurance Agency and Paul Dowell Accounting Company. About the time telephones were being installed at the beginning of the century, the Cumberland Telephone and Telegraph Company occupied a portion of the second floor above Smith's and what later became Rone's and Ruby's.

The Great Atlantic and Pacific Tea Company (A and P) opened a store (D-106) here in about 1929. Its debut in Murfreesboro was not hailed with much exuberance by either the merchants or the shopping public. Gradually that store and H.G. Hill began to receive more acceptance.

Miller-Jones Shoe Company arrived at that location in 1950. In 1963, Ruby's moved to D-106. Ruby's was a dress shop operated by two sisters-in-law whose names were Jimmie and Ruby Cowan. Jimmie Cowan is now the sole proprietor of that popular and successful business.

The Cowans have played a prominent part in the businesses on the Square since May 5, 1950. On that date, Cliff and his wife Jimmie came from Lebanon to open a general dry goods store in the old Woolworth building on the north side of the Square. They bought out the Evon Shoe Store operated by Evon Harris. After three years in that location, they moved to the old H.G. Hill store next to the Hub Store on the west side (F-101). H.G. Hill moved to the 300-block on East Main in 1953. That new location is where Jr's Food Town is now operating. Cliff continued on the west side until 1969. In the meantime, Jimmie, as mentioned earlier, entered into the partnership in 1963 with her sister-in-law. Cliff, in 1969, leased the large former Charles Store (E-2 and 4) on the north side of the Square. Cliff retired from business in 1983, after thirty-three years on the Square. Cliff states that his wife looks forward each morning to opening her store on the Square. She likes the daily associations with her customers and the business of which she is the principal architect.

Donald and Martha Ann Knight began an extensive restoration and renovation on their two buildings (D-104 and 106) more than three years ago. Dawn Eaton and her Main Street staff rendered considerable design and planning assistance to the project. A passerby has to admire the traditional preservation that has been incorporated into those buildings.

The same passerby will note many other instances around the Public Square of that same contribution and cooperation with the property holders as they pridefully strive to enhance the appearance and quality of the Square.

★ ★ ★

Hubert Elrod operated a shoe store at D-108 in the 1920s. His business was supplanted in the late 1920s by Buchanan and Tarpley Drug Store. It was a busy drug store and a popular meeting place for such men as E.E. "Pluck" Miller, Constable J.H. Bowling, Henry Huddleston, Sr., Deery Riggs, Leslie Merrill, "Cap" Ransom, Cullom Alexander, Dr. John Cason, Jack Todd, Tom Hord, Dr. Gilbert Gordon, and several others. Although the store had a soda fountain, Coca Cola chairs, and tables in the front section, the men liked to congregate on the sidewalk in front of the store. "Cap" Ransom has been mentioned before in this story. A black male attendant rolled "Cap's" wheel chair to the drug store. "Cap" kept a Scotch plaid blanket around the lower part of his body. Cullom Alexander lived on East Vine Street, below the Fire Hall. He had served several terms as trustee for Rutherford County. Cullom was a man to be admired in many ways. He had been stricken with paralysis at an early age and had lost the use of his lower limbs. Occasionally he used a wheel chair that was propelled by two hand cranks that Cullom manipulated. However, his usual ambulation was by pushing down on the sidewalk with his hands while at the same time he would project his legs forward. To protect his palms, he would strap a five-inch, hard rubber cushion to each hand. In that manner, he could cover distance almost as fast as the normal pedestrian. On account of such abnormal use of his arms, Cullom had developed a thick chest with muscular arms. He usually wore a gray Stetson hat on his frequent trips to the Square. From his constant smile and his optimistic demeanor, one would never think that Cullom dwelt overmuch on his physical plight.

John and Bill Shacklett alternated behind the popular soda fountain. James Keys Buchanan ("K-Buck") and Thomas M. Tarpley had formed their partnership in the early 1920s. Their first drug store had been on the northeast corner (E-2) of the Square. In the mid-1920s, they moved to the east side (D-108). Mildred Jordan owned the property in 1924. Her grandfather, whose surname was Barton, had participated in the partnership of Barton and Ridley, who had built these five identical stores (D-102, 104, 106, 108, and 110) in the last quarter of the nineteenth century. The property passed to Mildred's daughter, Margaret Buchanan, in 1945. Margaret became the wife of Avent Dismukes in 1948. Margaret sold the building to Milan and Ivan Brown, who operated Brown's Shoe Store in the next building (D-110).

When James Buchanan died, Charles Moudy bought the Buchanan interest in August, 1953. The partnership of Tarpley and Moudy lasted until 1961, when Mr. Tarpley died. Charles bought Tarpley's interest and continued the drug store operation until 1983. At that time, he sold the business to Milton Beckman, who was there for a short while. The Brown brothers, Milan and Ivan, sold the property to Wendell Rowland, who in turn sold it in 1987 to Ann Holland and Mary S. Hutchison. Those ladies operate Studio V at that location. Studio V is a dance studio where children are taught modern dance, ballet, tap dancing, and gymnastics.

★ ★ ★

There was a shoe store (D-110) on the northeast side of the Square in the 1920s. The property was owned by Foster Jones. The business was called the Allen-Robertson Shoe Store. Frank and Horace Allen made up the Allen half of the partnership. Those two men became better known as the operators of Allen Service Station on West Main Street. Frank Allen was the father of Frances Allen Hobgood.

The Brown brothers arrived in town in the spring of 1931. They opened a shoe store (D-110) on May 1, 1931. The two older brothers were Milan and Ivan. They were the partners in that enterprise that was to last until 1978. Wilson, their younger brother, was an employee until his death in the 1950s.

Brown Shoes soon became the number one shoe store in Rutherford County. Even the Brown (no relation) Shoe Factory in St. Louis recognized the large sales volume that the brothers were producing. The shoe factory displayed its recognition by lending the Brown brothers money for additional inventory and fixtures and also gave the brothers a tremendous boost in advertising by sending its famous trademark and boy mascot Buster Brown to Murfreesboro. Buster with his huge bow tie, red tam, and pantaloons, appeared with his dog "Tige" on the stage of the Princess Theatre several times and greeted customers at Brown Shoes on Friday and Saturday.

Although that and other promotions helped the business to prosper in those Depression Years, its main forte was the combined personalities of the brothers. They greeted every customer with a sincere cordiality that never failed to register. Also, they had a return merchandise policy which Sam Walton of Wal-Mart may have copied. They initiated a twice yearly sale program which became an institution in the minds of their customers. Those sales were on the first Tuesday in January and the first Tuesday in July. The store was thronged on those two days, when all shoes were marked down an average of 50 percent.

I asked Ivan Brown to compare the prices in 1931 of high quality shoes with the same quality in 1978, the year that he retired. He said that shoes like the E.T. Wright brand sold for $13.95 in 1931 and at $70.00 in 1978. Among the popular clerks at the store over the years were: John Hayes, Prater Dickens, "Doc" Burns, and Jack Harney.

Ivan and Milan bought the property from Foster Jones in 1943. In 1975, it was time for Milan to retire, so he sold his share of the partnership to his brother. Ivan continued the business until 1978, when he followed Milan into retirement. Brown Shoes was sold to William Boone, Miller Rucker, and Fred Shumate. That last partner bought the interests of Boone and Rucker in 1980. The name of the present store is Renato. Fred Shumate is the owner of both the business and the building.

Chapter XIII

Northeast Side Square—North Church (East Side)

A handsome stranger in town walked slowly around the courthouse. It was a spring day in approximately 1923. The man appeared to be about twenty-four years of age and five feet ten inches in height. His hair was black and slightly curled. Of muscular build, he walked with a light, springy step. The young man walked over to the middle of the north side of the Square and looked up at the white clock tower with the weather arrow on top. He then walked back and into the courthouse. An official led him up three flights of steps to emerge on the roof and at the base of the clock tower, which occupied his attention.

The stranger left the courthouse and walked into several of the stores around the Square. At each store, the man informed his listeners that he was known as the "Human Fly." He produced newspaper articles which confirmed that he had climbed several buildings and landmarks in other cities. Each conquest required much skill, risk, adeptness, and daring. The "Human Fly" let it be known that he would climb the courthouse to the top of the clock tower if a small amount of money was collected to compensate him for the daring act which he would attempt. The money was collected, and the word spread around the Square that the "Human Fly" would attempt the dangerous climb the following evening.

As dusk fell upon the town the next day, a fire engine parked on the east section of the grassy plot surrounding the courthouse. A powerful searchlight, mounted on the fire engine, focused on the white columns of the east entrance. After conversing with some of the crowd gathered to witness the feat, the young man began his climb.

It was still a mystery as to how he would climb the main building. Those doubts were soon dispelled. With an almost unbelievable agility, he stood between the two right fluted columns, placed his right foot two feet above the base of the right column and leaned toward his left hand which was on the left column. He raised his left foot to the same level as his right and thus he had gained two feet on his remarkable ascent. It was in this manner that he continued his climb to reach the Corinthian caps on top of the columns. The protrusions on these caps made convenient foot- and hand-holds as he reached the gabled ledges above. With amazement, the tense crowd saw him grasp one of the ledges, lift his left leg to the ledge, and scramble his entire body to that level. He then gained the top of the gable and was then upon the gravel-covered roof. He waved to the people from the east parapet. The "Human Fly" then began his climb up the clock tower. He reached the narrow ledge above the columns supporting the clock dome. He then perched himself at the six o'clock position of the east clock and again waved at the crowd. The people were now worried about the outcome of the daring feat for which some of them had paid to witness. They had acquired a rapport for the handsome young man. The climb slowly continued. He chose the scaly curved surface between the south and east clocks for the next stage of the ascent. Drops of rain could be seen in the beam of the search light. The man gained the upper curved section above the clock level and put his hand over the flat surface which is the base of the next set of columns which support the helmet-shaped top underneath the arrow. People in the crowd now began to hold their breaths more often. Amazingly, he gained a purchase with both hands and raised his legs to the flat surface. At that less-hazardous stage, he waved again to the crowd, which began to breathe more easily. There was still the helmet top to surmount and finally the weathervane arrow. As he began his final assault, the people began to restrict their breathing again. He clasped one of the columns with his legs, grasped the next ledge, raised his body again, and was able to grab the base of the arrow spindle. Then he was able to gain the very top and hold to the weathervane. The "Human Fly" had accomplished what seemed to be an impossible feat. The crowd applauded and began to breathe normally again. The "Fly" waved from his perch. It seemed that a victorious smile could be seen on his face in the glare of the searchlight. The young man had certainly demonstrated his daring, his skill, and his almost fly-like abilities.

All that remained was his descent, which should have been easier. The light reflected from the wet surface of the clock tower. The "Human Fly" shinnied down from the columned section. His feet made contact with the sloping section above the clock level. Releasing his grasp of the upper ledge, he turned to crouch and regain his balance. Suddenly, a foot slipped on the wet metal surface. Instinctively, he thrust upward both arms in a vain effort to seize a handhold. His body plunged to the roof of the courthouse. The crowd below was shocked into a few seconds of silence. After several minutes, some men could be seen bearing the body of the young man through the east door of the courthouse. After an examination and some discussion, the body was taken across the street to Sweeney's Funeral Parlor on the east side of the Square (D-112).

A search of the man's clothes revealed no name or address. On the following morning, passersby could view the corpse through the plate glass window of Sweeney's. The body was in a glass-covered casket that was slightly tilted toward the window. The body was on display for five days in hopes that someone would come forth to identify the stranger. Some of the hundreds who viewed the body said that "it was the most beautiful corpse that they had seen."

There is a small site on the north side of Evergreen Cemetery which has been designated as the pauper's section. This is where the young man who called himself the "Human Fly" was buried. There is no marker on his grave.

Sweeney's Funeral Parlor occupied the next building (D-112) north of Brown's Shoe Store. P.K. Miller was formerly a partner in the concern. That establishment closed about 1928.

★ ★ ★

The content of the new red sign above the door of the recently vacated building read:

CLARENCE SAUNDERS
Sole owner of my name

Clarence Saunders lived in Memphis. He was a grocery marketing genius with ideas several years in advance of the time of acceptance. His new store on the Square would employ a minimum of clerks. The customers were to pick up a wire basket on entering the store. Prices were posted on each item. The shopper would simply place his or her purchases in the basket and walk to the cashier and check-out counter. Unfortunately for Clarence Saunders, the people of Murfreesboro were not ready for the new concept. They were accustomed to personal attention from the clerks. Also, many customers bought on credit. Then that was another chain store which had come to town. Chain stores were frowned upon in those days. Clyde Rushing was manager of that store, where he gained enough experience to open his own store on Mink Slide a few years later. Saunders closed that and other stores which he was operating about two years later. It was said that the entrepreneur went broke two or three times but finally became a successful businessman. It was Clarence Saunders who built the famous Pink Palace in Memphis, which is one of the city's main tourist attractions.

Cannon's Quality Market came next to that location (D-112). E.C. Cannon was a descendant of one of the first families arriving in Middle Tennessee. It was his family for whom the new village of Cannonsburgh was named. Mr. Cannon was a good businessman and operated a successful store. Fred Smotherman was manager of the meat department. St. George Jones, Sam Lasseter, and Sam Lane were some of the clerks employed there. The store was closed in the mid-1940s when its location and the next two addresses northward were remodeled to become the new Woolworth store. E.C. Cannon accepted a position as the head of the Murfreesboro Chamber of Commerce, which was then located in the Mason Court Building. Mr. Cannon's son, Ed, Jr., played left end on the Central High football team that won the Little Tennessee championship in 1933. Ed was killed in combat while serving as an Air Force navigator in World War II.

In 1924, Blumenthal and Becker had operated a jewelry and watch business (D-114) for several years. Mr. Becker was the sole proprietor shortly after that date. His daughter, Helen, married Alf Huddleston, who became a prominent Murfreesboro attorney and eventually the City Attorney. Mr. Becker's wife operated a popular private school on College Street during the 1920s. In the mid-1920s, Becker sold his business to T.L. Huddleston, who was the brother of Alf, Henry, and Robert. Mr. T.L. was the father of Tom, Jr., and George. George may be better known as a Webb School and Vanderbilt alumnus than he is as the local Amoco distributor. Mr. Huddleston closed his jeweler's business in 1929. He eventually became an oil distributor. A shoe store occupied his space next for several years and until the Woolworth store came.

★ ★ ★

The W.T. Gerhardt Tailor Shop was next door (D-116). Mr. Gerhardt was a city councilman and followed Al D. McKnight as mayor of Murfreesboro. In those days, a tailor performed a much needed service and was in a profession that usually proved to be most remunerative. Many people who frequented the shop recall Mr. Jenkins sitting cross-legged on a table performing his tailor work. Mr. Jenkins was the father of Dr. Charles Jenkins, the dentist on Lytle Street who has been practicing since 1947. Mr. Gerhardt owned the building (D-122) which Sam DeGeorge had occupied since 1914. He requested that Sam move his restaurant business to the space (D-116) where the mayor was then located. The mayor would move into his own building (D-122). Those moves were accomplished, and Sam DeGeorge remained in that location (D-116) until the mid-1940s when Woolworth moved into the three-store building (D-112, 114, 116).

F.W. Woolworth and Company had been on the north side of the Square for at least fifteen years. The famous five-and-ten-cent store was restricted in its floor space. The three-store building had been owned by George W. Howse for many years. He will appear later in this account. His daughters, Elisobeth and Florence, inherited the property on the death of their father. Elisobeth was the wife of attorney Granville Ridley and Florence was the wife of Dr. B.N. White. At some time in the early 1940s, Mrs. Ridley purchased her sister's half interest in the property. The building underwent extensive remodeling in the mid-1940s in order to prepare for the advent of the famous Woolworth store. That business remained there until about 1965, when Fred-s replaced the five-and-ten-cent store. That store continued here until about 1985, when it moved to larger quarters in Georgetown Shopping Center. The Music Shop, owned by Marvin Burton, moved into the large building in May 1987. The Music Shop is a full-line music store, carrying guitars, amplifiers, televisions, stereos, sheet music, band instruments, and music instructions.

The property is now owned by Florence Ridley, Sue Ridley, and Mildred Stewart. They are the daughters of Elisobeth Howse Ridley and the granddaughters of George W. Howse.

★ ★ ★

The Rutherford Guidance Center is located in the building (D-118, 120) formerly occupied by the Princess Theatre. The movie house had been there several years and moved to the corner of North Maple and College Streets in about 1927. The white glazed tiles and facade decorations on the upper section of the old theatre are still visible. Oscar Altman was the theatre manager then and remained in that capacity until the late 1940s.

Motion pictures are a relatively recent historical development. By 1904, small theatres for the exclusive exhibition of motion pictures, called nickelodeons, had opened their doors. Nashville's first nickelodeon, the Dixie, opened in 1907 under the management of Tony Sudekum and his father, Harry Sudekum. Those two men formed the nucleus of a corporation called the Crescent Amusement Company, which was chartered in July 1911. It grew to become one of the largest independent theatre chains in the southern United States with ownership of seventy-seven theatres.

It was in Murfreesboro that the Crescent Amusement Company chose to locate its first theatre to be built outside Nashville. Ada Ewing owned two buildings at the addresses 118 and 120 North Church Street. On January 1, 1914, she leased the buildings to John Gray, a baker, and to a Mr. Trail, who operated a barber shop. Later in that same year, she leased the two lots to the Crescent Amusement Company with the provision that the lessees would erect a "building to cost from twelve to fifteen thousand dollars or more" on the two lots, which meant that the existing structures would have to be demolished. The Crescent Amusement Company obligated itself to remove the tenants occupying the lots at the company's expense.

The new Princess Theatre housed an auditorium and a balcony (for black patrons) designed to seat 620 moviegoers, a projection room containing two projectors, a small stage and dressing rooms off the stage to accommodate the vaudeville players who performed on the stage at times. Jesse C. Beesley bought the property on February 15, 1921, for $13,500.00. Mr. Beesley at one time owned the *Daily News Journal* and the local electric power company (later bought by the Tennessee Power Company). He continued the original lease agreement with the Crescent Amusement Company until sometime between 1923 and 1925. On June 23, 1923, the Sam Davis Opera House, located on the corner of College and Maple Streets, was sold to the Crescent for fifteen thousand dollars.

In the autumn of 1925, Cecil Nighman Elrod entered into a lease agreement with Jesse Beesley. Mr. Elrod incorporated Cecil Elrod's French Shoppe and thus began one of Murfreesboro's finest exclusive ladies' ready-to-wear fashion stores. Mr. Elrod's wife, Sarah Elrod, "was instrumental in bringing to Murfreesboro new clothing lines which eventually became some of the top lines in ladies' apparel." As early as 1925, the Elrods were selling fashions imported from France. The French Shoppe soon became known for its exclusivity, not only in Murfreesboro, but also in the surrounding areas of Middle Tennessee.

Cecil Elrod, Jr., was responsible for opening the first radio station in Rutherford County. WGNS, the "Good Neighbor Station," operated on the second floor of the French Shoppe and shared the floor space with insurance offices.

The station first came on the air for a trial two-hour broadcast on December 21, 1946, and signed on for full-time broadcasting on January 1, 1947. WGNS became known for its live broadcasts and interviews with Jimmy Rodgers, Pat Boone, and Elvis Presley. Carl Tipton with his Mid-State Playboys began his career at the station in 1948. The popular announcers John Hood and Jerry Brown began their radio careers at WGNS. The radio station moved to another building when Cecil H. Elrod sold WGNS to William Vogel in 1960.

The third generation of the Elrods became involved in the ownership of the Elrod's French Shoppe building in April, 1971 when Cecil ("Buddy") Elrod, III purchased the business from the founder and his grandfather, C.N. Elrod. "Buddy" added such fixtures as Italian chandeliers and oriental rugs in order to accent the French Shoppe's image of elegance. Unfortunately, Cecil "Buddy" Elrod, III found it necessary to close the French Shoppe due to financial difficulties.

The J.C. Bradford Company made the Elrod Building its first location in Murfreesboro in 1978. In December, 1979, Charles and Fred Farrer bought the building to convert it into a modern office building. After a few years, the Farrers sold the building to the City of Murfreesboro, the present owner.

It was the second floor of that building that provided the birthplace of Dawn Eaton's Main Street Program. The entire building is now occupied by the Rutherford County Guidance Center. This is a community mental health center which provides services to patients in Rutherford, Cannon, and Williamson counties. It is a private non-profit organization.

★ ★ ★

As mentioned earlier, Sam DeGeorge sold his interest in a restaurant on the east side of the Square (C-105) to his brother John DeGeorge in 1914. Sam moved northward to a location (D-122) in the next block. Sam and his wife, Rosa, continued to operate a successful business. Being next to Princess Theatre was a definite plus for them. The theatregoers usually had an appetite when the movie was over and the DeGeorges remained open to serve them.

When the DeGeorges moved to another location (D-116), Mr. Gerhardt moved his tailor shop to his own building from where Sam had moved (D-122). The mayor occupied the rear section of the store while Mr. McGhee operated a watch and jewelry store in the front section. That arrangement lasted until 1961, when Mr. Gerhardt retired. Fagan Shoe Store was the next tenant, then City Finance was there for about ten years. Hut's Restaurant was there for a short while. Then attorneys Granville S.R. "Buck" Bouldin and his son, Sumner, came to that location in 1987.

W.T. Gerhardt had built the two stores (D-122 and D-124) in the early 1900s. Like so many other buildings around the Square, that property has remained within the family for three generations. Mr. Gerhardt bequeathed (D-122) to his daughters, Martha Walker and Frances Clayton. They in turn passed the property to J.K. Clayton, Jr., and his sisters, Bettie Clayton Cook and Laura Keeble Clayton

★ ★ ★

The next building (D-124) was sold in 1953 to Laura and Mary Keeble. The property was bought by J.K. Clayton, Jr., and Betty Clayton Cook in 1971 by prearranged contract.

Smith and Fletcher Toggery occupied the next store northward (D-124) during the 1920s. It was a popular store for men's tailor-made suits and accessories. The well-dressed man in that time would insist upon a suit that was tailor-made. With the help of Aubrey Smith or Dudley Fletcher, the customer would select a fabric and color from large books of swatches that the Toggery kept on hand. Very meticulously, one of the partners would take many tape measurements of the customer's shoulders, arms, legs, neck, girth, height, etc. This information was carefully posted on a comprehensive order form which was mailed usually to a New York, Philadelphia, or Chicago concern. The suit would be tailored according to the measurements and the customer would receive his new tailor-made suit in about three weeks from time of ordering at a cost of about $40-$50.

Aubrey and Dudley were partners until the mid-1940s. Dudley continued the toggery until 1956.

James K. "Cap" Clayton owned a financial loan company located at the rear of the Murfreesboro Bank and Trust Company on North Maple Street. When Dudley Fletcher closed his store in 1956, Mr. Clayton moved his business to that location (D-124). The name of "Cap" Clayton's firm was Personal Loan and Investment Company. Mr. James K. Clayton, Sr., died in 1963. His son, James K. Clayton, Jr., is serving his second term as Circuit Court Judge. The Personal Loan and Investment Company is still located at the same address (D-124) and is managed by Tom Kendrick.

★ ★ ★

Mrs. Willie Haynes Hunt operated a millinery shop next door (D-126) during the early 1920s. She was followed by Mrs. W.H. Trail in the same business. There were several milliners around the Square in the latter part of the nineteenth century and in almost all of the first half of the twentieth century. Although those ladies made many of the hats they sold, they carried custom-made hats in their inventories.

After the two milliners at that location (D-126), there came the popular Ideal Barber Shop, which is still present and is called Ideal Hair Styling. That firm is believed to have been in business since 1922. Charlie Batey and Walter Taylor opened their new barber shop on the northwest corner of the Square. In 1948, the shop moved to its present location at 126 North Maple. At that time, Allie Taylor bought his brother's share of the partnership. That was when Walter Taylor became a game warden. W.E. Watts joined the partnership at about that time and sold his share to Eural Sauls in 1956. That was also when Charlie Batey retired and sold his share to S.A. "Red" Givens. Eural sold out in 1958. "Red" Givens bought the property that same year. After several years, Terry and Mike Givens bought the shop. In 1971, Harold and Mike Givens bought the property and have conducted their partnership since that year.

Among the barbers connected with Ideal at various times over almost seventy years are the following: Joe Davidson, Eural Sauls, W.E. Watts, P.W. Carter, Walter Taylor, Charlie Batey, Clarence Lenoir, Allie Taylor, Geoffrey Marable, Tom Butler Drake, Will Ed Blair, and S.A., Terry, Mike, and Harold Givens.

Between the two addresses (D-126) and (D-128), there was and is a set of steps rising to the second floor of the Jackson Building. During the 1920s, 1930s, and 1940s, that upper-story was occupied at varied lengths of time by several lawyers, among whom were C.C. Jackson, Barton Dement, Frank Hargis, Howell Washington, and his son John Washington. Les Fite with his insurance company was there for several years. He had formerly been a partner in the firm of Smotherman and Fite. The Ed Delbridge Studios were there before Ed moved to what became the Delbridge Building at 200 East College.

★ ★ ★

Maude and Emma Earthman had a millinery shop (128) during the 1920s. They were more involved in the reparation and design of ladies' hats than in the sale of new ones.

The Charles L. Briley Plumbing Company came to that address (128) in the early 1930s. That firm was to become Murfreesboro's number-one plumbing company. Charlie, with his wife, Laudis, and their three sons, Marvin, Clayton, and Ed, built a successful business which soon began to handle a line of electrical appliances. The Goodyear Tire Store was next door on the corner at the 130 address. When the tire company vacated the building in the late 1940s, the Brileys expanded into that building.

Soon after radio station WGNS began operation in 1947, the Briley Company began a novel and popular radio program which was on the air five mornings each week. The name of the program was "Swap and

Shop." The program became a favorite medium for the disposition and acquisition of needed items. The Brileys left that address in 1960, moving into the second block on West Main Street. Charles L. Briley died in 1969.

Maude's Beauty Shop moved to 128 when the Brileys moved. Pauline Sisco bought the beauty shop in 1965 and is still busy at that address twenty-six years later.

★ ★ ★

Charlie Nelson operated a pool hall at 130 North Maple during the 1920s. As related earlier, Charles L. Briley expanded into that store following the removal of the Goodyear Tire Shop.

Ruth Dial operated the Flower Center until about eight years ago when Sara Cogdill became the new owner of the business. On our mental stroll from 102 to 130 North Maple, it should be noted that that important block in the annals of the Square begins and ends with a florist shop in 1991.

Attorney John Washington began his law practice in 1946 on the upper floor of the Jackson Building at 128 and 130 North Maple Street. He is well acquainted with the history of the building and has made certain pertinent facts about the property available to this writer.

The building on the corner of East College and North Church streets was once the Methodist Church. According to a plaque mounted on the north side of the building, the church was built in A.D. 1848 and was remodeled in A.D. 1872. The story goes that H.C. Jackson was a contractor who was given the contract to erect a new church building across the street, which was to house the Methodist Church, which exists there today. The new church was built in 1888. In return for the contract services of Mr. Jackson, he was to receive the old house of worship across the street as compensation. In 1924, the tax records at the courthouse showed that that property was owned by H.C. Jackson. In 1989, the tax records showed that Walter J. Key et al. of Jackson, Tennessee, owned the property. Those were the heirs of H.C. Jackson, the builder. Joe Swanson bought the Jackson building in 1989. It was remarked at that time that the property had remained within the same family for almost one hundred years. The old church house predates the city's most famous architectural heirloom, the Rutherford County Courthouse, by ten years.

View from roof of courthouse of Confederate statue and East Main Street. Note at left the five buildings of similar architecture belonging to Barton and Ridley.

View of northeast side of Square showing the five similar Barton-Ridley buildings, circa 1900. Note two story brick at left which later became Woodfin & Moore and presently houses the Front Porch Cafe.

Rosa DeGeorge, wife of Sam DeGeorge, in restaurant on northeast side Square, circa 1920.

Mr. and Mrs. A.L. Smith, long time merchants on the square

THE Elrod

BUILDING

Old theatre building that became Cecil Elrod's French Shoppe.

1938 ad from Cecil Elrod's French Shoppe.

cecil elrod's french shoppe

presents

A Tennessee College private

.... Sale ....

Silk Stockings

Sheer 2 + 3 thread
Double gauge

59¢

regular price $1.00

2 prs. for $1.00

Ultra smart shades..........

Here are silk stockings that many women have eagerly sought but have never found...until now! So very sheer you can scarcely see the ribs and you will be surprised at how well they wear.

An ideal gift for Graduation No 9 pencil

mail your order or call 382

1938 ad from Cecil Elrod's French Shoppe.

E. LYTLE ST.
MT. ZION BAPT. CH
SHEET METAL SHOP
L.O.D.F. LODGE
MARBLE WRKS
D.
GARAGE
GARAGE
CUMB. TEL EXCHANGE
PARSONAGE
METH. CH.
METH. CH
HAYNES HOTEL
N
221
211
209
222
216
214
212
227
212
211
226
218
130
120
118
116
102
COLLEGE
120
A-119-B
117
115
113
111
109
107
105
101
BATTERY STORAGE
WALL PAPER PAINT
BANK
HARDWARE
DRUGS
DRUGS
N. MAPLE
N. CHURCH
28
26
24
22
20
18
16
14
12
10
8
6
4
2
PUBLIC SQ - N

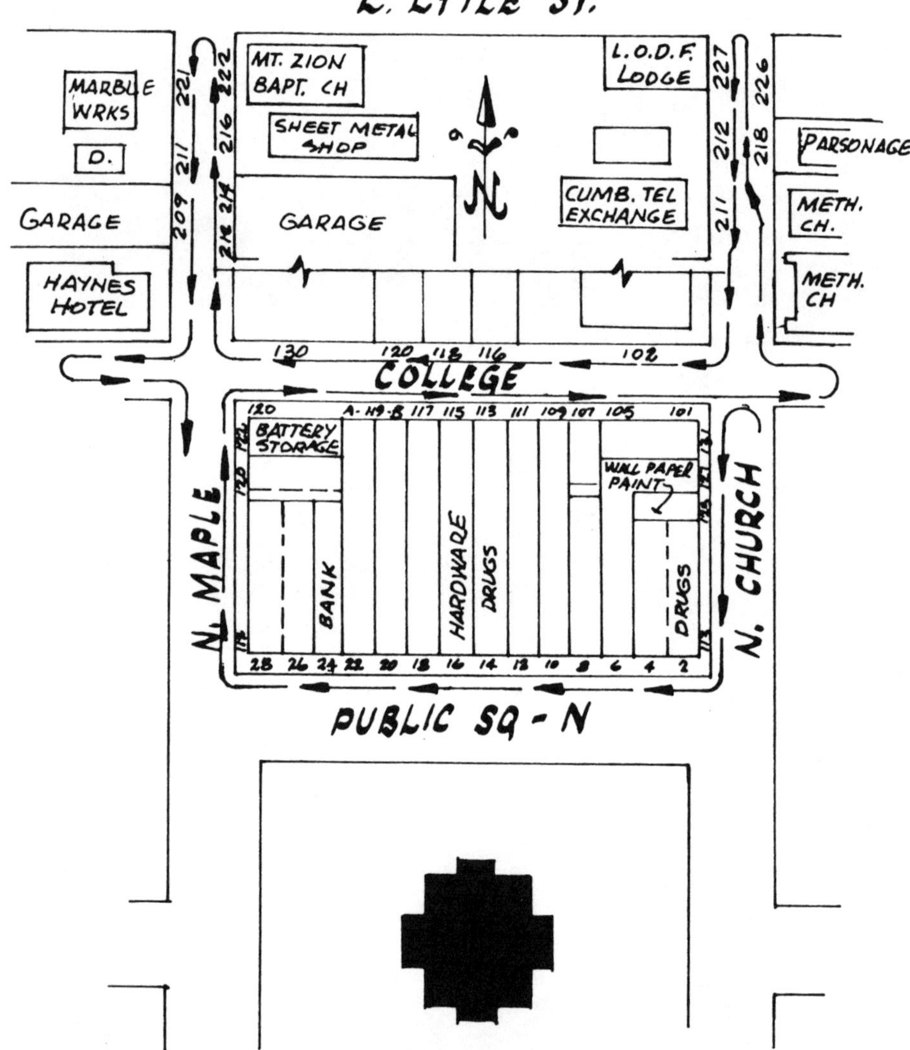

SECTION - E

Chapter XIV

North Church (West Side)—North Side Square

Across Church Street from the Flower Center is the newly rejuvenated Wiseman Building. Its address is 131 North Church. The lower floor of that attractice building contains the offices of attorneys Jim Wiseman and his wife Sally Schneider.

Jim arrived at Middle Tennessee State University from Tulsa, Oklahoma in 1971. He taught security and safety courses at the university while attending law school in Nashville. Sally Schneider, a native of Tullahoma, was studying law at the same school during the same period of time. The two met and soon were married.

Jim and Sally bought the corner property from Wendell Rowland in 1988. After several conferences with the staff of Main Street and after receiving much input from the architectural design service which Main Street provided, they embarked upon an extensive renovating program. The sub-ceiling was removed revealing the original embossed tin ceiling which was installed when the building was first erected. The entire ceiling was sand blasted and received multi coats of off-white paint. The wood paneling and sheet rock were removed in order to leave exposed the old brick and mortar walls on two sides of the building. A handsome staircase was installed which rises to the second floor which has not been renovated. Formerly, an enclosed stairwell outside the metes and bounds of the structure was used for access to the second floor which housed several offices.

The Wiseman-Schneider rejuvenation is a splendid example of how imaginative design and renovation can transform an old dull building into a new life of inviting and distinctive quality. It is also another example of the increased pride that property owners have exhibited on and about the Square in their buildings during the past few years.

The Wiseman Building won the Main Street Governor's Award in 1990 for excellence in design and revitalization.

The 131 North Maple Street address was known as the Cannon Building for more than fifty years. It was owned by Otho Cannon who was the brother of former Square merchants Tom B. and Ed Cannon. Mr. Otho has been mentioned previously in regard to a billboard and sign business which he operated for many years.

W.R. Coleman came into possession of that corner building (131) and the buildings on both sides (123 North Church and 107 West College). His heirs sold the three buildings to Wendell Rowland in 1988. It was Wendell, who lives in Shelbyville, who sold the corner to Jim Wiseman shortly thereafter.

The Bill Carey Realty Company occupied the lower floor for nineteen years (1968-1987).

Kate Coleman operated a beauty parlor there in the early thirties. She sold her business to Corrine and Florine Pearson who operated there for several years.

Among those who had offices on the second floor of 131 North Church Street were Howell Washington, John S. Bell, Collier Crichlow and the Selective Service Draft Board in World War II.

★ ★ ★

Caldwell and Associates occupy the building next door (125). The 125 entrance was formerly an inside entrance to the second floor of the Cannon Building. The stairwell has been removed and the building is now arranged for two-tenant occupancy. The 125 address gives access to a large L shaped interior which extends behind the 123 office space. The entire building and the business of Caldwell and Associates is owned by Ashley Earl (Bob) Caldwell. They are consulting engineers who handle environmental and civil engineering projects. Bob Caldwell bought the double wide building in 1990 from Wendell Rowland who, as mentioned earlier, bought the three-building corner in 1988.

Bob has performed much innovative interior rearranging to accomplish the dual purpose of providing inviting space for a prospective tenant as well as furnishing suitable quarters for his professional group. He has installed two quarter-shaped green awnings which lend distinctive accents to what would otherwise have been a flat front structure.

Oddly enough, that building is accustomed to containing an L-shaped interior section or being a part of an L-shaped building. Referring forward to the part of this account which deals with the north side of the Square and particularly the Woolworth store (E-6), it may be noticed that the five-and-ten-cent store extended back almost one hundred feet to where it made a ninety degree turn to exit on North Church Street. The base of the original L section is now part of the building which is used by Caldwell and Associates.

Like the other two buildings on that corner, those two addresses (125 and 123) were bought by W.R. Coleman in 1945. His heirs sold the property to Rowland in 1988. It is better known as the home of the C.B. Leatherman Dry Goods Company which was there for approximately forty years. That firm has appeared in two other locations in this account - on the south and north sides of the Square. The Leathermans (Charles B. and Charlie, Jr.) were well known and highly respected merchants on and about the Square for almost eighty-five years. Their tenure on the Square ended when Charlie Leatherman, Jr. died in the mid-nineteen eighties. The business was closed in 1986.

L.H. Wherle had a paint store in E-125 during the early thirties. The Parsley brothers operated a fruit stand there around 1935. Montgomery-Ward had a mail order store there in the late thirties and early forties. The Middle Tennessee Electric Membership Corporation had an office there during the mid forties.

★ ★ ★

The double store on the northeast corner of the Square has the lowest number addresses of all the stores on the Square (B-2 and 4). That store with the yellow brick front was originally known as the Palmer Building. Horace was the son of the Civil War general, Gen. Joseph B. Palmer. J.B. Palmer was the namesake of his famous grandfather. Horace and his son owned the property around the turn of the century. They sold it to John M. Butler, who has already appeared on these pages and will appear again. Mr. Butler sold the corner store to Pearl Ransom Kerr (Mrs. B.B. Kerr) in 1922. The present owners of both 2 and 4 are the heirs of Mrs. Kerr, which include her son B.B. Kerr, Jr.

During the early 1920s, the divided store was occupied by Buchanan and Tarpley Drug Company on the corner (E-2), and C.B. Leatherman Dry Goods on the west side. Those two businesses moved and the entire building was leased to Charles Stores, which owned several department stores around the country and was headquartered in New York. That was a popular ladies', men's, and children's clothing store, which catered mostly to middle- and lower-income pocketbooks. Charles remained there until 1969, at which time the business was closed. Cliff Cowan leased the store that year and continued a dry goods operation until his retirement in 1983.

Alan Loveless leased the entire building in February, 1983. His photographic studio was and is located on East Clark on a plot of ground which contains a pond, an island, a gazebo, his studio, and home. The uptown studio would afford added exposure for his business. The show window in number 4 (west side) contains framed picture examples of Loveless Photographics.

Big and Beautiful operated by Virginia Phillips came into number 2 (the corner) and remained until 1987. Henry Phillips used that space a short time while his present building was undergoing a remodeling process. Ribbons, Etc. came next and was followed by Ribbons and Crafts. Then there was Marlene's Bridal and Formal Wear, operated by Marlene Holt.

Bridal Reflections, operated by Carolyn W. Parrish, is now the business that occupies that northeast corner of the Square. They offer a collection of bridal gowns, bridesmaids' and party dresses, sequined and special dresses for special events.

The F.W. Woolworth five-and-ten-cent store was a popular business on the north side of the Square (E-6). It could not be accused of false advertising. It really meant that its merchandise was within the price range of five and ten cents. In looking back from the time frame of 1990, one finds it almost impossible to imagine that a large store could be filled with popular wares to be obtained at such prices. In 1924 and for several years of non-inflation, the "5¢ & 10¢" logo appeared on the store's red sign in gold letters.

Woolworth's was an L-shaped building which fronted on the Public Square and exited on North Church Street. The business remained in that location until the early 1940s, when it moved to a new building on the east side of the Square (D-112, 114, 116).

In 1924, the building was owned by James K. Clayton. Later, it was owned by attorney Wendell T. Rowland of Shelbyville. He bought the property from Mrs. J.K. Clayton in 1981. Rowland has recently sold it to Ron Wilson and his son Howard, who are both attorneys in Shelbyville. The building is presently undergoing remodeling to accommodate the law offices of the new owners. It appears that they intend to preserve the glazed white brick on the upper section that was applied when Woolworth arrived in the early 1920s.

When the Woolworth store left in the late 1940s, Evon Harris moved his Evon Shoe Store into the place. That business was short-lived. Cliff and Jimmie Cowan moved there in 1950 from Lebanon. Their dry goods store moved to the west side of the Square after three years.

Joe Wolfe is intimately acquainted with the Square. He was a merchant on the Square for thirty-three years. Even after retirement in 1971, Joe is at the City Cafe six mornings per week and keeps abreast of just about all that is going on about the Square.

Joe arrived here in 1938 from Nashville as manager of the new Davis Store at 107 on the west side of the Square. The women's wear store moved from that location in 1946 to number 18 on the north side. Joe continued to head the store until he decided to enter his own women's ready-to-wear store. That he did in 1953 when he chose to open his new store at number 6 (the old Woolworth's store) on the north side of the Square, which had been recently vacated by Cliff and Jimmie Cowan. Joe remained there until 1965, when he returned to his old position as manager of the Davis Store, which was continuing its occupancy of 18 on the north side.

Joe Wolfe is eighty years of age at the time of this writing. He talks fondly about his fifty-three years of memories about the Square.

The Cato Corporation of Charlotte, North Carolina, became the next tenant of number 6. It was a ladies' ready-to-wear store and operated there for several years. The North Side Restaurant came next and remained there until recently.

The Wilson-occupied law offices promise to be a fine feather in the cap of the Murfreesboro Square.

Next comes address number 8 on the north side of the Square. The logo of that store in 1929 was W.R. Bell Jewelers, 50 years on the Square. Bell Jewelers can easily claim the accolade of having been on the Square longer than any other business. Actually, this statement could hold true for the entire city.

W.R. Bell began his jewelers business at that address in 1879. It is believed that a Roulet operated a similar business here before Mr. Bell arrived. Roulet married the daughter of John Cedric Spence, a prominent Murfreesboro citizen and historian.

Besides jewelry, Will Bell carried watches, clocks, silver, pianos, and organs in the early days. His son Jim Bell assisted his father and continued the operation of the business after the death of his father. Upon the death of W.R. Bell, the property passed to his daughter, Frosty Bell. Frosty was a wonderful, loving woman. During the 1930s, she ran a dance school. Later she had a craft shop in the old Dixie Hotel. Finally, she found her niche in life when she began more than three decades of volunteer work at Rutherford Hospital. From the moment she began her service at the hospital, her daily routine was a life of giving.

When Jim Bell left the jewelry store in the early 1950s, Mr. and Mrs. John Dixon became the new owners of the business. In 1973, Blake and Lee Tidwell became the new owners.

If a turn-of-the-century customer could walk into the store today, he or she would notice that the fixtures, which include the walk-in vault, mahogany wall cabinets, display cases with cabriole legs, lead glass windows, and even the distinctive store front, have not changed in the ninety-one or more years. The present owners, Blake and Lee Tidwell, seem to be proud of the store character and stewardship which they have inherited. Their two children, Lisa and Greg, are certified gemologists and assist in the business.

Blake Tidwell deserves much credit for his leadership in the Main Street Program which has resulted in an entirely different picture of the Square. More later about his and other chairmanships of this program.

Upon the death of owner Frosty Bell, Blake J. Tidwell et al. became the new owners of the venerable store and business.

★ ★ ★

Murfreesboro, in the late 1920s, had three stores that were units of a national chain of stores. They were J.C. Penney, F.W. Woolworth, and McClellans. H.G. Hill came later, followed by A and P, and M.P. Brothers. As mentioned earlier, the grocery chains were frowned on for several years, but not the three department stores named above.

J.C. Penney was firmly and popularly ensconced on the Square (E-10 and E-12) in those years. It was a double store, two-storied, and large by Murfreesboro standards. The store had an interesting and unique system of handling all sales transactions, of which all were cash. There was an office mounted in the middle of the second floor. From there, cables proceeded to several stations on the lower floor. When a sale was made, the saleslady would place the cash and invoice into a wooden cannister, which was then propelled on the cable to the cashier in the central location. If change was required, the cannister came charging back with the amount needed. It was interesting for a kid to watch all of those trollies going back and forth.

Another very interesting feature at that store was for the young people. During the pre-Christmas weeks, a girl or boy could walk up two flights of steps and gaze upon a large room filled entirely with toys. There were dolls, wagons, tricycles, cribs, erector sets, tinker toys, popguns, B-B guns, model cars, trucks, airplanes, wind-up and electric trains, real model working steam engines, and many other items that would whet the toy-loving appetites of all the kids who walked dreamily down the aisles.

In the late 1950s, it seemed appropriate for Penney's to expand into larger quarters. The Haynes Hotel on the northwest corner of West College and North Church streets had been demolished. This allowed the construction of a large two-story building with a full-size basement plus several offices placed on the rear of the property. The complex was named Penney Plaza. It was a busy area until the 1960s, when shopping centers, with plenty of parking, began to arrive.

In the late 1970s, J.C. Penney closed its doors after almost sixty years of contributing much to the shopping attraction of the Public Square.

The building in 1924 was co-owned by two separate entities. (E-10) was the property of Mrs. C.F. Partee. The (E-12) portion of the building was owned by George W. Howse. Both properties have remained within the same separate families. Al Partee, Jr., owns (E-10), and (E-12) was until recently the property of the Elisobeth Howse Ridley heirs.

Penney's made an unusual arrangement with the owners of the two stores when they leased the buildings. They promised to rebuild the existing masonry wall when or if they left the two stores. When J.C. Penney finally did leave the premises in the late 1950s, the owners elected to accept an amount equal to the estimated cost of replacing the wall.

In 1990, the two buildings became the property of one owner. Al Partee, Jr., bought E-12 from the daughters of Mrs. Ridley: Florence, Susan, and Margaret.

During the late teens and early 1920s, E-10 was occupied by the Cannon Dry Goods Company. The business owner was Tom B. Cannon, who was the father of Tom and Juliet Cannon. Tom is probably Murfreesboro's most vocal University of Tennessee alumnus and Kappa Alpha fraternity member.

Mr. Cannon vacated the store in 1924. Shacklett, Staley and Sanders Dry Goods became the new tenants in E-10. They remained until J.C.

Penney's expanded into E-10. At that time, Shacklett, Staley and Sanders closed its doors, one of the several victims of the Great Depression around the Square.

The west side store E-12 was occupied by another clothing store in the same time frame as above. The owners then were Ephraim Foster Lytle and Al Lytle Partee.

The present tenant of the old Penney double store building is Martin Drugs. That tenant came here in July, 1971. Between the times of J.C. Penney's departure in 1959 and Martin Drugs arrival in 1971, the store was occupied by Graber's, a department store carrying ladies', men's, and children's ready-to-wear.

Jesse Messick began his sojourn upon the Square January 1, 1962, as a pharmacist at Frank Martin's Drug Company on the east side. Upon the death of Mr. Martin in 1965, Jesse and Bob Farmer entered into a partnership and bought the assets of Martin Drugs. They moved to the present location of Martin Drugs. Jesse bought the one-half interest of Bob Farmer in 1975. Jesse Messick passed away in April, 1988. His wife, Martha, capably manages the large store, which also includes a U.S. Post Office.

Jesse was an enthusiastic promoter of the Square. He was very much involved in the Uptown Merchants Association which preceded the Main Street Program. Jesse envisioned and worked toward the accomplishment of a Square which Murfreesboro boasts today. He originated Murfreesboro's greatest annual celebration—Uncle Dave Macon Days—in 1976. He was voted Rutherford County's Retailer of the year in 1975. Jesse served six years as County Commissioner.

Gladys Dement loved the Square, the store owners, and the people she frequently met in the restaurants, the barber shops, the courthouse, and in Jesse Messick's store. She was an informed politician and a great worker for the candidate that she supported. Gladys seldom missed a day in making her rounds on the Square. On Uncle Dave Macon Days, Gladys would accompany Jesse Messick in the lead vehicle of the parade. She also accompanied him in the Christmas parades. Gladys is now in her late eighties and resides at the Community Care Rest Home.

It has taken many Jesse Messicks for the Square to get all of the way from Mink Slide to Main Street. Jesse should occupy a seat on the front row.

★ ★ ★

B.B. Kerr has appeared on these pages in two locations, both on the southeast side of the Square. In an earlier year, B.B. Kerr was operating a drug store in number 14 on the north side. He was there in the early 1920s in his store that extended from the Square back to College Street. Mr. Kerr was the owner of the building. Toward the end of the decade, he moved to the east side. The partnership of McCord and Harris came to number 14 next and remained into the late 1950s.

The drug store did a thriving business with its pharmacy, soda fountain, sandwiches, cosmetics, paints, and wallpaper.

Following McCord and Harris Rexall Drugs, there came Sears Catalog store. That store moved to Jackson Heights Shopping Center after about ten years. Then to the address (E-14) there came Scotty's, a firm which sold pre-packaged drug items.

In 1978, Ed Netherland, and Richard and John Rucker, Jr., bought the property that extended from the Square to College Street. The building underwent an extensive renovation that produced several office suites in the long rectangular structure. Later, Ed sold his share of the front half of number 14 to Richard and John Rucker, Jr. By a deed of partition, Ed would own the north half fronting on College Street. The Ed Netherland Insurance Agency occupied that address until 1985, when Eddie Seddon's Cumberland Title Company moved there. Ed moved to the west side of the Square at the site of the old Hub Store. In 1985, Eddie Seddon bought Netherland's interest in the College Street property.

The rejuvenated front half of the old Kerr, McCord and Harris, Sears, and Scotty building is now occupied by four attorneys—Kent Coleman, Richard Rucker, John Rucker, Sr., and John Rucker, Jr.

John Rucker, Sr., can easily claim the title of dean of Murfreesboro attorneys. He has been engaged in the practice of law for fifty-seven years. He has been introduced earlier on these pages, but the loyalty of John, his two sons, and their maternal forebears to the legal profession and public service deserves further mention.

The mother of John Rucker, Sr., was the daughter of John E. Richardson, who began his practice of law in Murfreesboro in 1878. John, Sr., began his legal practice with his grandfather in 1934, as related on an earlier page. John Richardson married Annie Lou McLemore of Williamson County. She was the daughter of Judge W.S. McLemore of that county.

The great uncle of John Rucker, Sr., was the Hon. James D. Richardson, who served in the lower house of the State Legislature, later as Speaker of that body, and later as a State Senator. In 1876, he was elected to the U.S. House of Representatives. He was also a distinguished writer of legal treatises.

John Rucker, Sr., served as General Sessions Judge in Murfreesboro from 1948 into 1962. He was State Senator from 1977 through 1989.

Kent Coleman bought Richard Rucker's interest in the property; so now, in 1991, Coleman and John Rucker, Jr., are the partners who own the south half of number 14.

Chapter XV
North Side Square—North Maple (East Side)

Murfreesboro has had its share of Horatio Alger, Jr., stories. The Square has had numerous examples of men who, upon arriving in town, were virtually penniless. Through hard work and prudent business management, they prospered and became relatively rich according to the standards of the town. If their individual stories could be written, their biographies would involve the same pathos and drama as were contained in the success stories written by the famous author mentioned above. Their stories would have such elements as sweat, tears, romance, long hours, dedication, honesty, and honor. In each success story, there would be found an intertwining and binding thread in their fabric of a heartfelt obligation to serve.

Charles Hall Byrn was one of the primary success stories of his time. Born near Milton in 1856, he came to town in 1877. He began working for William Street at his hardware store on the north side of the Square for a salary of eight dollars per month. After a few years, he became a partner in the firm of Street and Byrn at the address of 16 north side Public Square. A few years later, he became the sole owner of the business. After the turn of the century, Mr. Byrn was the owner of another hardware store on the west side of the Square, at which we will arrive later. In about 1915, he initiated what may have been the first automobile dealership in town. His dealership was located with entrances on both College and Maple streets. The Maple Street frontage was just north of what became the Princess Theatre and the College Street entrance was about 150 feet west of what is now Linebaugh Library. That dealership eventually became Byrn and Reagor Motor Company and finally was operated by Roy Byrn, a nephew of Charles Hall Byrn. The car that the original dealership handled was the T-Model Ford, the car that remained black and without a self-starter until 1925.

C.H. Byrn was one of the primary founders of Tennessee College for Women. The original board of directors of the college met at the home of Mr. Byrn at 346 East Main Street in the initial meeting that resulted in the founding of the college. One of his daughters, Annie Byrn Roberts, still lives in the house of Queen Anne architecture that Mr. Byrn built in 1903.

Mr. Byrn died in 1929. He was the father of five daughters and one son. They were as follows: Sarah (deceased 1915), Annie Roberts, Lucille Reagor, Allie Ledbetter, Ida Lee Evans, Virginia Sanders, and Charlie Byrn, who served as postmaster during the 1940s and 1950s.

The C.B. Leatherman Department Store followed the C.H. Byrn Hardware at number 16. Charles Leatherman was a highly respected and familiar merchant on the Square from 1900, when he had a store on the south side of the Square. Upon his death, his son, Charles, Jr., moved the business to what is now number 8 behind the old Charles Store building. With more than seventy-five years of business leadership on the Square, the Leathermans became a household name of trust and dependability throughout the county. The Glamour Shop was to come to number 16 as a ladies' ready-to-wear business.

Matt Murfree, III, et al. purchased the property in 1978 from Virginia Sanders and Ida Lee Evans, two of the daughters of C.H. Byrn. In the following year, a complete exterior and interior renovation of the building was accomplished. A first-class job of traditional and colonial architecture was employed throughout, with the primary accent being a visible framed view of the courthouse just across the street. The members of that busy law firm are: Matt Murfree, III, James C. Cope, Mark S. Moore, Roger W. Hudson, and Darrell L. Scarlett.

★ ★ ★

At the address of number 18 on the north side of the Square in 1900, a sign on the upper section of the front read: L.R. Jacobs, Undertakers. Mr. Jacobs had just moved to town from the south end of the county. He was the great-grandfather of John B. "Bubba" Woodfin. Mr. Jacobs was the first of four generations of the same family who conducted an undertaking business in Murfreesboro. To this family belongs the superlative of having been in the same business longer than any other family in Murfreesboro and possibly in the county. It is rare and most noteworthy that a member of each generation for ninety-one years will choose to follow in the steps of his father and forefathers.

L.R. Jacobs operated an undertaking and general merchandise establishment in 1893 in Beech Grove. "Bubba" Woodfin relates that in those times and for several years thereafter some people would select the casket they preferred from the stock on display, take it home, and bury their own dead. He has retained yellowed invoices dated around the turn of the century that show funeral services priced from $4.00 to $50.00. It seems that undertaking firms in those days carried a line of furniture and were also engaged in cabinet-making.

The daughter of L.R. Jacobs married John T. Woodfin. John Woodfin formed a partnership with H.C. "Dick" Moore in about 1910 and began operating the business that had been founded by Woodfin's father-in-law. In 1913, the building at number 18 on the Square suffered heavily from a devastating cyclone on the night of March 21st. The firm moved into the old Elks Club building on College Street. It remained at that location until 1949, when John Woodfin, Jr., sold his father's interest to H.C. "Dick" Moore. Mr. Moore continued at the same address until the early 1960s. John, Jr., built the Woodfin Memorial Chapel in 1949 in memory of his late father.

John B. had assisted in the business since the age of thirteen. He returned from a stint in the armed forces in 1956 and became a member of the staff. His father, John T., died in 1973, and "Bubba" succeeded him as president. In 1980, Jerry D. Lowery joined the staff and became vice-president of the firm of Woodfin Memorial Chapel. The firm has kept a subsidiary undertaking parlor in Smyrna since 1954. The people at Woodfin's can well be proud of their unusual longevity and the dedication to business and service as displayed by their predecessors.

Shacklett, Cason, and Rogers Dry Goods Company was in number 28 on the corner of the Square and North Maple Street in 1911. The Shacklett contingent's given name was Arthur. He was the father of John, Dr. Bill, Dick, Sara and Dr. Bob Shacklett. The Rogers partner was Edgar Rogers, who was the father of Frances, Octavia, and Edgar ("Sonny") Rogers, Jr. "Sonny" was killed in action during World War II. He was one of the trio for whom the local V.F.W. Post was named. Those three were J.W. Reeves, Edgar Rogers, and Roger Smith.

In 1914, the firm was operated by E.H. Tatum and Arthur Shacklett. In 1922, the Tatum-Shacklett partnership became Shacklett, Staley, and Sanders. That was the Aultman Sanders who later managed Aultman's Jewelers on the east side of the Square. In that same year, the firm moved to number 18, where they remained until 1928. McCord Furniture Company had just moved from number 18 to the northwest side of the Square. In about 1928, the store moved to number 10 on the west side of Bell Jewelers, as mentioned previously.

Johnson Shoe Company came to this address and remained for several years. Davis Stores came in the late 1940s with Joe Wolfe as manager. Joe resigned from the business in 1953 to open his own ladies' apparel in the old F.W. Woolworth store in number 6. The Draper and Darwin Company was next in number 18. The register's office shows that Margaret Cannon was the owner of that property in 1924.

In 1970, the county bought numbers 18 and 20. On those two sites was constructed the imposing five-storied Judicial Building.

★ ★ ★

In 1900, the two addresses, 20 and 22 on the north side of the Square, were occupied by Smith, Cason and Kittrell, a dry goods store. The Elrod Bros. Department Store was in number 20 in 1924. Number 22 was the location of McClellans, a variety store. The Elrod brothers moved out of their space, with Cecil opening the French Shoppe on the east side and Paschal Elrod moving to a building in the 100-block on East Main.

In 1924, the double store was owned by Mrs. Florence Bilbro (E-20 and E-22). McClellans on the Square in 1924 was similar to F.W.

Woolworth, except for the more expensive range of merchandise carried by the former. McClellans also had a long, red sign with gold letters across the upper portion of the two-story building (E-20 and E-22). Their logo in gold letters indicated that their maximum range of prices was $1.00. This was a double building with two front doors. It was a vibrant business on the Square throughout its longevity. It closed its doors in the early 1970s. The building was demolished and in its place and on the site of number 20 was built the Grecian architectural five-storied Rutherford County Judicial Building.

★ ★ ★

The Murfreesboro Bank and Trust Company occupied E-24 in 1924. Plans were already underway for the next two buildings (E-26 and E-28) toward the corner to become a part of the new expansion program for the bank. That acquisition would almost triple the bank's square footage, especially since the acquired buildings were three-storied.

The bank was organized and chartered July 8, 1905, with a capital stock of $50,000. The first officers elected were: B.F. Moore, president; G.S. Harding, vice president; and Leland Jordan, cashier.

In 1906 the capital stock was increased to $75,000, and in 1920 the capitalization was $100,000. A dividend of six percent was declared every year until 1915, when the rate was increased to eight percent. In 1917, the dividend was fixed at ten percent. A twelve percent rate was shown in 1921. A statement of April, 1923 shows that the bank's capital stock was $100,000, surplus $100,000, deposits in the amount of $1,436,209.98, and total resources of $1,850,720.07.

Robert T. "Bob" Bell had the designation of cashier of the bank in 1923. In that office, he was also the chief executive officer. Until his death in the early 1950s and under his leadership, the bank enjoyed a phenomenal growth. That occurred even during the lean and economically dangerous years of the Great Depression. It is still remembered by some of the oldtimers about town how the bank weathered those ominous few days in 1932 when the First National Bank around the corner closed its doors. The Murfreesboro Bank and Trust Company's customers were rightfully anxious about their deposits and began gathering early before the bank opened. As if by some pre-designed plan, an armored car arrived at the side door on Maple Street. Uniformed men began stacking bags and packages on a cart to be wheeled into the just-opened side door. The customers began lining up before the teller's cages to withdraw their deposits. The story goes that Mr. Bell stood on a stool and announced that the money was available to cover whatever withdrawals the customers wanted to make. With this announcement and the obvious sight of all of the money arriving, the people were calmed and began to have second thoughts about withdrawing their money. Thus, the run on the bank was averted. That incident became a vote of confidence in the bank, which providentially contributed to its ensuing growth.

Homer Powell was a teller in the bank during the 1920s and until he was appointed cashier in 1929. He played a prominent part in the operation of the bank during the next two decades.

Upon the death of Mr. Bell, his son-in-law, Al Mifflin, received the mantle of chief executive officer. Al was the affable outgoing executive who kept the bank on an even keel with continued growth throughout his tenure and until his death in 1970.

Then came Jack Weatherford to take over the helm of a successful bank that had been so closely involved in the business and economic life of Murfreesboro for over threescore years. Jack began his leadership in 1970, and retired as CEO in 1988. At that time, Jack Holden took over the reins.

In 1977, the Murfreesboro Bank and Trust Company bought the fifty-year-old James K. Polk Hotel on the corner of East Main and North Spring streets. It also bought the adjoining former Nelson home, Wade home, the Delbridge and Professional Building properties which resulted in the bank's ownership of about nine tenths of the entire block. The bank built its present elegant commodious building on that site.

The bank became a part of the Third National Bank in Nashville in 1985. Shortly thereafter, Sun Trust of Atlanta purchased the assets of the Third National system.

When the bank moved to its new prestigious quarters, its former home of almost seventy years was sold to Rutherford County and now houses the busy offices of Ed Elam, who is the Clerk of Rutherford County.

It was in the general area of numbers 18, 20, 22, and 24 that a public market was located in 1834. It was at that place that the slave auctions were held until the Civil War. Across the street was the Public Well, the well that is mentioned in John Cedric Spence's *Annals of Murfreesboro*, a book recently published by the Rutherford County Historical Society.

There were two more addresses past the Murfreesboro Bank and Trust Company—26 and 28. Number 26 became occupied by the Ideal Barber Shop in 1922. Walter Taylor, who later became game warden, was one of the barbers there. The shop later moved around the corner and into the west side of the bank and thence, after a few years, into its present address on the northeast side of the Square. The Office of Veterans Affairs moved into that space in the mid-1940s and remained for a few years. The bank decided that the area was needed for the growth that it was experiencing and it soon expanded into 26 and 28.

Number 28 was on the corner. It was occupied in the early 1920s by the Lytle Clothing Company. Ephraim Foster Lytle and his son Julian conducted that business.

R.T. Groom—"Nothing but Insurance." That was the name and logo of a company that was one of Murfreesboro's most successful insurance brokers for sixty-five years. Robert T. Groom opened his company on the north side of the 100-block of West Main in 1919. His tile-imbedded name is still in the sidewalk in front of where his office was (F-24). Mr. Groom was a sincere man who was able to convince his customers that he championed them in any difference between them and the underwriter. His chief secretary was Miss Lockie Smith, who became known as one of the best secretaries around the Square. The chief salesperson was easy-going Frank "Fatty" Stephens. Frank was never offended when a prospect declined to buy insurance from him. He just kept going and going and going back.

The Groom Insurance Company moved from West Main in about 1930 to number 28 where Lytle Clothing Company had recently been. They remained there until 1949 which was the year that Robert T.Groom died. Buford Turpin had married Mr. Groom's daughter, Margaret. Buford and Bob's son, Tom Groom, had been working in the company so they moved into the Scott Building on College Street. Shortly after the move, the company's name was changed to Groom and Turpin. When the Scott Building was demolished to make room for the new Cavalry Bank in 1972, the partnership moved to Penney Plaza where they remained until the company was sold to Farmer Brothers in 1984.

The Rutherford County Clerk's office occupies that northwest corner of the Square at the present time. The county bought the property from the Murfreesboro Bank and Trust Company in 1978 and moved the clerk's office from the courthouse in February of 1979. Ed "Sonny" Elam has held his office since 1974. J.P. Leathers holds the record for having served as Rutherford County Clerk for more years than any other person. He served eight terms or thirty-two years—from 1918 to 1950. Fount Pitts came next, serving from 1950 into 1962. Ben Hall McFarlin began his three terms in 1962, and served to the beginning term of the present county clerk, Ed "Sonny" Elam.

This concludes a past and present tour of the Square's north side, a side which has provided exciting, high quality professional services, shopping, and banking for the residents of Rutherford County. Its property owners continue to proudly renovate and face-lift their buildings. During the 1920s, 1930s, and 1940s, it seemed that the north side attracted the largest crowds on Saturdays except for the harvest time Saturdays. Those were the days that Mink Slide attracted the most people. The black people filled the sidewalk, the street, and meandered onto the courthouse yard and other portions of the Square; but the Slide was where the action was.

It is time now to turn the corner and walk about one hundred feet to the side door of the early site of Murfreesboro Bank and Trust Company. Through the double doors and to the right was the personal loan department of the bank. Jack Lee became the manager of that office during the late 1940s. On the left of the side entrance was the insurance company operated by J.K. "Cap" Clayton and John Nelson.

It was through double doors that the second- and third-story office holders made their entrance. Some of the many people who occupied those offices over the years were Jesse Huggins, Eugene "Burrhead" Hargis, Ed Rhodes, "Ebbie" Miller Insurance, Dr. George Stephenson, dentist, Tommy Martin Insurance, David Hall Accounting, Dr. Mel Roberts, chiropractor, Pruitt and Davidson Insurance, and Tennessee Welfare Departments (Mrs. Thelma Woods). Boy Scout Troop 105 used a large room on the third floor for several years beginning in 1930.

Few loads of cotton on Square, circa 1925.

Policeman in left foreground was Police Chief "Jep" Hall, grandfather of author.

C.H. Byrn, owner of two hardware stores on Square and one of the town's first automobile dealers.

Jesse Messick, well known druggist, leader in Uptown Merchants Association, County Commissioner and founder in 1976 of "Uncle Dave Macon Days."

Gladys Dement beside Jesse Messick in parade on Square. Gladys was probably the Square's most frequent visitor as well as its best known political prognosticator.

Murfreesboro Bank & Trust Co. as it appeared in 1909.

Northside Square, circa 1923.

Occasion for largest crowd to ever gather on Square.

Chapter XVI

West and East College

Emerging from the side door of the bank, the tour resumes and proceeds to the right. The next door address is E-124. That location is occupied by the Mid-Tenn Coin and Jewelry Company. Its owners are John Parker and Ken Fanning, and they have been there since 1980. They buy and sell coins and jewelry. Also, the firm does appraisals of such items and sells metal detectors. The present owner of the property is Melinda Young Sherer of Atlanta. She is the granddaughter of R.Y. "Bob" Martin, who owned the building for several years. Bob was a highly visible figure in Murfreesboro during the 1930s, 1940s, 1950s, and early 1960s. He owned the Gulf Oil Distributing Company for many of those years. He also owned and operated the Murfreesboro Golf and Country Club on the Shelbyville Road for several years. Bob Martin served as state representative of Rutherford County during a portion of the early 1940s.

In 1923, that property was owned by Leland Jordan. He was the cashier of the Murfreesboro Bank and Trust Company when it was first chartered in 1905. In those early years, the building fronted on West College Street and its address was 120 College.

The building was occupied by the Murfreesboro Battery Company, which was owned by Tom Dement. Mr. Dement was mayor of Murfreesboro during a portion of the early 1930s. His chief assistant in the business operation was Lytle Thompson. Lytle went on to own his own battery and ignition business which was located between West College and West Lytle streets. Dement and Stephens operated a service station there for awhile after the Murfreesboro Battery Company closed.

The Sue and Willie Service Station and Restaurant was the next business located on that corner by which passed the busy 41 Highway. Myrtle, Sue, Willie, and Bonnie Anderson moved from Crossville to Murfreesboro during the late 1930s. Their business did so well that they decided to move two blocks west on College Street to a large lot which would accommodate a restaurant and space for the large trucks that would frequent their operation.

Shortly after the S. and W. Restaurant moved from 124 North Maple Street, Dura Cook began her operation of a popular restaurant on that corner. Later the Murfreesboro Bank and Trust Company leased the corner for its expanded operation. The next building eastward is the rear of the Judicial Building which was formerly McClellans. Earlier, it was Shacklett, Staley and Sanders. Both businesses fronted on the Square.

★ ★ ★

The next address on West College Street is E-115. It formerly fronted on the Public Square and its address was number 16. Its former tenants were C.H. Byrn Hardware Co., C.B. Leatherman Dry Goods Co. and others. Nowadays, the entire building from front (E-16) to rear (E-115) is occupied by attorneys Matt Murfree, III, James C. Cope, Mark S. Moore, Roger W. Hudson and Darrell L. Scarlett. The property is registered to Matt Murfree, III.

★ ★ ★

The next address on West College Street is E-111 and is occupied by the Cumberland Title Co. That building also formerly fronted on the Public Square and was the home of Kerr Drug Store, McCord & Harris and others. Now the Square side is occupied by the law offices of John Rucker Sr., John Rucker, Jr. and Kent Coleman.

The Cumberland Title Co. is owned by Edward Seddon and Patrick L. Vaden. The partnership also owns the property in which it operates.

Forty years ago and until 1961, Eddie Seddon was the executive director of both the Murfreesboro Urban Renewal (Bottoms) Project and the Murfreesboro Housing Authority. In order to appreciate the immensity of the project and the wonderful improvements that it made to that blighted area of the town, one would have had to visit the almost fifty acre area before the mid-point of the century. Ed Bell wrote candidly in the forties that "the Bottoms is a low section of shanties, floods, poverty, misery and sin where mainly whites live."

The project was recognized by the Federal Government as the largest per capita urban renewal project in the nation at that time. At completion, the Murfreesboro Housing Authority comprised two hundred apartment units and one hundred and fifty individual housing units. Present day Judge Whitney Stegall was also connected in that huge effort which was to be the first effort to bring the town from "Mink Slide" of those days to the "Main Street" of today.

★ ★ ★

The next address (E-111) West College Street was formerly a portion of the rear entrance to the J.C. Penney store. Its address numbers on the Public Square were 10 and 12. The front portion as mentioned earlier is occupied by the Martin Rexall Drug Co. and is operated by Mrs. Jesse Messick.

★ ★ ★

The rear section (109 West College Street) is occupied by M J's Hair Styling Boutique. The M J initials are the first letters of the beauty operator's name, Mary Johnson. She has been at that location for almost two years. Al Lytle Partee, Jr. is the owner of the entire property which houses the drug company and the boutique.

E-107 West College Street is owned and occupied by attorneys George White and Larry Tolbert. George White and Ed Netherland bought the property in 1989. With architectural and design assistance from Dawn Eaton's Main Street staff, the two partners completely renovated the building while managing to preserve the traditional integrity of the structure. Ed sold his interest in the property in 1990 to George who shortly thereafter sold one half interest to Larry Tolbert who occupies an office suite therein.

The address (107) is better known as the Rion Flower Shop. Mattie Rion and her staff were there from 1937 until the mid-nineteen eighties. Mattie is ninety-one years of age, but her memory capabilities are as sharp as one much younger. She is retired and the Rion Flower Shop is operated by her daughter Martha Ann Rion Moffett. The business is now located on South Academy Street across from the East Main Street Church of Christ. Two long-time staff members are Sara Rion Abernathy and Virginia Overall Rawlins.

The Jaggers-Wade Flower Shop was there for several years before the Rions. The Corrine and Florine Beauty Shop was there before moving to the corner of West College and North Church Streets. Also located there during the late twenties was Jimmie Haynes and his Jimmie's Place. He later moved to the southwest corner of College and Maple Streets.

Continuing east on College Street, the tour passes the Wiseman Building, crosses Church Street and resumes behind the Flower Center (D-130) on East College Street. These are the offices of Dr. William C. Smith. He is a Doctor of Optometry. Dr. Smith is a native of Smithville, Tennessee, who came to Murfreesboro eleven years ago. His first office was in the middle of the block on Bell Street behind Dr. Sam Hay. The doctor moved to his present location the following year in 1980. Dr. Smith also has an office in Eagleville where he practices two days each week.

Dr. Paul Lynn was an optometrist who had maintained offices on North Spring Street. He had been practicing since 1948. Dr. Lynn moved to 102 East College Street in 1960. He practiced optometry there until his death in 1980.

There is a marked contrast between the handsome modern appointments in the interior of Dr. Smith's offices and the ancient brick walls of the old Methodist Church which was erected there in 1847. The building later became the old Jackson Building and is now owned by Joe Swanson.

The next address eastward (106) was a vacant lot in 1923. Dr. David Ferrell was to erect the two story building now located there in the nineteen forties. Tom Lane was the contractor and Harold Garland subsequently bought the property when Dr. Ferrell decided to move his dental practice to another city. The building became known as the Ferrell Building.

Leo Ferrell was a well known photographer in Murfreesboro during the early part of this century and into the early nineteen forties. He was the father of Dr. David Ferrell. David now resides in Richmond, Indiana.

Attorneys Whitney Stegall and Dick LaRoche came to the 106 location in 1951. They practiced there for twenty years. Margie Pitts was employed by Stegall and LaRoche as a secretary. She later attended law school and is now a practicing attorney in Marietta, Georgia.

Joe Dearman and his wife Florine operated an accounting service in the rear of the upper floor section.

James "Doc" Garner came to the Ferrell Building next with his First Realty Company. "Doc" had operated a prescription shop in the James K. Polk Hotel for several years. Mr. Garner bought the building in the early seventies. Among those who occupied the newly remodeled building were Dr. Lloyd Smith, dentist, Dr. W.J. Schoenberger and Harry Hassell, pastor of the First Presbyterian Church.

Steve Ruckart bought the Ferrell Building from James Garner in 1981. Steve came to Murfreesboro from Oak Ridge, Tennessee in 1973. He graduated from Middle Tennessee State University in 1977.

In the ten years that Ruckart Associates Inc. have been at that location, they have become the largest independently owned life and health insurance company in Murfreesboro. The insurance company occupies the entire upper floor of the Ferrell Building. They have six local agents who have offices there. They are affiliated with 50 agents in Middle Tennessee.

Steve Ruckart is a personable young man. Under his leadership Ruckart Associates should have a successful future.

The Crisis Pregnancy Counseling Center has its offices downstairs in the front section of D-106. Cliff Sharpe is the executive director of the center.

Equifax PMI (Physical Measurements Inc.) occupies the rear section of the downstairs. They perform medical examinations for insurance companies.

★ ★ ★

The next building (110) is relatively new, having been built in 1979. It has accommodated an insurance agency, a beauty parlor and most recently, an antique refinishing shop. The place is vacant at the present time.

114 East College Street is the present address of the Front Porch Cafe. In 1907 the building was the home of the Elks Club. In April of 1914 the undertaking firm of Woodfin & Moore bought the property. Their building on the north side of the Square had been severely damaged in the cyclone of March, 1913.

The Woodfin & Moore partnership was dissolved in 1949 and H.C. "Dick" Moore retained the building in which to continue the operation of the Moore Funeral Home. John Woodfin founded the new funeral home at the location where the present Woodfin Memorial Chapel is situated.

Mr. H.C. Moore remained there for several years. He sold the property to Dr. David T. Dodd in 1966. Dr. Dodd gave the building a good renovation, adding decorative appointments and fashioning the building into a restaurant. John and Alma Jean Cook opened a restaurant there later in the year of 1966. They were there for approximately a year. Dr. Dodd sold the property in 1968.

Eventually in December, 1988, the former Elks Club, funeral home and restaurant site was sold at auction by the Mid-South Bank and Trust Company. The Wright Properties became the new owners of 114 East College Street. The building is now occupied by the Front Porch Cafe. The owners are Russell Gannon, John and Debbie Barner and Ty Osman.

★ ★ ★

Proceeding past Beckman's Prescription Shop to the corner of East College and North Spring Streets, this armchair tour would cross to the opposite corner northward to the address of 123 East College Street. In 1823 and for over a century thereafter, the old two story plain front brick house located there was known as the Wendel house. When it was demolished in 1945 it was probably the oldest house in Murfreesboro.

The Wendels were prominent in the professional, political and social activities of the town from almost its beginning to the end of the first quarter of the twentieth century.

Dr. B.W. Rawlins bought the Wendel property in 1945. He erected the yellow brick building standing on that corner during the same year. It has been a popular and almost always-leased professional location since its erection. It has housed the offices of Dr. Rawlins, Dr. James Scott, Dr. R.A. Nausley, Dr. Gilbert Gordon, Dr. Joe Knight, Dr. C.A. Heffington, Dr. R.H. Hackman and attorney Jack Heffington.

Since the death of Dr. Rawlins, his wife, Virginia Overall Rawlins, has leased the building to its various tenants. She sold the property to the present occupants, the Clark Maples Realty & Auction Company, in 1988. Virginia Rawlins' son, Benjamin Wade Rawlins, is the chairman of the board, president and chief operating officer of the Union Planters Bank headquartered in Memphis.

The building at 123 East College Street was a handy and timely purchase for Clark Maples. His office and sales staff had been increasing until they were bursting at the seams in the brick two story house next door (115 East College Street).

★ ★ ★

The building at 115 was built in 1936 by a family whose name is believed to have been Mintlow. A partnership composed of Whitney Stegall, Dick LaRoche and Dr. George Stephenson bought the residence in 1963.

The building housed the law offices of attorneys Stegall and LaRoche and the dental office of Dr. Stephenson. They were there for several years. John O'Brien became the next owner of the property and he moved his real estate operation into those quarters. John was there for about ten years when he sold the property to Clark Maples in 1980.

Just recently in March of 1991, the First Methodist Church bought the property from Maples. He will be moving his company into the large next door building which he owns and which contains 6200 sq. feet.

★ ★ ★

There was a large frame structure between 115 East College Street and the First Methodist Church. It was a tall and deep two-story building which was, in 1907, the closest semblance to a hospital in town. It contained eight beds. The doctor in charge was Dr. Vernon King Earthman. He was the father of Harold Earthman who became a Congressman in the late nineteen forties. Harold "Doc" Earthman served as a state legislator, county judge and the chairman of Rutherford County's One-Gallus Foxhunters.

The former hospital became the Dixie Hotel in the late teens. Virginia Hale and her sister became the owners of the property. Miss Hale was the seventh grade teacher at Crichlow Grammer School during the late twenties. She later married attorney Frank Hargis. In 1944, the Dixie Hotel was sold to my parents C.B. and Sarah Hall Arnette. They leased the hotel to Mr. and Mrs. R.L. Grandstaff who operated it for several years.

The First Methodist Church bought the property in 1957 from Annie Lou Mason, Sara Elizabeth Pearson and C.B., Jr. who were the children of C.B. Arnette. The former hospital and hotel building was demolished and is now a parking lot for the adjacent church.

Chapter XVII

North Church—West College (North Side)

The tour continues past the church with a right turn at the corner. In the middle of the block on North Church Street in 1924 was a two story brick house with a large porch. That was the parsonage of the First United Methodist Church. If a pedestrian were strolling by the house on a summer afternoon in 1924, the chances were that the pastor David Hinkle and his wife would be sitting on a canvas covered glider on the porch. In 1928 the occupants of the glider would have been Pastor John Baggett and his wife. Their children, John, Jr. and Eva, might have been on the porch also. In 1932 the new pastor of the church and the new family on the block would have been J. Robert Parsons, his wife and son, Bob. Bob was president of the C.H.S. Senior Class in 1935. He studied medicine at Duke University and is still practicing in Huntington, West Virginia.

Beyond the parsonage was a frame house on the corner of North Church and East Lytle Streets. The tour goes no farther on North Church Street, but crosses to the opposite corner, turns left and heads toward the Square.

★ ★ ★

On the corner at North Church and East Lytle was a two story, square, stucco building. Cedar boxes were manufactured downstairs and the upper floor was used as a meeting place for the I.O.O.F. (colored) Lodge. The address was 227 North Church. Later, Aubrey Smith occupied that place with a cleaning establishment.

★ ★ ★

The next address southward was 217 North Church Street. A quaint, low, two story ancient brick house was on the large lot in 1924 and into the early nineteen fifties. That was the Burgdorf home.

Louis J. Burgdorf was the publisher of the *Home Journal* around the turn of the century. His wife, Amelia, lived to the age of ninety-nine years, most of which were spent in that house in front of the Methodist Church. Louis and Amelia had four sons and three daughters. Frank Burgdorf has already been mentioned in connection with Goldsteins.

George Burgdorf was the publisher's grandson and was connected with the *News Banner* in the late twenties.

The telephone company bought that property, demolished the house, and erected a large brick building on the lot.

★ ★ ★

The next address is 211 North Church Street. The Cumberland Telephone Company was located there in 1924. The large two story brick is still standing and is occupied by the Miller-Loughry Insurance Company.

Dr. W.C. Bilbro owned the building in 1924 and leased it to the telephone company. In the twenties, the switchboards were usually manned by a staff of ten operators. Their salaries were about $8.00 per week. In 1942, the telephone company had nineteen operators and three supervisors. The beginning operator's salary in those days was $12.00 per week.

The telephone company remained there until 1954. The back rooms of the large building were used for repairing and testing telephones. The number of operators continued to increase. The company changed from the manual system (number please ?) to the dial system. The large brick structure was built next door and the company moved out of 211 North Church Street.

Ewing Smith bought the 211 property in the late sixties. Attorneys Ewing Smith, Tommie Smith, Bill and Nancy Sellers moved into the building in 1970. They were there until 1974 when they moved into a suite of offices in the new Cavalry Bank Building.

Ebbie Miller brought his Edward E. Miller Insurance Agency into the remodeled old telephone building in 1979. On July 1, 1988 Andrea Loughry became a member of the insurance firm. Edward E. Miller, III is also a partner in the agency.

★ ★ ★

Proceeding about one hundred feet to the corner of West College and North Church Streets, the next address is 102 West College. That was the site of the U.S. Post office in 1924 and back into 1919. That is the date shown on the cornerstone of the building. It is noted on a map in 1914 that a livery stable was on that site.

Among the postmasters who have served at the post since 1924 were J.V. Braswell, Neil Elrod, J.C. Elrod, Beulah Hughes, William Earthman, Charlie Byrn, Norman Hutchinson and David Huskey. Strangely enough, for the day and age in which she served, Postmistress Beulah Hughes was a Republican. That was when Rutherford County was about 99% purely Democratic.

Robert Lasseter was connected with the *Rutherford Courier* in 1942. He wrote in a column one day that it was shameful that Murfreesboro was bereft of a library. He decried that the children of the town were not afforded access to books. A man in Tampa, Florida read the article. His name was Henry Linebaugh. He had been reared in Murfreesboro and had gone to Florida to engage in fruit picking. Florida had been good to him. He had prospered. He felt that his hometown should have a library. With those thoughts in mind, he informed Bob Lasseter that he would contribute $5,000.00 to the formation of a library. It was to be in memory of his mother Mattie V. Linebaugh.

With the proposition from the Linebaugh benefactor, Bob started the ball to rolling. He formed a board of directors with an office on the third floor of the courthouse. The Mattie V. Linebaugh Library came into being, and was located in the old Hale house (also Dr. Kirtley home) on the former Tennessee College campus. The library soon outgrew those quarters and moved to the old Elks Club on North Spring Street in August, 1953. Emma Weitzel left $30,000.00 in her will to the struggling library which continued to grow. By 1961, it had outgrown the Elks Club building. The post office building on West College Street became available in 1961. In that year the General Service Administration gave the property to the library.

Myla Parsons processed the first book at the newly-formed Mattie V. Linebaugh Library in 1947. She had been teaching English at Christiana High School while serving as librarian at the school. She was approached by Bealer Smotherman who was Rutherford County School Superintendent, to serve as librarian at the new library. She served fifteen years, until 1962, in that capacity. It was a hard struggle during those years but the Mattie V. Linebaugh was on a firm footing when Briley Adcock took over the reins in 1962.

In the early days of the library, many contributed much of their time to help the library to survive. An example of those people was Alberta Spence who volunteered her assistance until funds were available to pay her.

The future looks bright for the library today. It has been awarded $1.4 million by the Christy-Houston Foundation. Its new quarters will be in the new city center. Bob Lasseter would applaud this.

Behind the old Post Office was the office of Dr. Eugene P. Odom. Dr. Odom came there in 1947 from his one-year-old practice in Smyrna. He was there for ten years. In 1957, the doctor moved to his present location on the corner of North Tennessee Blvd. and Greenland Drive. His son, Dr. Stephen Odom has his medical practice in the same building.

Upstairs in that building was the Knox Business College which was operated by Elsie Knox.

★ ★ ★

Just west of the Post Office in 1924 was the Putnam Overall Manufacturing Company. The firm operated one hundred fifty machines and was reputed to be the largest clothing manufacturer from St. Louis to the coast. It was the largest plant in Tennessee that made a complete line of working-men's clothes.

Established in 1907, they manufactured a complete line of men's and boy's corduroy, gabardines, moleskins, khakis, cotton check suits, men's and boy's coveralls, overalls and jumpers.

The president of the overall factory was Mr. G.A. Maxwell. He and his family lived in a handsome limestone rock house in the nine hundred block on East Main Street. That had formerly been the home of Dr. and Mrs. W.C. Bilbro.

There came next to that address at 116 West College Street the Murfreesboro Federal Savings & Loan Company. The year was 1941. They had moved from the old Jordan Hotel on East Main Street. Ernest Jordan was the bank's manager, William Mason, Jr. was the chief bookkeeper and Mr. Jordan's wife, Amy, assisted. Ernest and Amy had an apartment over the bank. The company had been founded in 1929 as the Murfreesboro Building & Loan Association. They had weathered the depths of the Great Depression and, still operating with a rather spartan existence, they had a new name and a new location. World War II came with its restrictions on any kind of construction, but the institution made transactions, gained the confidence of more depositors, increased its staff and, at war's end, was able to assist the many first-time homebuilders in Rutherford County. Mary Mason, William's wife, came aboard along with Lillie Mae Hoover, the wife of J.T. Hoover, the owner of the Hoover Paint Store. Ben Batey came in 1946. John Alsup, Gladys Jones, and Jack McHenry came later.

The bank did exceptionally well through the years. The directors began to think in terms of expansion in 1970. By 1972, they had purchased all of the property in the southwest quadrant of the block to make room for the construction of a five story finely architectured building. It would be, at that time, Murfreesboro's most expensive building. The cost was to be two million dollars. The new building was completed in 1974 and the forty-five-year-old loan association became known as Cavalry Banking. The institution has two branch offices in town—Memorial and South Tennessee Blvd.

The presidents of the bank since its inception have been: Ernest Jordan, Hollis Donnell, Ben Batey and Ed Loughry, Jr. Some of the directors who served in the earlier years were: Will Bell, Ellis Gray, Clyde Fite, Harry Scott, John Nelson, Cary Knight and Burns Carroll.

Ewing Smith had his law offices on the second floor of the building for several years.

★ ★ ★

The addresses 118 through 126 West College Street in 1924 were occupied mainly by a garage and hardware storage facility. The property was owned by C.H. Byrn who has been mentioned previously. The portion fronting on West College extended back in an L shaped manner to exit through a similarly large frontage on North Maple Street. That was the building in which Mr. Byrn operated his automobile dealership during the teens.

John Cedric Spence kept a journal of Murfreesboro dealing with almost all of the last century. He bought a fine house which was located in that section of West College Street. He had just bought a tract of land extending from North Maple Street to North Walnut Street, and adjacent to the north side of Soule College. That lot was to become the site of the handsome James Moore home and eventually the Discovery House. Mr. Spence moved the house from West College Street to his lot on North Maple Street which was quite a feat for those days.

Mr. Clyde Reagor was a partner in a Buick dealership. Mr. Reagor was a son-in-law of C.H. Byrn, and Roy Byrn was a nephew. They occupied the building which fronted on West College and North Maple Streets. When the partnership was dissolved in the early thirties, Mr. Byrn occupied the North Maple address and Mr. Reagor the West College address. Clyde Reagor began the Reagor Tire Company in 118, 120 and 122 West College. He installed gravity flow gasoline pumps in front of the building. I can recall that he was the only man selling gasoline in town who served his customers attired in a fine felt hat, gold frame rimless spectacles, coat, tie and a clean white shirt. He was a most mannerly man. Mr. Reagor later moved two blocks west. After his death, his wife Lucille Reagor, continued to lease the location until the Murfreesboro Federal bought the property in 1972.

The Great Atlantic & Pacific Tea Company (A & P) came there in the late nineteen thirties and remained until 1950. Wayne Dickens was the store's manager.

When A & P left that address in 1950, the Tip Top Barber Shop moved into the right side of the building. A & P moved to North Maple where the First American Bank is located.

★ ★ ★

The 118 West College Street address was occupied by the Tip Top Barber Shop from 1950 into 1972. The shop moved to the south side of the Square in 1972. The Murfreesboro Savings & Loan Co. had bought all of the property on the southeast quadrant of the block and all of the buildings thereon were to be demolished. Some of the barbers who worked there during those years were: T.B. Gilley, Eural Sauls, Hall Todd, Joe Davidson, Will Ed Blair and Godfrey Marable.

Dudley Fletcher operated a men's clothing store there until 1962.

Tom Cannon and Tom Groom came to West College Street next with an exciting store named Tom-Tom's High-Fidelity Shop. They handled high fidelity and stereo equipment plus records, tapes and accessories. They were there from 1962 into 1966.

Attorneys Wilkes Coffey, Dick Kidwell and Judge Campbell had offices there until those buildings were razed.

Harry Scott and Aubrey Smith established a cleaning service in the next addresses 124 and 126 West College Street. Eventually the partnership was dissolved and Aubrey Smith opened a cleaning business on the corner of North Church and West Lytle which was mentioned earlier. Harry Scott leased the cleaning business later to Reed Brendle. After a while, Mr. Brendle moved to another location and Mr. Scott remodeled to accommodate several offices. Among those who occupied offices there over a span of years were: Groom & Turpin Insurance Co.; Harry Scott Realty; Gilbert McClanahan, Contractor; Attorney Jack Todd; J.R. Young Insurance Co.; S.A. Todd, Realtor; and Hughes Real Estate Co.

Attorneys Ewing, and Tommie Smith and Bill and Nancy Smith Sellers had, as already mentioned, occupied the upper floor of the Murfreesboro Federal building at 116 West College. They moved to the building next door to the Princess Theatre in the late forties. The address was 128 West College Street. In 1971, they moved to the old telephone building on North Church Street. That last move occurred just before those buildings were razed to make room for the new Cavalry Bank building.

During the late twenties, Tom Ferrell had a barber shop in that building. One of the popular and well known barbers there was Barney (Big Boy) Dunaway. Upstairs there were offices occupied by Oscar Morgan, Jesse Rutledge and Eugene "Burr Head" Hargis.

★ ★ ★

The last building in this block on West College Street was known in the first quarter of this century as the Sam Davis Building. It housed what was known as the opera house in 1924. Shortly thereafter, it became known as the Princess Theatre. That theatre had just moved from its location in what became the Elrod Building on the east side of the Square. Oscar Altman was the manager then and remained in that capacity through the forties. Subsequent managers to the present time have been Mr. Hawk, Sanford Cox and Joe Tomlinson. The property was owned by the Princess Amusement Co. (Crescent Amusement Co.)

During the late nineteen twenties, each Saturday had the alternate showings of Tom Mix and Buck Jones films. "Hoot" Gibson, Ken Maynard and Jack Daugherty showed occasionally. William S. Hart was a favorite cowboy star in the early twenties. The admission was ten cents for those under twelve years of age. Popcorn with lots of real butter was five cents. The "tear-jerking" movies in the early thirties were "Trail of the Lonesome Pine," "Little Shepherd of the Hills," and later "Smiling Through" with Norma Shearer.

Quite often there were good quality stage shows, beauty contests, and other attractions that would still be appreciated today.

The following headline was in the *News Journal* issue of December 16, 1931: Princess to Open Tonight With New Talkie Equipment. The feature attraction was "Cuban Love Song" with Lawrence Tibbett.

A headline in the April 1, 1936 issue of the *News Journal* announced the opening of Murfreesboro's new Ultra Modern Theatre. Excerpts are given:....entirely new structure throughout from the basement to the roof....seating capacity of one thousand....ultra-modern exterior will be faced with structural glass of varying iridescent colors in keeping with cosmopolitan theatres of today....building will be air-conditioned throughout....balcony has 200 seats....separate colored balcony will seat one hundred and fifty persons...the stage will accommodate stage productions as well.

The Princess Theatre was the main entertainment center in town until the fifties. With the advent of television and drive-in movies, its attraction began to dwindle. However, the company that owned the Princess evolved into the company that owned the drive-in theatres. The owner of the Princess Theatre property during the twenties, thirties and forties was the Crescent Amusement Co. of Nashville. They became the Martin Amusement Co. in the early fifties and also eventually became the owners of the two local drive-in theatres which had been owned by W.D. Hamaker and Vernon Hickson.

Doris "Blue" J. David was the perennial ticket taker and order-keeper from the early twenties into the early sixties. Gilbert McClanahan, James Barrett and Walter Coleman were some of the projectionists through the years.

Within the theatre and next to the corner was a small square space which was called the Princess Sweet Shop. Sewell Manley was owner of the shop for several years.

The old Wendel home on corner of North Spring and East College Streets. Presently the location of Clark Maples Realty and Auction Company.

Princess Theatre at corner of North Maple and West College Streets.

Site of former Post Office which later housed Linebaugh Library. Picture circa 1900.

Putnam Overall Manufacturing Co. which later housed Murfreesboro Federal Savings & Loan Company. Razed in 1972.

Chapter XVIII

North Maple—West College

Turning right at the Princess and walking about one hundred and twenty-five feet, the tour comes to 212 North Maple Street. In 1924 that was the Byrn-Reagor Buick dealership and garage. A showroom was on the north side of the building. It was a huge building which accommodated a large repair shop and spaces for used cars. As noted earlier, the building had an entrance on West College Street. Also as mentioned before, the Byrn-Reagor partnership was dissolved in the thirties. The Roy Byrn dealership continued there until the late nineteen fifties. Then a large new building with showrooms, repair shop, offices and sales lot was arranged on West College Street south of the old State Farm building. Mrs. Annie Byrn Roberts was owner of the property until it was sold in 1972 to the Murfreesboro Federal Savings & Loan Co.

Leaving the Byrn building and past the gravity-flow pumps, the next address in 1924 was 220 North Maple Street. There was a narrow deep building which had a sheet metal shop within. The building was situated on a large lot. That large lot was to be utilized at the end of the twenties when a large building the width of the entire space was erected. The structure had a tall rounded roof which was supported by long wooden girders.

That was the newest and most modern service station in town. It was called Tom, Dick and Eph's Service Station and Garage. Those were the Carney brothers who had initiated the enterprise. They were there for several years.

The Bob Overall Motor Company was to come to that large garage building during the mid forties. The next business there was the Southern Furniture Company which came in 1959. It was operated by Curtis Hutson and James Rowland. They bought the property from Mr. Roberts of Monteagle. The building burned in 1972 and the property was sold to the Murfreesboro Federal Savings & Loan Co. the same year.

★ ★ ★

The corner address was 226 North Maple Street. That was the meeting place of the Mt. Zion Baptist Church (Colored) in 1924. According to the Mt. Zion church historian, the congregation began meeting some time before 1884 in a rented old frame building on the lower end of South Maple Street. Even then it was known as the Mt. Zion Missionary Baptist Church.

In 1884, the present church building with the gothic windows was erected on the corner of North Maple and West Lytle Streets. It has had some additions and renovations during its one-hundred-and-seven-year history. Pastor John Ratliff is the nineteenth pastor to serve that historic congregation since its inception.

★ ★ ★

Across North Maple Street from the Mt. Zion Baptist Church was the Turpin Marble Works in 1924. A passerby at that time would observe a large lot that appeared to be a small cemetery. There was a small office building in the center of the lot. Actually, it was a firm which cut, carved and lettered marble and granite tombstones. David Nugent had been the former owner of that business. Turpin Bros. & Company were the owners in 1924.

A Woco-Pep service station was to come to the address of 221 North Maple Street several years later. W.C. "Tick" Brown and Mankin "Mack" McKee were partners in the operation of the popular and busy station for several years. It was to become a Union 76 gas station later. Then the Carpet Center came and they are the present occupants.

The property has been owned for several years by Anna Lee Davenport. She sold it in 1990 to Morris Publishing Co. of Columbus, Georgia (Mid-South Publishing Co.).

★ ★ ★

The next lot southward from the corner at address 215 North Maple Street contained a dwelling. The owner of the house in 1924 was James W. Donnell.

The Murfreesboro Laundry came to that place in the early nineteen twenties. The business was operated by Albert King, Jr. The laundry employed quite a few women. In its heyday they had about fifty employees. There were panel trucks that were used to pick up and deliver the customers' clothes. That was at a time when there were few powered washing machines and no dryers. By the forties more people could afford those appliances and by the fifties most households had at least a clothes washer. Consequently, the need for a laundry diminished to such an extent that the business closed in the late sixties.

Mr. Albert King, Jr. sold the property in 1968 to Curtis Hutson and James Rowland who operated the Southern Furniture Co. across the street. They operated the laundry for two or three years and sold the property to the Mid-South Publishing Co.

There were three dependable sounds that could be heard around and off the square during the twenties, thirties and forties. On the hour and half hour for seven days a week there was the tolling bell in the clock tower of the courthouse. The Sunshine Hosiery Mill and the Murfreesboro Laundry both had steam whistles which sounded off punctually at 7:30 a.m., noon, 12:30 p.m. and 5:00 p.m. There were two other most penetrating irregular sounds. One was the deep throaty-to-treble fire alarm at the ice plant and the others were the steam locomotives arriving and departing from the railway depot.

★ ★ ★

One of the greatest entrepreneurial stories to come out of the first third of this century involved James Cason, Edward E. "Pluck" Miller and Ephraim "Eph" Hoover.

James Cason built a large brick garage at 209 North Maple Street during the teens. He bought four Reo chassis' with engines etc. and installed wooden bodies on them which had been made at the old Dupont powder plant in Old Hickory. Those pre-Greyhound buses carried sixteen passengers each.

Edward "Pluck" Miller was born in 1903 on the site of where Indian Hills Golf Club is now located. After graduating from Webb School, "Pluck" worked at various jobs. By 1923 he had managed to save about three thousand dollars.

Ephraim "Eph" Hoover had been running seven passenger sedans on round trips to Nashville. "Eph" was "Pluck's" brother-in-law. With "Pluck's" three thousand dollars, they formed a partnership. Their first station in town was at the old Jordan Hotel. Their bus line was called Miller Safety Coach Lines. The standard passenger fare in those days was fifty cents one way.

Cason's bus line was called the Puckett Auto Co. Both lines—Millers and Casons—were running on the hour to and from Nashville from 7:00 A.M. to 5:00 P.M. Business was good for both lines. Each bus was filled every trip, but neither line was showing a profit. Mr. Cason approached the two brothers-in-law with the proposition that they should consolidate. They agreed and a new bus line was formed. It was called the Union Transfer Co. The new bus line had its garage and ticket office at the Cason garage at 209 North Maple Street. Its Nashville terminal was at the Maxwell House on Fourth Avenue and Church Street. An alternate drop-off and pick-up place was at the Hermitage Hotel on Sixth Avenue. The partners soon extended their lines to include Huntsville, Columbia, Shelbyville, Birmingham and Knoxville. Instead of the Reo and Studebaker vehicles, they were now using White Motor Co. twenty-eight passenger buses that were painted gray. People in the transport business were now noticing the three small-town partners.

"Eph" Hoover had been operating a small truck line during the early twenties. He was using Mack trucks with solid rubber tires and chain drives. His trucks were operating between Murfreesboro, Nashville and Woodbury. Shortly, his trucks were going to Knoxville. "Pluck" Miller also became involved in that operation. Before 1929, "Eph" traded his interest in the bus line for "Pluck's" interest in the truck lines. Ephraim Hoover became the sole owner of Hoover Truck Lines. The rest of the Hoover venture is history. Hoover Truck Lines became one of the largest if not the largest truck line in the U.S. transport industry.

In the late nineteen twenties, the Interstate Commerce Commission began regulating the new bus line routes. They began granting franchises to the lines then operating on certain routes. That regulated the industry and protected the operators and the public from fly-by-night and unsafe competition.

In 1929, the Consolidated Coach Co., a branch of the new Greyhound Bus Lines, which was a subsidiary of the Pennsylvania Railroad, talked to Cason and Miller of paying them $1,000,000 for their franchises and their rolling stock. The Great Depression put a damper on those negotiations for awhile. However, the Consolidated Coach Co. was back again in 1930 with almost the same amount that they had offered the previous year. The partners accepted.

To realize the immensity of that transaction in small-town Murfreesboro, one would have to consider that one million dollars in 1930 would equal more than ten million dollars in 1991. That kind of money was beyond most peoples' comprehension in those days. Another admirable consideration here was the youthfulness of Miller and Hoover. The latter was not much older than Miller. "Pluck" was twenty years of age when he began his bus line odyssey in 1923. In 1930, he was a highly successful business man at the age of twenty-seven. Another noteworthy consideration was the fact that these three men were embarking in the early twenties on a venture of high risk with little or no experience ratings for bankers to ponder upon before granting any backing for their enterprises.

Edward E. "Pluck" Miller is eighty-eight years of age. He enjoys reflecting upon those conquests of the past. He enjoys pointing out the wall plaques proclaiming his service as city councilman, bank and hospital director.

James Cason continued to lease the station at 209 North Maple Street to the Greyhound Bus Lines that would keep stopping there for many years and into the fifties. The old bus station was to be demolished later to make way for the new Penney Plaza.

★ ★ ★

The last property in the block was the Haynes Hotel. It fronted on West College Street which was the old Dixie Highway (later highway 41) which ran from Chicago to Florida. For the first quarter of this century, it was Murfreesboro's finest hotel and one of the finest small town hotels in Tennessee. Its most distinguishing features were the three white railing porches that extended around two sides of the three story building. There were white rocking chairs on all three levels.

The hotel was built just before the turn of the century by James Monroe Haynes. He was the grandfather of James Brevard Haynes, who lives on the old homeplace on the Lebanon Road. Mr. Haynes lived in what is now the Woman's Club building in 1900. He later lived in what is known as the Beasley-Keathley house beyond Middle Tennessee Christian School. His farm was on both sides of the road and extended northward to Haynes Drive. He died in 1910.

Ferdinand Washington Miles bought the hotel and operated it until the early nineteen thirties. As a boy, I can recall visiting Mr. Miles' grandson Bob at the hotel. The elderly Mr. "Ferd" and his wife would be sitting in rocking chairs on the east side porch in the afternoon. He was smoking a cigar. His wife had her hair pinned on top of her head. They both passed away in the early thirties. They had been intimately associated with the hotel business in Murfreesboro, having owned both the Jordan and Haynes Hotels.

Mr. "Ferd's" son, Harry Miles, became the next manager of the hotel. He had just returned with his family from Cleveland, Tennessee where he had operated the Cherokee Hotel. In the latter forties, his sister, Mrs. Eugene Guill, became involved in the operation of the hotel.

During the early fifties highway 41 was rerouted to what is now Broad Street. That, of course, had a negative effect on the amount of business that the hostelry could expect from tourists. That situation was also devastating to the James K. Polk Hotel on East Main Street.

The property was sold in the latter nineteen fifties to James Cason of California who was the son of James Cason, the former bus line and station owner. The J.C. Penney building was erected on the site. Also, a row of offices was erected behind the Penney building. That was called Penney Plaza. Its address was 207 North Maple Street. That rectangular property was still a part of the James Cason and son's property which included the old bus station already mentioned. The registered owner is Anthony J. Leimas Trustee, et ux, Ellie J. of Palm Springs, California.

J.C. Penney closed its doors in Murfreesboro in the early eighties. The large building was vacant for quite some while. Hope-Vere Anderson bought the Penney building property in 1988. The upper floor has been rented to a company which is named Wholesale Furniture. Hope-Vere has a large antique shop in the basement. This has been the history of the James Monroe Haynes to Ferdinand Washington Miles to Harry Miles and Bessie Miles Guill to James Cason to Hope-Vere Anderson property.

★ ★ ★

Slightly to the left of the Haynes Hotel and on the same lot, as it fronted on West College Street in 1924, there was a small building which housed an upholstery shop. The next lot westward was vacant in 1924. In the early nineteen thirties, the Jackson brothers moved their Chevrolet dealership to that relatively large lot. Their move is noted in the portion of this story which deals with West Main Street. They moved in 1958 to a larger lot and a new building on West Broad Street. The Jackson Bros. Chevrolet building was demolished and the lot became part of the new J.C. Penney building and Penney Plaza complex.

★ ★ ★

The McClaran and Posey Realty and Auction Company occupies the next lot on the corner of West College and North Walnut Streets. Don McClaran and Eldridge Posey are the partners in the enterprise.

The address 224 West College Street was a dwelling place in 1924. The property was owned by James Cason and sons. In 1943, the Sinclair Oil Company bought the lot and erected a service station on the corner. S.F. "Simp" Houston was the Sinclair oil distributor in Rutherford County for many years.

Wade Williams became the first operator of the new station in 1943. Mr. Williams began to specialize in the sale of truck and passenger car tires and soon rented a large building across North Walnut Street in which to operate his large post-war tire business. John Shearron bought the property in the early seventies and sold it to Preston Sweeney and James Rowland who remodeled the former service station in which to operate a realty company. The partnership sold the property in 1983 to Eldridge Posey and Comas Montgomery. Posey bought Montgomery's one half interest in 1985. Eldridge conducted his realty business there until 1989, when he sold one half interest in the business to Don McClaran.

★ ★ ★

Across West College Street is the 225 address of the Rutherford County Board of Realtors. A general business service is provided its members which involves coordination of multiple listings, the projection of good will within the industry and the provision of up-to-date educational tips and trends to the membership.

Later in this story, the partnership of Osborn-Harrell will be mentioned. They moved their hardware store from 121 North Maple Street to 225 West College Street in 1959. This was a new building, was much larger, had front off-street parking and had a building fronting on North Walnut in which to expand.

Shortly after the move in 1959, the long-time clerk, Forney Hoover, became a partner in the popular hardware store. Mr. Osborn died in 1965 at the age of seventy-two. Henry and Forney continued the operation together until Mr. Harrell died in 1975. Forney carried on the business until 1977 when the business and property were sold to Elgin Achord. Mr. Achord was there until 1980, when he moved the business to a new store in front of Stones River Country Club on Broad Street. Mr. Forney Hoover passed away in 1989.

Ferrell Holloway bought the property at 225 West College Street in 1980. He renovated the store to accommodate the operation of a children's ready-to-wear as a specialty and later added ladies' ready-to-wear to his inventory. He closed the store in 1988 and sold the property later to the Rutherford County Board of Realtors.

Cason's Garage with fleet of buses, circa 1925.

Cason's Garage after Cason and Miller had sold to Greyhound, circa 1930.

Haynes Hotel on corner of West College and North Maple Streets. Razed in about 1955.

Westside Square 1923.

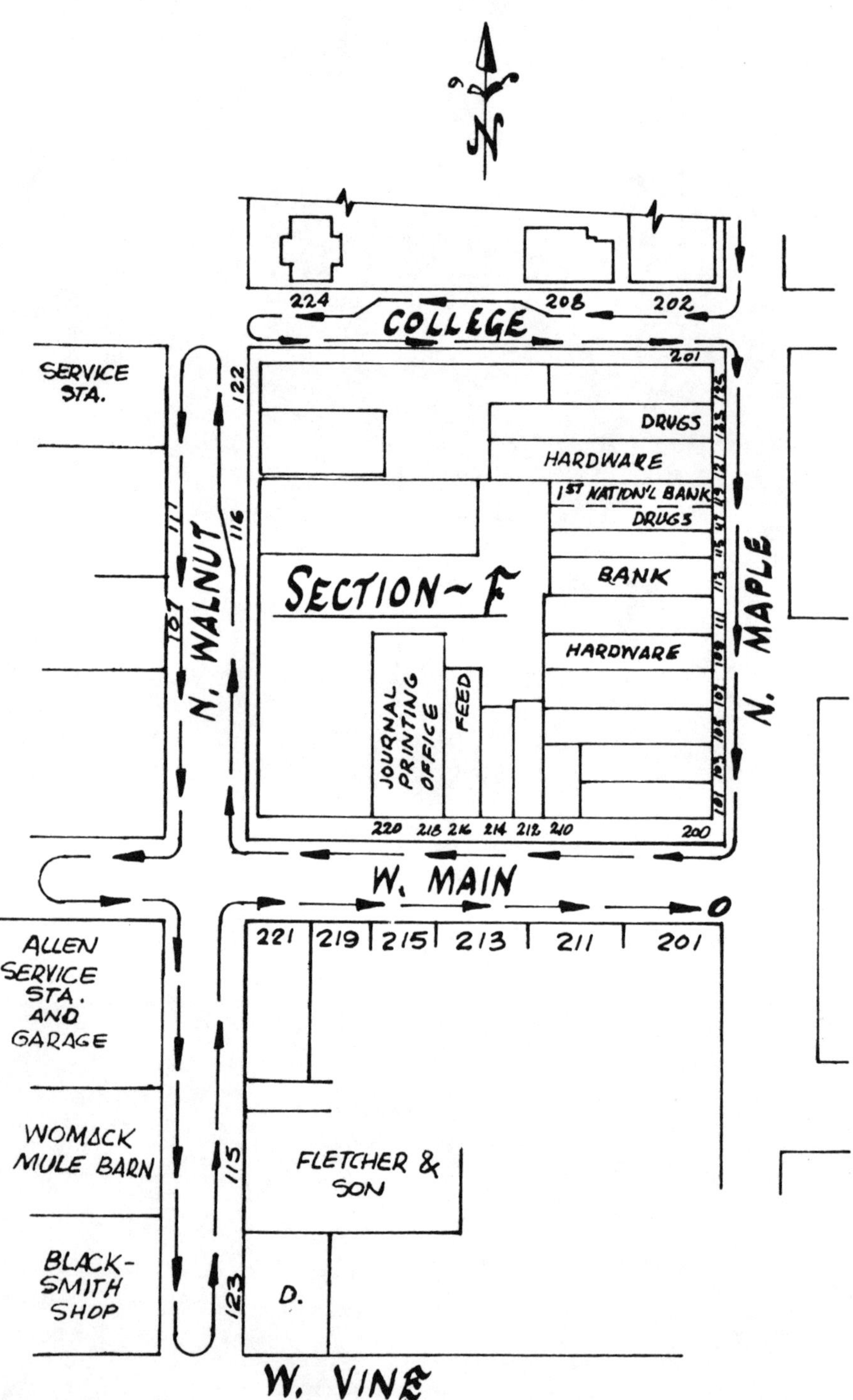
N
224
208
202
COLLEGE
201
SERVICE STA.
122
DRUGS
HARDWARE
1ST NATION'L BANK
DRUGS
BANK
HARDWARE
SECTION ~ F
JOURNAL PRINTING OFFICE
FEED
111
116
107
N. WALNUT
N. MAPLE
220
218
216
214
212
210
200
W. MAIN
221
219
215
213
211
201
ALLEN SERVICE STA. AND GARAGE
WOMACK MULE BARN
BLACK-SMITH SHOP
115
FLETCHER & SON
123
D.
W. VINE

Chapter XIX

North Maple (West Side)—West Side Square

Ingram Blanks Collier was one of the top merchant princes in Murfreesboro in the 1860s and 1870s. Born in 1840, he died in 1879. During his short lifetime, he amassed quite a fortune for those times. He married Louisiana Jones in 1869. Carmine Collier was born to that union.

I.B. Collier became a cotton broker at an early age. Much of his time was spent traveling on riverboats to New Orleans and back to Nashville. In 1869, he built the three two-story brick structures numbered right to left 125, 123, and 121 on the section F map. Those buildings were to serve as cotton warehouses. Large double doors were installed in the front of each warehouse.

Mr. Collier served as mayor of the town during the term of 1869-1871. Ingram and his wife, Louisiana, strangely enough, both participated in the founding of the First National Bank in 1869. The address of the bank was F-119, next door to Collier's warehouses. Mr. Collier was the first cashier of the bank.

His daughter Carmine was born in 1872. She never married. Her father planned in the mid-1870s to build Murfreesboro's most handsome and imposing mansion. He died just as the first floor of the house was raised. That great three-story house of Italianate architecture was completed in 1880. It is located at 511 East Main Street.

Mr. Collier's widow was not interested in completing the house, but the executors of the estate compelled her to carry out the original plans. Louisiana married Col. Horace Ready in 1882. He died in 1905. The mother and daughter, Carmine, continued to live in the house until the mother's death in 1924. Miss Carmine refused to remain at the residence and lived for a while with Sarah McKelley King's parents. Later, she moved to a three-story frame residence on East Lytle Street.

I saw Miss Carmine several times in the 1920s and 1930s as she walked on East Lytle Street and while eating at Miss Betty Ferrell's boarding house. She was gracious; she had pleasing facial characteristics, a nice complexion and an ever-present smile. Known as an eccentric lady, she was probably better known as the richest person in town. A story about the lives and experiences of the riverboat traveler Ingram Blanks

Collier, Louisiana Jones, who insisted on affixing the name Jones on business documents, and their eccentric daughter Carmine, should have all the elements of interesting reading.

Upon the death of Miss Carmine in 1954, her uptown properties were inherited by her two cousins thrice removed, Sarah McKelley King, Martha McKelley Meeks, and their mother, Lutie Osborn McKelley. Sarah received address 123 North Maple, Martha, 125, and Mrs. McKelley, 121. Later, Sarah King purchased Martha Meek's building (125) and her sister's interest in (121) upon the death of their mother.

The Collier buildings are another remarkable example of how more than several properties about the Square have been retained within the same families. In the instance of Ingram Blanks Collier's uptown buildings, those properties have remained intact for 122 years. In 1991, (125) is owned by Sarah King et vir and Witt King, (123) by Sarah McKelley King, and (121) by Walter Hughey King, et al.

Address F-125 was occupied by the Busy Bee Cafe in 1928. That corner was a prime location in those days. The busy 41 highway came past on College Street. The Busy Bee was operated by Dominick and Rosa Meshotto, who have appeared on these pages before in regard to the DeGeorges. Dominick's brothers and sisters provided all the help that the Busy Bee needed. They were Vance, Sam, Mary, and Clara. The Meshottos were there until about 1935. (*See note at end of Chapter)

Jimmie's Place was the next restaurant on that corner. It was operated by Jimmie Haynes, a World War I veteran, a good restaurateur, and an avid fisherman. He was the father of Ann Marie, Ben, Dan, Evelyn, and Jane Haynes. Mr. Haynes was there until about 1941, when he moved his business to a place next to the old Highway Patrol office on West College.

Eddie Griswold moved his restaurant operation from the 100-block on East Main Street to that corner. He was there until the early 1950s.

Al Sullivan and his wife, Mary, came next to that place from Memphis. Al bought the restaurant from Griswold, gave it a thorough face lift and generally refurbished it. The Sullivans brought a new sophistication to the restaurant business in Murfreesboro. Their business flourished and prospered so well that they eventually moved to the Murfreesboro Motel, which provided large restaurant quarters for the expanded business. Shortly after opening, Al and Mary were gratified to have customers waiting in line to be seated at almost every meal.

John and Alma Jean Cook were the next restaurant operators to come to the 125 address. They later moved to the newly remodeled building which had formerly been occupied by Woodfin and Moore.

Don's Kitchen Corner was the next occupant of 125. That was a popular restaurant for several years. The next occupant was David Clark. David was followed by the Town Square Cafe, which is the present business in that 122-year-old building. The cafe is operated by Thomas E. and Pearl A. Crips and Irene Carter.

It appears that McCord Furniture Company came to address 123 North Maple in 1928 from the Square's north side.

In 1948, the H.A. Todd Furniture Company moved to 123. The firm had been operating near the Slide, just north of where Holden's Hardware is now located. The name of the business in the late 1920s was Todd and Huddleston Furniture Company. Mr. Todd bought Caesar Huddleston's interest in 1935. His son Charles returned from army service in 1946 and soon took over the active managership of the business. In 1960, Charles moved the operation into a new building which he had built next to the Episcopal Church on East Main Street. He retired in 1986, selling the property to the church. It seems that the H.A. Todd family can claim the record of having remained in the furniture business longer than any other family in Murfreesboro. Charles's grandfather had a furniture store on the Square's south side in 1900. Norris Lovvorn operated a pool hall at that address for a short while. He has appeared earlier on these pages.

Earl Bailey's Fabric Center moved to 123 in 1960. That business prospered so well that Mr. Bailey found it necessary to move into much larger quarters. He solved his dilemma by moving to the new shopping center on Memorial Boulevard and into the large building next to the one then occupied by Wal-Mart.

John Burkhart came next to 123, with a store that handled men's and women's clothing. Dee's Furniture Store came next and was followed by the Bushido School of Karate, which eventually moved to the country club center on Broad Street. The building at 123 is vacant at present.

★ ★ ★

The next building south on North Maple Street (121), had a long history of housing hardware businesses. James Sidney Braswell and W. Eugene Mullins formed a partnership and began a hardware business there in the early 1920s. They were there until about 1940, when George Osborn bought the interest of Mr. Braswell. Osborn and Mullins operated until 1939, when Mr. Mullins died. Henry Harrell came next on the scene when the new partnership prompted the firm's sign to read Osborn-Harrell Hardware Company. Forney Hoover began working for the hardware firm in 1936 as a clerk and accompanied the partners, George Osborn and Henry Harrell, when they moved to the brand new store at 225 West College Street.

When the hardware store moved to West College Street, the Murfreesboro Barber College came to that address (121). The business remained there twenty-nine years (1961-1990). The building is vacant at the present time.

★ ★ ★

As mentioned earlier, Ingram Blanks Collier and his wife, Louisiana Jones, were instrumental in founding the First National Bank in 1869. It was located in the next building southward (F-119). That bank was an integral part of the Murfreesboro banking community for sixty-three years.

In 1932, I was a sophomore at Central High School. On January 25th of that year at 1:30 p.m., I was in a science class taught by the perennial sponsor of the senior class, Miss Perry Williamson. A note was handed to Miss Perry as she sat at her desk. She glanced at it and immediately told someone to take charge of the class. She dashed out and was gone for less than an hour. Upon returning, she was pale but composed—composed enough to resume teaching. We found out later that the note which was handed to her read: "First National Bank has closed its doors."

The January 26, 1932, issue of the *Home Journal* contained the following statement in regard to the bank:

"Yesterday, the directors of the First National Bank, of Murfreesboro, decided in the interests of their customers to temporarily close that institution.

"During the period immediately prior to this week the demands upon the bank for funds accumulated more rapidly than the bank could realize on its paper, and for that reason the board felt it would be to the best interest of all concerned to take this action.

"It is hoped that with the cooperation of their customers that institution may be in position to re-open soon and to continue its service of so many years to Murfreesboro and Rutherford County."

The sixty-three-year-old bank did not re-open. The year 1932 was in the midst of the Depression. However, the auditors found after several months that the bank could have remained open and survived had not the run on deposits developed. As it was, the defunct bank was able to pay all customers 85 percent of their deposits.

John Jenkins came next to this location (F-119) with his five-pin bowling alley. This building was rather narrow and would accommodate only one alley. Later, John moved to the 100-block on East Main, as mentioned earlier. Present almost every afternoon at this place among others were Johnnie Malone, Lee McCartney, Oscar Morgan, and Oscar Barrett.

The popular Men's Shop has been in 119 since the 1940s. Sanford Cox was the first owner of the business. Emory Sumner bought the Cox ownership in 1951. Then came Ira Cravens in 1954. J.M. "Buck" Deavours came here in October, 1958 as a partner with Cravens. In 1970, "Buck" bought Cravens' interest and was the owner not only of the business but also of the property for twenty years. On January 1, 1990, James E. Alford, who had been assisting in the Men's Shop, bought both the business and the property from Deavours. Although "Buck" has retired, he still tries to keep current on his sales technique by working occasionally at the store. It seems that that store has been a viable and successful enterprise for each of its owners for more than forty years.

In 1915, R.H. Stickney and R.W. Vickers began a drugstore business in F-117. Mr. Vickers owned the building at that time and for several years thereafter. He also conducted a real estate business in an office on the second floor.

In 1920, Ed Griffis bought the interest of Mr. Vickers and thus began the long and well-known partnership of Stickney and Griffis. They remained in F-117 until about 1924. At that time, they moved next door to F-115. In 1924, the Zeitlins came to Murfreesboro and to the Square. They began a clothing business in 117. They were there for several years and are believed to have moved to Nashville. They had two sons, Victor and Bernice, and a daughter whose name was Clara.

Then a Singer Sewing Machine sales and repair office came to that address in the early 1950s. Virgle Young bought the property, did extensive remodeling, and leased the building to Murfreesboro Bank and Trust Company. The bank initiated its new trust department in that building, and David Hopper was appointed manager. When the bank moved to its new quarters on East Main, attorney Thomas Haynes bought the 117 property in 1979. He accomplished a first-class exterior and interior renovation to the building, which has complimented the entire west side of the Square. Sharing offices with Tom Haynes are Royce Taylor and Rosalind Akin.

Jim Crichlow and DeWitt Smith were the owners of F-115. That is where the Stickney and Griffis Drug Company was to move in about 1924. Their sign was to remain above the entrance of the store for fifty-nine years, until 1983.

I recall visiting the book department of the store in the late 1920s and early 1930s. The store kept all of the issues in hardback of the Tom Swift series. There must have been more than twenty of them. The books sold for fifty cents each. The store kept a soda fountain and short-order counter. There were the familiar Coca-Cola tables and chairs on the left of the store's entrance. That was one of the favorite teen-age gathering places in town. Harry Gannaway was the well-known pharmacist who worked there for many years.

Mr. Ed Griffis died in 1978. Mr. Stickney continued opening the store until 1983. An auction was held at which all of the furniture and fixtures were sold. Mr. Stickney died in 1985.

A health food store was in 115 until about 1986. The A and B Sound and Light Company came next. When it moved after a short while, Encore Performance moved into the old drugstore building. That is a family hairstyling salon, operated by Mike and Jan Morton. Five operators are involved in the salon.

The property at 115 is owned by Matt Murfree, III, et al. and Robert Bell Murfree. It was transferred from their father, Dr. Matt Murfree, Jr., who had inherited it from his father, Dr. Matt Murfree, Sr.

The next door southward (F-113) was the home of the Stones River Bank and Trust Company. The bank was organized in 1872. It remained in business until the late 1920s, when it merged with the First National Bank. C.B. Bell was the cashier and W. Burton Carnahan the assistant cashier during the bank's latter days. Its ancient steel door vault is still in the basement.

Next came to 113 a Walgreen Drug Store managed by a Mr. Maxwell. Watt Harrison, already a well-known druggist in town, bought that drug business in 1944 and was there until November, 1979. That drugstore also had a well-manned soda fountain. There were then two locally owned drug stores side by side on the west side of the Square. Evidently, there was plenty of business, for both businesses seemed to prosper.

Joe Adams operated a restaurant there from November, 1979 until May, 1980. Salads and More came December, 1980 and remained until June, 1986. The restaurant was managed by Frank and Edna Coffman.

Ron and Annette Swartz came next to 113 in November, 1987 with their Amanda Jane's Restaurant. That became a popular luncheon place for the office people around the Square. Ron and Annette specialized in soup, salads, sandwiches, and baked goods. Outside catering was and is one of the main thrusts of the business. They moved in August, 1990 to the Heritage Square Shopping Center on Northfield Boulevard.

After Amanda Jane's moved, the present occupant, Lighting Design and Sales, came to that address. Bob M. Pruitt is the manager of the business. It specializes in light bulb sales and lighting maintenance for commercial and industrial buildings, parking lots, and so forth.

Matt Murfree, III and Robert Bell Murfree are also the owners of that building (113) which was passed from Dr. Matt Murfree, Sr., to Dr. Matt Murfree, Jr., and thence to his two sons.

An observer will note that the roof line of the building (113) is considerably lower than the other buildings in that block. There are some who believe that a street or alley once went through there from the Square to Walnut Street.

*Rose Ann Meshotto Smith has called this writer to supply more information about her father Dominick and mother Rose Meshotto in regard to their occupancy and ownership of a later restaurant located four doors down the street at (F-119) North Maple Street. The Busy Bee moved here in the summer of 1934 and bought the building in December of the same year from The First National Bank. The popular restaurant was here until April 1944 at which time the Meshottos sold the building to W.R. Coleman.

Chapter XX

Northwest Side Square

Howse and Butler occupied F-111 in 1912. The partners were George Howse and John Butler. Both of those men have been mentioned previously in these pages—Mr. Howse on the east side and Mr. Butler on the south side and also the latter's connection with the First National Bank. The firm handled feed, seed, candy (in buckets), bulk white and brown sugar, salt, sack goods, and other items. The business apparently flourished until the Depression years. The partnership was dissolved, and John Butler moved to the south side in the early 1930s.

The M.P. Brothers Grocery Company moved to that address when Howse and Butler closed. That was a chain store headquartered in Nashville. Tommy Martin, the man who has been a member of the Mutual of New York's Million Dollar Round Table probably longer than anyone else, was manager of the store from 1933 into 1935. He states that the Brothers store was at that place until 1943.

Dixie Auto Store came next in 1944. That store was owned by Economy Sales and Supply Company of Pulaski, Tennessee. The parent corporation retained ownership of the Murfreesboro store until 1975, when it was sold to the Bill Hunter Furniture Company. Meanwhile, James Whitley became manager of the Dixie Auto Store in 1946. At Whitley's suggestion, the auto store was changed to a furniture operation in 1957. Virgil Jones, Raymond Todd, and Hal Harding were connected with the store during some of those years. They moved to much larger quarters on South Church Street in 1967.

In that year, the County Clerk's vehicle registration division became the next tenant and remained there until 1983. Ben Hall McFarlin was County Clerk at that time.

That was the year that the legal firm of Smith and Sellers moved to F-111. In 1923, the building's owners were Jim Crichlow and DeWitt Smith. The present firm of Smith and Sellers bought the property from the Crichlow estate. The ownership is now equally shared by William T. Sellers, Nancy Smith Sellers, and Ewing Smith, Jr.

The building underwent extensive remodeling and renovating when the new owners purchased it. Almost the whole interior was removed, leaving only the walls and roof. The exterior bricks were cleaned, windows and doors replaced with new trim, and a new face lift of traditional architecture was added. A handsome stairway to the second floor, which contains offices, was also installed. The lack of utilization of the second floors in many of the buildings around the Square is a problem that needs to be addressed in the future.

The founder of the firm of Smith and Sellers was Ewing T. Smith, Sr. He began the practice of law in 1920 and continued until a short time before his death in 1980. Mr. Smith was a lawyer who lent much credit to the legal profession in Murfreesboro. Although constantly busy in the courtroom and in his offices, he shunned the limelight and accomplished much by remaining behind the scenes.

If a lawyer were judged by the number of his progeny and their spouses who continued in the legal profession, then Ewing T. Smith, Sr., would probably rate as the number-one progenitor of attorneys in the state of Tennessee. The names of those who continued in his footsteps are Nancy Smith Sellers, Bill Sellers, Ewing Smith, Jr., Millie Smith Dufour, Alfred E. Dufour, Steve Dufour (these three of Aiken, South Carolina), Ewing T. Sellers, William T. Sellers, Jr., Cynthia Sellers Forrester (Nashville), and Sandy Smith Benson, who is almost ready to hang out her shingle in Nashville. Incidently, Ewing Smith's wife, the woman who kept things together and going in the busy law offices, was the aunt of Sara McGuire, who married Ed Bell, the storyteller of Murfreesboro and the author of "Main Street to Mink Slide."

★ ★ ★

The next-door hardware location was both owned and operated by Charles H. Byrn, who was encountered earlier on the north side of the Square as the owner of another hardware store. Store number two was at the address of F-109 in 1923.

Charles Newton Haynes operated a hardware store at F-101 in 1921. That corner address later became the Hub Store. Mr. Haynes moved his business in 1923 to 109, which had been vacated the same year. Mr. Byrn retained his ownership in the building, and at his death in 1929, the ownership was transferred to Annie Byrn Roberts and Allie Byrn Ledbetter.

Mr. Charlie N. Haynes was joined in the hardware business by his son, William Tillman Haynes. The store prospered, and its inventory increased to such an extent that all three floors were utilized. In 1946, two important changes in ownership were effected. C.N. Haynes retired and sold his interest to his son Tillman. Later in the year and upon the return of W. Tillman Haynes, Jr., from the navy, Tillman, Sr., transferred one-half interest in the store to his son.

The store's inventory continued to increase. The owners added new lines of china, crystal, and ceramics to the shelves and counters in 107. The upper floors in both buildings, plus the basements, were occupied with merchandise. They began the sale and installation of well pumps which were presided over by Ray Bugg.

Mr. Tillman, Sr., retired in the late 1970s and transferred his partnership interest to his daughter, Martha Ann Haynes Knight. Mr. Haynes died in 1985. Tillman, Jr., retired from the business in 1983. At that time, he sold his one-half interest to his sister, Martha Ann, and her husband, Donald Knight. Tillman became actively connected with the Murfreesboro Bank and Trust Company as a stock and security advisor. He died in 1986. Both Tillman, Sr., and Tillman, Jr., were generous in their philanthropy to worthwhile causes. They were especially interested in Stones River Manor, a retirement home that is sponsored by Churches of Christ. Tillman, Jr., was a valued member of the Board of Directors of the Rutherford Hospital, and a director in the Murfreesboro Bank and Trust Company.

In 1989, Donald and Martha Ann Knight bought the large building which formerly housed the Frank's IGA Market on Memorial Boulevard. They vacated both addresses on the Square (F-107 and 109) and moved their large inventory to the new address. They have retained ownership of the building at 107, which is presently vacant.

It is a far cry from a staid hardware to an exciting and modish restaurant with musical entertainment and a Greek atmosphere. That is what has been accomplished at 109. The Mediterranean Restaurant is owned by 28-year-old Mike Skordallos, who hails from the isle of Cyprus. Mike's restaurant was first located down the street at 103. He bought the property at his present location January 1, 1990. After extensive remodeling, renovating, and decorating with fluted Greek columns, a new stairway to a private upper floor dining room and a piano lounge, the restaurant reopened in the fall of 1990. It has a seating capacity of two hundred people. The Mediterranean presents both European and American cuisines.

Mike Skordallos first arrived in Murfreesboro as a student at MTSU. He says that the town kind of grew on him. Standing amidst the Greek columns, the vases and large pictures of his island heritage, he states that Murfreesboro reminds him of a nice, quiet, small town. With an ever-present smile that includes his eyes, he goes on to say that the Square is a part of the town rather than a shopping mall. Mike Skordallos says that he wants to be a part of the history of the town.

F-107 has been mentioned earlier in its relationship with Haynes Hardware Company, which purchased the building in 1946. It was owned in 1924 by John Butler, who owned several other properties about the Square until the Depression Years of the early 1930s.

Ernest Hooper recalls that his father Edgar Walter Hooper was engaged as a partner in the Butler-Hooper Men's Clothing Company during the 1920s until 1927.

The firm of Harrison and Alexander was there into the early 1930s and until Robert Harrison built the large, yellow brick feed, seed, and hardware store on West Vine Street.

The Davis Store, with Joe Wolfe as manager, came to that location in 1938 and remained there until Tillman Haynes bought the building in 1946.

★ ★ ★

Harrison and Spain Grocery Company occupied F-105 in 1900. In 1923, it was still a grocery, but the owner of the business was Beecher Horton. The owner of the property was T.G. Ivie. He ran a produce operation on West Main Street during the 1920s.

Mr. Horton's store was a busy place throughout the 1920s and 1930s. John L. Batey was one of the main clerks there for many years. Gus Mears was associated with the store through the 1920s and most of the 1930s. Former Squire Granville "Sump" Dismukes worked there during some summer vacations. James Hunt was also there for several years.

Mr. Horton sold his interest in the store in the latter part of the 1930s to Roy Norris. Mr. Norris sold a one-third interest in the business to his brother-in-law, W.B. "Bill" Carlton in 1938. Bill was an officer in the 115th Field Artillery and was called to active duty in 1940. He retained his interest in the store until his return from the armed services in 1945. At that time, he sold his share of the partnership to Mr. Norris. Bill worked in the educational section of the Veterans Administration until 1951, when he was again called to active duty. He retired with the rank of colonel in 1967 and now resides in Fayetteville, Tennessee.

Meanwhile, the Norris Grocery and Market (a meat section was added in 1939) continued to grow. Carmack Caffey worked there as a butcher for several years.

Roy Norris retired in 1954. His location had served as an important grocery store on the Square for over half a century. Turner's Department Store moved into the vacated grocery store at F-105 in 1955. That was a ladies' and men's ready-to-wear store with a dollar basement. Those people moved in 1958. Cliff Cowan, who has been introduced several times on these pages, had become installed next door in F-103 in 1953. Mr. Cowan bought the Turner stock in F-105, added more inventory and let his given name be the new trademark for this business. Cliff's became a successful store on the Square, remaining there until 1969, when Cowan moved both stores (Cowan's and Cliff's) to the former Charles Store location on the Square's north side.

Kirkpatrick's Shoe Store became the next business to move into F-105. In 1985, Kirkpatrick sold the building to Bill Carey, who shortly thereafter sold it to Logan Hickerson, et al., Gregory Peck, Lon Nuell, and Raymond Gibbs.

The old building underwent a thorough and almost complete renovation and remodeling at the hands of the new owners. An exposed and inviting stairway was installed, which served both the upper floor and basement. Office suites were partitioned on all floors of the building.

A novel and commendable piece of architectural work was produced on the front of the building. The whole front was removed with the exception of a steel beam extending between 103 and 105 at a height of about fourteen feet above the sidewalk, and the old metal encased cornice that ran between the two buildings. The structural engineer, who was employed for the building's architectural design, happened to see some cast iron columns that were being removed by a wrecking firm on the site of the new Nashville Convention Center. He was able to procure two of those columns which Hickerson brought back to Murfreesboro. They were installed beneath the old horizontal beam between the two neighboring buildings. Three new windows were placed in the upper section. The new owners sought to bring to address 105 an architectural design and appearance that would have been contemporary with the 1890s and turn-of-the-century architecture. The new owners have been most successful in restoring the design flavor of that bygone era.

The firms which have offices in 105 are as follows: attorney Raymond Gibbs, attorney Bonita Tucker, Gregory Peck & Associates, Seyco (Tommie and May Seymour Computer Services), Dilcher Engineering (sales representative of industrial ovens) and Smith, Seckman Reid, Inc., Consulting Engineers.

★ ★ ★

The Clayton and Draper Shoe Store was in 103 on the Square's west side in 1900. In 1923, J.K. "Cap" Clayton operated the store. Mr. Clayton has been noted in several locations thus far in this story. The Clayton family has accounted for several important personages in the history of Murfreesboro and particularly the Square. "Cap" Clayton was the owner of both the business and the building at 103. He departed the building at the end of the 1920s when he leased it to the H.G. Hill Store, which was headquartered in Nashville. The well-known and recently departed Frank Clardy was one of the first managers of that store. Hill's remained there until 1953 when the business moved to its new supermarket building in the 300-block on East Main.

That was when Cliff Cowan came to 103 on the west side. The Cowan sign was installed on the upper section of the store's facade. The transition from a grocery market to a ladies' and men's ready-to-wear store required much remodeling, which Cliff accomplished. In 1969, the two side-by-side Cowan stores on the west side moved as previously noted to the former Charles Store.

The next occupant of the 103 address was Vester and Charlene Waldron, who were there for a short while, disposing of a stock of clothing which they had acquired. Then there came the Kentucky Finance Company, which eventually moved to East Main Street. The Bailey Mortgage Company followed the finance company.

The Mediterranean Restaurant made its Murfreesboro debut at 103 in 1988. With its European flavor and style, with its European and

American cuisine, and with its waiters' hospitality and black ties, the restaurant did well from the beginning. It did so well that the young owner, Mike Skordallos, felt the need for expansion and bought the 109 address in the same block.

Logan Hickerson bought the 103 address in 1988 from the James K. Clayton estate and did some remodeling to the building. It should be noted here that the owners of 105 of which Hickerson is a partner and the owners of 101 (Steve Waldron and Sandra Taylor) arranged that the basements of all three buildings (101, 103, 105) should be interconnected. That complies with the fire codes, and, in addition, the occupants of the lower floors have a direct access to the West Main sidewalk. At the present time, 103 is vacant.

★ ★ ★

At the turn of the century, the sign on the corner building (F-101) read Naylor and Rucker Groceries, Boots and Shoes. That was an unlikely combination of items offered for sale. Possibly it was prophetic of one of the items which that store was going to offer for the greater part of the twentieth century. That item was boots. More about this later.

John Cox was the owner of F-101 in 1923. There was a hardware store located there which was operated by Reed & Haynes. The partners were Ellis Reed and Eugene Haynes.

Solomon "Sol" Arbit arrived on that corner in 101 in 1932. He soon had a huge inventory of ladies' and men's clothing and shoes on all three floors of the store. The property remained in the ownership of the Cox family until the late 1940s when Mr. Arbit bought the building. In 1955, Sol informed his son Hal that it was time for him to take over the business. Sol wanted to retire. Hal and his wife, Marilyn, operated the business for the next twenty-eight years. Hal carried the same categories of merchandise as his father, with the exception of ladies' clothing.

Hal states that the Arbits sold Duckhead overalls in the 1930s for 98¢. Men's suits could be bought for as low as $8.00; men's shoes for $5.00. During the 1950s, $20.00 would buy a man's suit.

The business was called The Hub Store. All who tuned in to WGNS or WMTS on wet or snowy days during the Arbit years would hear the familiar cry from the announcer: BOOTS, BOOTS, BOOTS, in a stentorian volume. The store would be deluged with boot customers on those days. Needless to say, the store did carry the largest inventory of boots in town.

In 1983, Hal Arbit sold the F-101 property to the Hub Building partnership, a Tennessee general partnership consisting of Edward H. Netherland, Steve Waldron, and Sandra Taylor. The new owners decided to give the old corner building a thorough renovation and face lift. This they did while at the same time preserving the traditional character of the structure. An elevator at the West Main Street entrance was installed. The basement was partitioned into offices. The first and upper floors were entirely new with office suites arranged to accommodate the requirements of the individual owners. The interior brick walls were left exposed in order that the historical heritage of the building would remain apparent.

The basement area is occupied by the law offices of Gerald Melton, Public Defender. The top floor is occupied by attorneys Sandra Taylor, Steve Waldron, and Terry Fann, each of whom is engaged in a separate practice. The Square entrance level is occupied by the Ed Netherland Insurance Company.

Carol Simpson is the office manager of the last-named firm. She comes from Raleigh, North Carolina. She states without prompting and with much enthusiasm that, when she first came to Murfreesboro, she felt as though she had come home.

Chapter XXI

West Main (North Side)

It is now time to consider the first two blocks off the Square of West Main Street. That would be a familiar sight and walkway for Ed Bell. His steps would be a bit more jaunty as he returned to his newspaper office from the Square. His coat pockets contained some notes which he had written on his customary stroll from Main Street to Mink Slide. When he arrived about 250 feet down the street at the *News Journal* office (F-218), he would write the story that was already forming in his mind from the notes he had taken.

Immediately behind the Hub Store, or what was to become the Hub Store later in 1932, there was in 1924 a barber shop in the right front side of F-208. The shop had two barber chairs. The front barber and owner of the business was a colored man whose name was Sam Woods. When this story was dealing with the lower part of Mink Slide, Sam Woods was encountered in his shop at B-123. He was in a more sophisticated area later, but the price of his haircuts was still twenty-five cents. The second barber chair was tended by a white man whose name was McGee.

On the left side of the building was a restaurant which expanded to the rear of the small barber shop. The restaurant was operated by Ross Pitts and his family. Mr. Pitts had two sons, Raymond and Stanley, and a daughter, Hazel. She later became Mrs. Floyd Lamb. Raymond and Stanley were star players on Central's football teams for several years. Raymond retired from the armed forces as a colonel. He passed away about three years ago. Stanley resides in Murfreesboro. In those early days on West Main, the family resided in an apartment above the restaurant. They were at that location until 1929, when Mr. Pitts became a policeman on the local force. The family then moved to a house on North Maple Street.

Ella Williams, the wife of Houston "Cutie" Williams, operated a restaurant at F-208 for a few years. Then there came the Lyric Cafe. Following the Lyric, there was "Ma" Smotherman, who continued the restaurant tradition at that address. Later, there was an insurance company there. Attorney Jo Atwood had a law practice there from 1987 and into 1989. Dr. Scott Cranford, an optometrist, established an office there and is the present occupant of F-208.

C.R. Cawthon was the owner of the building and the next three buildings westward during the 1920s and well into the 1930s. Matt Murfree, III and Robert Bell Murfree are the present owners of that property. They purchased it from their father, Dr. Matt Murfree, Jr., in 1981. He had inherited it from his father, Dr. Matt Murfree, Sr.

★ ★ ★

The next address is 212 West Main Street. The name of the business located there in 1924 was Travis and Gregory. The early thrust of the business was hardware and shoe repair. Will Travis handled the hardware department and Tom Gregory the shoe department. Burns Phillips of Shelbyville became connected with the business in the late 1920s or early 1930s. Burns was a master leather worker and harness maker. When he came to the store, the firm attracted new customers who were involved in harness racing and show horses.

In 1943, Mr. Travis sold his interest to Mr. Gregory. Mrs. Gregory handled the bookkeeping and also the hardware sales. Among some of the store's employees were Ross Knox, John Travis, the Rooker boys, Paul Brown, and Jimmie Martin. When Sewart Air Force Base opened in the early 1940s, Mr. Phillips became foreman of the fabric and paint section at the base. When the base closed after World War II, he returned to the shoe and harness shop. When Sewart was reactivated, he returned to his former job there and remained until his retirement in 1969.

Mr. Gregory closed the shop in 1958. He continued in his shoe repair in a shop back of his house for several years.

★ ★ ★

Tillman Haynes, Sr., bought the property at F-212 in the mid-1930s. The former owner had been C.R. Cawthon. Mr. Haynes kept part of his store inventory there for several years while having occasional sales of that merchandise.

The City Finance Company is the present occupant of the lower floor of 212. L. Byrne occupies an office on the second floor of the building. He is involved in the sale of medical supplies. Betsy Turner and Associates occupy the other offices on that floor. They are a court reporting firm which has recently moved into the building. The other court reporters besides Betsy Turner are Lisa Reeves, Dawn Williams, and Pam Rhody. The present owner of the property at F-212 is the 212 West Main Partnership, c/o Logan Hickerson.

★ ★ ★

On the sidewalk in front of F-214 is imbedded the name of R.T. Groom. He was mentioned earlier on the northwest corner of the Square. He came to 214 in 1919. His logo stated "Nothing But Insurance." His business was there until 1930.

The Western Auto Store, in the person of Roy Dennard, was the next business to occupy that location. Mr. Dennard had been connected with the N. C. & St. L. Railroad for several years. He chose to accept the first Western Auto Store franchise in Murfreesboro. It became a successful business. In 1954, Mr. Dennard bought the former *News Journal* (originally **Home Journal**) building and moved his business to that place. It was a larger building that suited the requirements of the expanding business. John Sant Amour came to the store in 1951. He had married Emily, the daughter of Roy Dennard. John became connected with the new Singer plant on Highway 41 in 1956. He returned to the store in 1978. In 1980, the business moved to the former C.H. Briley location in the next block westward. The partnership of the present business is John and Emily Sant Amour and Lois Bugg.

When the Western Auto Store moved from 214 in 1954, the next tenant became the Lewis Appliance Company. That business was owned by Emmitt Lewis, who had recently operated an appliance and general store on the Manchester highway. Mr. Lewis was a busy, aggressive man who did a good volume of business. He was assisted by his two sons, Russell and Jim, and eventually by his son-in-law, Ed Jones.

In 1973, Mr. Lewis gave the business to his son Jim and his son-in-law, Ed Jones. They remained there until 1978, when the partnership bought and moved to a location around the corner on North Walnut Street. In the meantime, Emmitt Lewis sold the 214 property in 1978, which he had bought from Roy Dennard. The buyers of the property were John Pittard and David Loughry. They were the registered owners in 1990. The new owners effected a handsome face-lift to the building's front exterior and partitioned the large open spaces within into imposing office suites. Attorneys John Pittard and Lance Selva conduct their law practices in that building.

★ ★ ★

Charles R. Cawthon owned F-216 in 1924. It was the fourth consecutive building that he owned in that block. The Depression Years in the early 1930s were difficult years that drastically reduced the fortunes of many business people in the town, and were years that required many negative adjustments in the lives of those people. These pages have only hinted as to how the Depression adversely affected the people of Murfreesboro. Mr. Cawthon ordered an auction to be held on each of his four properties on West Main Street.

Mr. E.C. Fite, Sr., was the buyer of address 216 on West Main Street at that auction which was held in 1934. "Cousin" Abner Dement had a grocery store there in the 1920s and until 1929. At that time, Mr. Fite moved his feed store from Depot Hill to 216. A hand-operated elevator was installed, which allowed the large upper floor to be utilized. Clyde Fite recalls that his father gave him and his younger brother Neil the responsibility of attending to two hundred Hollywood white Leghorn hens. Those hens ranged over the entire second floor of the building.

Clyde says that the eggs, which those hens produced, paid the monthly rent of twenty-five dollars. The two brothers also had the job of cleaning the floor every Saturday.

Mr. Fite had the Purina franchise for Rutherford County. The famous checkerboard squares were painted on the building's exterior. Mr. C.R. Craddock rented a space in the rear of the store where he placed incubators for raising baby chicks.

Mr. Elmus Clyde Fite, Sr., retired in 1950. Clyde, Jr., bought the old Ransom building on South Front Street and began the operation of a large feed, seed, and fertilizer business, which also included an Allis-Chalmers dealership. Norman Hutchinson became a partner in the business in 1952. Clyde Fite was elected to the city council in 1946 and served until 1962, at which time he became City Manager, replacing Hubert McCullough. Clyde served in his new capacity until his retirement in 1989—twenty-seven years.

His brother Neil inherited the 216 store as his share of his father's estate. He continued to rent the building until 1960.

Neil Fite began driving for Greyhound Bus Lines in 1937. After five years, he began working in the company's offices in Nashville. After awhile, he was made manager of the East Tennessee district in Knoxville. After a few years, he returned to Nashville in an executive position. In 1959, Neil resigned from the Greyhound Company to accept a managerial position in the trucking industry. While beyond retirement age, he is still involved for three days per week in the trucking business.

McAdoo's Hardware Company came to 216 in the mid-1950s. He bought the property from Neil Fite and was there until about 1963. The store was sold to Edward Alsup, who operated a jewelry store there until 1967. In that year, he sold the property to Comas Montgomery, who is the present owner. Mr. Alsup had remodeled the building's ground floor and arranged five apartments on the second floor. The Domestic Loan Company was there for a while after 1967. The Bridle and Saddle Shop was next. Then there was the Tennessee Probation and Parole Office, which was followed by Dr. Scott Cranford, who has recently moved up the street to 208. The lower-floor offices are presently vacant.

★ ★ ★

The 218 building has a masonry sign imbedded in the brick wall that reads HOME JOURNAL BUILDING. The *Home Journal* paper was founded in 1890 by Mr. Chip Henderson, son of Mr. Reese K. Henderson. That paper was one of the ancestors of the present-day *News Journal.* Its other ancestor was the *Murfreesboro News* which was established in 1848 or 1849 by A. Watkins.

Louis Burgdorf published the *Home Journal* until his death in 1920. The plant was then sold to Andrew L. Todd and W.H. Trevathan. Jesse Beesley, Jr., bought the *News-Banner* in 1926. He converted it into a daily paper the following year. In 1931, Mr. Beesley bought an interest in the *Home Journal.* The *Daily News-Banner* was consolidated with the semi-weekly *Home Journal,* and the title of *Daily News-Journal* was assumed.

Few men have had the great positive influence on the State of Tennessee, Rutherford County, and Murfreesboro as did Andrew L. Todd, who for several years owned the building at 218 West Main Street. His merits and his attainments deserve a full-fledged biography. He served two terms as a member of the lower house of the State Legislature in 1913 and again in 1921, as speaker of that body; and he also served two terms in the State Senate, in 1915 and again in 1919 as Speaker of that body. He was the only man in Tennessee ever to serve as Speaker of both House and Senate.

In 1933, the *Daily News Journal* was leased by E.W. Carmack. A year later he bought the paper and published it until 1940. In 1940, Mr. Carmack sold the paper to Andrew L. Todd, who in turn sold it to Jack MacFarland and Major W.E. Rynerson, who constituted the Mid-South Publishing Company. The new company remained in 218 until 1951, when it moved to its present quarters on Walnut Street. In the meantime, it continued to use the building for storage of paper goods, etc.

As mentioned earlier, Roy Dennard of Western Auto bought the property in 1954. That business operated there until 1980, when it moved to 310 West Main Street. Bob Parks bought the property and later sold it to Hope Anderson, who converted the property into an apartment house. Hope-Vere Anderson is a former expatriate of Scotland. I had known him and his parents since about 1963 through my frequent trips to Scotland while purchasing antiques. It was through my invitation and offer of employment that he came to the United States in 1979. Hope attended Middle Tennessee State University, graduated, married, and eventually gained his green card as a new citizen of the U.S. He recently bought the former J.C. Penney building on the northwest corner of North Maple and West College Street.

During the time in which Andrew L. Todd owned the *Home Journal* Building, he occupied the second floor with a suite of offices. His son, attorney Jack Todd, occupied those offices before moving to the Scott Building on College Street.

★ ★ ★

Address F-224 West Main Street was an empty lot in 1923. There came later to that space a small service station that was called Consumers. The manager of the station was a man whose surname was Travis. There were several stations around town in those days that sold gasoline at a discount—usually two cents lower than the larger stations. Most of the discount stations sold only fuel and oil and sold no services. Consumers was later to move to a location just north of the Kingwood Church of Christ on Memorial Drive.

Joe Harrison bought the property from the Eph Hoover estate in 1960. Shortly thereafter, he built the present building that is on this location. The Fabric Center, owned by Earl Bailey, moved to the new building from 123 North Maple Street in 1966. Earl moved out in 1972, and Harry Friedman leased the building for the operation of a sporting goods and surplus store. Harry sold the business to John Friedman (no relation) in 1976. John was there until 1983 and sold out to Charles Friedman (no relation). The present name of the busy store is Friedman's Army Surplus. There is a friendly atmosphere there where the staff is anxious to help the customers. Mike Lorance handles the fishing tackle and gun department. Mike is blind. He is positively a marvel. He can meet a customer once and will recognize that person's voice three months later. He can disassemble a fishing reel, find the problem, and reassemble it without hesitation. He participates in fishing tournaments and asks no quarter from any contestant. Mike Lorance should be an encouragement to any person who feels shortchanged on any of their normal senses or attributes.

The property at 224 is now held in trust by the Mid-South Bank and Trust Company for the benefit of the children of Joe and Madilyn Harrison.

Chapter XXII

North Walnut—West Main

On North Walnut Street, behind the old Home Journal Building and what is now Friedman's, there was an empty fenced lot and an old brick building. Sometimes the lot was not empty. Sometimes the lot contained several roan horses. They were out for exercise for there was no grass on the lot. The horses were for the express use of certain military officers. The time was 1924.

That was the Headquarters Battery and Combat Training First Battalion of the 115th Field Artillery. Hefty Sgt. Walter Zumbro was the caretaker of the unit. Allie P. McAdoo was the stable sergeant. During the 1930s, Capt. Aultman Sanders was the unit commander. Other ranking officers during the early 1930s were Capt. James "Goat" Ridley, and Capt. Hubert L. McCullough. Tom Givan became a member of the unit in 1934. He recalls that his National Guard unit met once per week for drill, etc. Occasionally it met on the Square for close order drill.

On September 22, 1940, the members of the Guard unit were called for active duty in World War II. Most of those men were to take part in that war until 1946. On their return, the location on North Walnut Street was no longer to be used by the Guard. Instead, there was to be a new location and new building on the old Highway 41 for the use of the local Tennessee State Guard.

Mr. R.B. Womack owned the property on North Walnut Street which housed the Guard unit of the 1920s and 1930s. The fenced-in lot on which the cavalry horses exercised was used by Oscar and Everett Johns in the latter 1940s as a used car lot. They placed a portable office on the lot in which to do business.

Roy Byrn became the owner of that property, which has a street address of 116 North Walnut. He built two yellow brick buildings on the lot which was formerly used by the National Guard. The first building (116) was used by Joe Scomber for an antique shop in the late 1950s and early 1960s. He made regular trips to New York for the procurement of antiques. Auction sales were held there often. Eugene "Burr" Hargis, Don Durham, Tim Durham, and this writer assisted in the sales. When Joe Scomber moved out, the building was used by Richard Bailey as a warehouse for the storage of carpets.

The Lewis-Jones Appliance Company moved there in March, 1978 from the 200-block on West Main Street. They bought the property from Roy Byrn, Jr. The building was subsequently remodeled to suit their requirements. James L. Lewis and Edward H. Jones are very much there with a large inventory of Whirlpool and Maytag appliances. They probably carry a larger inventory of appliance parts than any other concern in Murfreesboro. Emmitt Lewis would be proud of his son, James L. Lewis, and his son-in-law, Ed Jones, who have so capably carried on the business that he began over forty years ago.

The next building on the east side of North Walnut Street has the address of 118. It is a yellow brick building, busily occupied by Eddie Alsup. The name of the business is Wholesale Tops. They fashion formica tops for the several local cabinetmakers. Mr. Alsup bought the building in 1983 from Mr. Achord, who had operated the hardware store on West College Street. The building (118) was used as an annex of the hardware store. The hardware store is treated in the section that deals with College Street.

The location of 118 North Walnut Street will be the northernmost limit of Walnut Street with which this story deals. Across the street, the first building behind the Firestone Service Station was 111 North Walnut Street.

★ ★ ★

The J.B. Cook Auto Parts Company is the oldest auto parts industry in Murfreesboro. It came here in 1938. It was first located at 119 West Main Street. After a short while there, it moved to the address at 111 North Walnut Street. Bob Gailey and Curtis Eaton were managers of the store for various lengths of time. Grady Wilkerson was an employee there for several years.

The next door southward on North Walnut Street is address 107. The occupant is P and P Printing Company. The owner is David Picklesimer. The firm came here August, 1990. That location is at the back of the old Hirshbrunner & Miles Dodge, Plymouth, Chrysler building at 302 West Main Street. Both 107 and 105 are parts of 302 West Main. The large building is owned by John Brockwell, who bought the property from the Eph Hoover estate in November, 1989. Mr. Brockwell has accomplished extensive face lifting, partitioning and remodeling to the old building, which once served as a livery stable. The 105 address is presently serving as a rear entrance to Brockwell's firm, which is named IDEAS. Hope-Vere Anderson used that building for several years as an antique shop and auction house.

★ ★ ★

The first two blocks off the Square on West Main Street could have almost been called "Gasoline Alley" in the 1920s. There were three automobile dealerships and five gasoline dispensing stations, three of which were in conjunction with the dealerships.

On the northwest corner of Vine and West Main streets, there was the Dodge, Plymouth and Chrysler dealership. It was operated by William Archibald Miles and Sam Hirschbrunner. Mr. Miles served several years on the City Council and was Mayor for two terms in the late 1930s and early 1940s.

The General Shoe Company came to that former Dodge, Plymouth and Chrysler place in 1941. It occupied the corner building, the former Earthman-Wilson Ford at 310 and all of the space between West Main and the Firestone garage on North Walnut Street. That company left in 1951.

Roger Sanders came next to the corner in 1953 with his Sanders Super Service Tire Company. Roger conducted a huge tire business there. His largest volume was with such trucking firms as Hoover, Wilson, and TCT. Mr. Sanders died in 1975. His secretary, Cora Cottar, closed out the business in 1976. The Eph Hoover heirs owned the property at that time. The next occupant was Jimmie Jacobs, who had a tire business there for a while. The next tenant was Roy Leathers, who conducted sales of miscellaneous goods there. Then there came Hope-Vere Anderson with his antiques and auction sales. The name of the present business is Ideas, a firm which does screen art and printing. That interesting firm also handles advertising specialties for schools and other organizations which may be involved in fund raising. The large building is owned by John Brockwell who bought 302 West Main Street from the Eph Hoover estate in November, 1989.

★ ★ ★

The next door and 310 address was the business home of Earthman and Wilson Motor Company in the 1920s and early 1930s. They had the dealership that sold the most cars in town—Ford. In 1924, a new T-Model Ford could be bought for fewer than $500.00. In 1927, a new A-Model Ford with rumble seat could be had for fewer than $400.00 f.o.b. Detroit. In the 1930s, the dealership moved over to West College Street. Hoover Truck Lines used the old Ford building as a Murfreesboro branch office for several years. Charlie Haynes had a cabinetmaking shop there in conjunction with his contracting business. Charlie was the number-one residential contractor in town for several years.

Charles L. Briley came to 310 West Main after several years at D-130 on North Church Street. Then there came the present tenant, the Western Auto Store.

★ ★ ★

The next address (320) is the Security Federal Building. About one-half of the building houses the Security Federal Savings and Loan Association. Several offices occupy the remaining space. That site was formerly occupied by the U.S. Post Office.

From 1914 into the 1940s, the 320 corner was the location of a flour mill. During its earlier stages, it was called the Hisle Roller Mills. It had moved from Walter Hill into Murfreesboro around 1914. The mill was a large three-story corrugated-metal-sided building. It was to be operated later and into the 1940s by James A. "Goat" Ridley. He was the father of James A. "Jimmie" Ridley, Jr., and Granville S. Ridley, III. During the period of Mr. Ridley's ownership, the name of the company was Murfreesboro Mills.

In 1923, the largest lumber and millwork business in Rutherford County was Maugan-Bell Lumber Company. It was there in the early 1920s and possibly earlier. It occupied almost one-half of the 300-block on the south side of West Main Street. During the early 1930s, the firm's name became Bell Bros. Lumber Company. The ownership was comprised of: Will Bell, Cliff Bell, Warner and William Hooper, and Gilbert Shearon. "Monk" Howard was a well-known office member. The firm went out of business in 1948. "Cap" Martindale was there for about two years with a lumber business. Among those who were employees of the Maugan-Bell and finally Bell Lumber Company were: J.J. Victory and his son J.W. "Red" Victory, Walter Singleton, Jack Winsett, Jimmie Hastings, Joe Nickols, Charlie Miller, Ed Vaughn, Floyd Rigsby, and Woodrow McClain.

Sterchi Furniture Company came next to that corner and remained into the 1980s. Heilig-Myers Furniture Company is presently located there. Next door at 309 is located the Mayo Paint and Decorating Company, Rowland and Associates and the CRM Insurance Company.

During the 1920s and most of the 1930s, that site contained the small building in which Squire J.P. Hicks held court. The squire had no formal legal experience, but he was the judge before whom those appeared who had committed felonies or misdemeanors. Short, rotund, and with a glistening bald head, he wielded much power in those times. The Alex Briley Plumbing and Electrical Company was there during the latter 1940s.

Next door and on the same site of the present 309 building was a small building that housed an automobile repair shop. That business was very capably handled by Raymond and Amon Bilbrey. They were there during the years from 1937 into 1974. Actually, Raymond left the partnership for a few years to work for Hoover Truck Lines. Oscar Sanders was in charge of radiator repair there for many years.

The business on the southwest corner of West Main and South Walnut streets was the busiest and most visible place in town. From early morning until late in the evening, the place was buzzing with activity. It was Allen's Service Station. The property owners in 1923 were

W.C. and F.E. Allen. Herman Rhodes, W.H. Davidson, and Horace Allen formed a partnership for the operation of the business. They were ideally suited for one another as partners.

The building was built for the purpose for which it was used. There were several gasoline pumps under the large overhang of the building. Each dispenser was the gravity flow type which required the attendant to manually pump the fuel from the underground tank up into a ten-gallon glass cylinder mounted on top of the dispenser column. The ten-gallon cylinder was graduated by visible one-gallon markers. All of this seems primitive by modern methods, but then the cars (mostly T-Models) did not require much fuel. They did not travel very far. The roads were bad and the tires were highly susceptible to blow-outs, punctures, etc. That last problem contributed to the high visibility which the station enjoyed.

If people drove their cars much in those years, they would have numerous tire problems. It was not uncommon for a motorist to suffer three or four punctures or blow-outs on a fifteen-mile trip. Usually, the driver would do the repair, but after a few of those happenings, the average driver became rather adept at that task plus the ability to care for the many idiosyncracies of the pesky critter—the T-Model Ford. Also, many drivers of that day were not very diligent about watching the fuel level of the gravity flow tanks of their cars. Those and other reasons were why Allen's Service Station was there.

On Sundays, an observer passing the station would notice a fleet of what was called "skeeters" parked across the street on Walnut. A "skeeter" was a stripped-down T-Model Ford on which a wooden cab with no doors and a flat wooden bed had been fashioned. That was the super emergency vehicle which Allen's sent for a motorist's rescue; and it was prompt and fast. A person called the telephone operator, gave the number which was 811, Allen's answered, and help was on the way. Most of the mufflers had been removed from the "skeeter's" engines. The stranded motorist knew he was about to be rescued several minutes before the "skeeter" arrived. The vehicles' wooden bodies were painted yellow with professionally painted red and black lettering. The entire fleet was operated by colored boys. They were good at their job, they were fast, and they all carried big smiles. Everybody in the county knew and appreciated the people at Allen's Service Station.

Allen's had the number-one tire dealership in the early 1920s. The station handled General Tires. The well-known logo around town was that of a child with blond hair, dressed in night clothes, yawning and carrying a burning candle in one hand. The caption read, "It's time to retire."

The south end of the station was leased by Jim Bynum in 1931. He had the dealership for the then very small car which was the American-made English Austin. Much fanfare preceded the introduction of the Bantam Austin, but it was soon destined to oblivion. The gravel roads were not suited for the narrow wheelbase of the car, and people really did not appreciate its small fuel consumption. Mr. Bynum later joined the Stephens Motors in the operation of a large station and garage on West College Street.

Allen's Service Station continued in business until 1946. That was when W.H. Davidson decided to enter the insurance business. He established an office on the second floor of the Murfreesboro Bank and Trust Company. His son, W.H. "Slick" Davidson, accompanied his father into the agency.

The next occupant of the corner service station was the gasoline business operated by Lynn White and Ernest Watson. In 1955, they sold out to Willie Keaton. Next, Cecil Harrell came there, followed by Ray Vaughn with his electrical business. Then came Dean Westbrooks with his cabinet shop. The building is now vacant.

Chapter XXIII

South Walnut—West Main (South Side)

Facing Walnut and at the back of Allen's was an auto repair and wheel alignment shop operated by Hatton Hopkins and Oscar Davis. Hal Harrison used a corner of the shop for generator, starter, and auto electric repair. They came there in 1949. Hatton Hopkins moved across Walnut to the corner of South Walnut and West Vine streets in 1966. He retired in 1968. The wheel alignment shop behind Allen's is vacant at the present time. Mrs. Frances Allen Hobgood owned the large corner Allen building until she sold it to Rowland and Hutson. Those partners sold the property to Ray Vaughn in 1967. Ray retired in 1982. He still owns the property.

★ ★ ★

R.B. "Dick" Womack had a huge brick front barn in the middle of the block between West Main and West Vine streets. A sign on the front of the building read: R.B. WOMACK Dealer in Horses and Mules. That was a prosperous business during the 1920s and part of the 1930s. Mr. Womack was a colorful man who made friends easily. I always appreciated his cheerful greeting. He was a director in the Murfreesboro Bank and Trust Company. Elvis Rushing bought the brick edifice in the early 1950s and used it for storage in connection with his grocery salvage business, which was located around the corner on West Vine. Elvis retired in the late 1970s and recently had the old horse and mule barn dismantled.

★ ★ ★

The last building in that block and on the corner of South Walnut and West Vine streets was a blacksmith shop operated by Dave Anderson, his brother Lewis Anderson, and Frank Bean. That was a busy place. Horses, mules, and ponies were usually tied to a wooden horizontal log in front of the divided shop. They were awaiting the shoeing process. The right side of the building was used for the repair of wagons and especially the repair of wagon and buggy wheels. They also specialized in the installation of new solid rubber tires on buggies. Those kinds of repairs required a craftsmanship that is seldom found in these modern times.

View of West Main Street from courthouse. Note grassy median down street.

R.B. "Dick" Womack at his mule barn on South Walnut Street.

On the opposite corner on South Walnut Street, there was a dwelling in 1923 (A-123). Mr. R.B. Womack was the owner in 1942 when he built the brick garage at 119 South Walnut Street. That was where Brockman "Brock" Sanders came with his Ford dealership when the new building was completed. Alex Briley also leased a portion of the building for his plumbing business. At the same time, Mr. Womack built the adjacent building on West Vine which became the Murfreesboro Produce Company and is now Neeley's Hatchery (A-218).

"Brock" Sanders remained there with his Ford dealership until 1948, when Ford informed him that the company required him to move to larger quarters and that he would have to carry a much larger inventory of Ford products. Mr. Sanders refused to comply with the new requirements and gave up the dealership in 1948. The new Ford place in town became the Weatherford Motor Company on West Main Street near the depot.

Meanwhile "Brock" Sanders remained at his shop on the corner of Vine and Walnut. The new name for the garage became Sanders Auto Repair. Alex Briley Plumbing Company moved in 1946 to a shop on West Main Street.

Mr. Sanders remained there until 1966. Among the well-known mechanics who worked with him were "Dutch" Waldron, Burley Hayes, and James Estes. In 1966, "Brock" retired and Hatton Hopkins came there from across the street. He retired in 1968.

The shop at 119 South Walnut is still named Hopkins Wheel Alignment and Brake Repair. It is now owned by Frank Walton. He bought the corner building and also the building which houses Neeley's Hatchery from Sara Sue Womack Warner (R.B. Womack's daughter) in 1976. The Hopkins name has been on Vine Street for forty-two years.

★ ★ ★

In the middle of that same block on the east side of the street was the large warehouse from which the J.W. Fletcher & Son Wholesale Grocery Company (A-115) conducted its business. It was there until the late 1920s when the wholesale company moved to South Front Street. From there, it moved in the mid-1930s to just beyond the passenger depot on West Main Street. Mr. J.W. Fletcher, Jr., died in 1975. The fifty-four year old business was closed. It was Rutherford County's only wholesale grocery business for most of its existence.

When the wholesale grocery left the space on South Walnut Street, the warehouse was vacant for quite some while. Mr. Womack bought the property and used the south section of the building to augment his horse and mule trade. The Tennessee Valley Authority (T.V.A.) leased that section in the late 1930s. Mr. Robertson leased the north section of the building during that period. He stored and sold coal from his location. In 1941, the Cohens leased the south section. Gerald Cohen recalls that when he returned from the service in World War II, he and his brother began to store furniture in the building. The Cohen brothers,

Mortimer and Gerald, soon had their large Home Furniture Company going. It took several buildings and thousands of square footage in floor space to store and display their huge inventory. They bought the property at the end of the 1950s. The buildings were rapidly deteriorating, so Gerald Cohen decided to demolish the buildings. Gerald sold the property in the mid-1960s to Leon Schklar, who owned Standard Auto Parts on West Main Street. That property is presently leased to the City of Murfreesboro for parking during its new construction period.

★ ★ ★

The Chevrolet dealer in Murfreesboro in 1924 was Jackson Bros. The name of the same dealership in Murfreesboro after sixty-seven years and after thousands and thousands of sales and almost uncountable services to its customers is still Jackson Bros. Chevrolet.

Five brothers, I.S. "Cap," Jerry, Horace, Joe, and Ralph came to Murfreesboro from Eagleville in 1924. They had been offered and had accepted the Chevrolet dealership for Murfreesboro. The Chevrolet auto was relatively a new car on the market with production having begun in 1913. It was to be General Motors' answer to the competition offered by Henry Ford's T-Model. It was a few steps above the Ford in that it had a transmission with a gear shift, it came with a self-starter, and it could be delivered in other colors than black. The Chevy cost only a little over one hundred dollars more than Ford, but the Ford continued to be America's favorite car by far until the early 1930s. However, Jackson Bros. did sell Chevrolets. The five Jackson brothers slowly but surely increased their sales volume and provided a trustworthy service to their customers.

They moved in the early 1930s from 231 West Main Street to West College Street, next to the then existing Haynes Hotel. That was a new building to which they moved. Their growth required much larger quarters. In 1958, with an expanded growth, it became necessary to move again to much larger quarters on Broad Street, where Mark Pirtle's is now located. The five brothers from Eagleville had come a long way. In 1970, I.S. "Cap" Jackson was the one remaining brother who retained the business. He recognized the need for again a larger building and sales lot. He purchased the several acres on which Rutherford County's oldest family owned dealership is now located. Jackson Bros. Chevrolet is still going strong at 1422 Northwest Broad Street. "Cap" Jackson died in 1977. His son, Jim, or "Uncle Jim" Jackson as he is more popularly known, still carries on the business in the same Jackson manner.

The original Jackson Bros. building, 221 West Main, was owned by Herman Jackson along with the G.B. Sawyer estate for many years. Various businesses were in and out of the corner location for several years. In 1951, the W.T. Lowe Auto Parts Company came there. The Joe Scomber Antique Shop was there for a while. Then there was W.D. "Dub" Humaker and his wife, Jim, who operated an antique and book shop there during the early 1960s. They were followed by White's Auto Parts Store, which was operated by Forrest McKnight. An egg and poultry produce shop was there for a time. Then Roy Leathers moved a used furniture store there. There have been some oriental restaurants there in recent years. The 221 West Main building is presently vacant. The property is owned Nghiep Nguyen, et ux.

★ ★ ★

Up the street a few steps to 219 West Main Street is the Murfreesboro Auto Parts operated by Horace W. "Bud" Burns. "Bud" came here in September, 1954 as an employee of the W.T. Lowe Auto Parts Company. He bought the business in 1968 and changed the name to Murfreesboro Auto Parts. "Bud" is now in his thirty-seventh year there at this place. He bought the building from the Elizabeth Shearron estate in July, 1982. H.W. Burns is a jovial, accommodating individual. It seems that this characteristic is necessary for success in any business, but sometimes it is sadly lacking.

Mr. R.D. Craddock was there for several years during the early 1940s. He bought the property during his occupation of 219. Mr. Craddock operated a chicken hatchery and feed business there. He moved there from three doors up the street at address 211.

★ ★ ★

Up a few steps and on a higher level is the address of A-215 and 217. The Home Journal Exchange is located there. It is operated by Doug and Mary Stem, who have been there for three years. They carry a large inventory of various and interesting items such as novelties, closeouts, and appliances, both large and small. They keep a neat and tidy store where all of the merchandise is plainly visible. Doug is a licensed auctioneer, having graduated from the Nashville Auction School in 1980.

That property was bought in the late 1950s by Leon and Edith Schklar. The store was occupied at various times by Stroud's Furniture Company, Jim Sidwell, James Rowland, and Home Furniture. When the Schklars bought the property, they expanded into the entire building.

Henry Cohen had operated a furniture store there from 1939 until the early 1950s.

That building or warehouse was double the size of the other stores in the block. In 1923, it housed a general feed, grain, fence, and lime sales. The business was operated by a partnership which was called Overall & Avent. The Overall contingent was composed of the brothers Asbury Stanley and Robert Floyd Overall. The other part of the partnership was James Avent. The firm operated a lime quarry at Summitville, Tennessee. The quarry used small donkey steam locomotives to transport the lime from the quarry to a loading area where normal size locomotives and freight cars would haul the product to distant points.

Overall & Avent had the largest wire fence house in Tennessee. They dealt exclusively in American fence and shipped large amounts to Western states.

Mr. Stanley Overall operated a large coal, sand, lime, and building material yard which was located just across the railroad tracks at the passenger depot. There were several warehouses located on the approximately ten acres of that complex. Stanley Overall died in the early 1930s. After his death, his son Bill operated the business. Bill passed away while still in his late teens, after the mid-1930s. His brother Robert "Bob" Overall ran the business for a few years. Bob was quite interested in the automobile business and became very widely known throughout middle Tennessee as an enterprising and highly competitive auto dealer.

The Overall properties and enterprises could easily be considered as one of the most extensive and prosperous in Rutherford County during the first third of the twentieth century. Leon Schklar bought the large store (215 and 217) from the Asbury M. Overall estate in the mid-1950s.

★ ★ ★

At the 211 and 213 addresses in 1923, there was a tall vertical sign in front of the building. The sign contained the name Cantrell. As yet the significance of this sign has not been ascertained. Mrs. Florence Bilbro was the registered owner of the two stores. She was the wife of Dr. W.C. Bilbro. They were the family for which the Bilbro Addition was named.

The Smotherman & Fite Insurance Company was in 211 for a while during the 1930s. Mr. R.D. Craddock brought his hatchery business there from across the street in the rear of Fite's Purina building. Later, at the end of the 1930s, the Craddocks moved down the street to 219 West Main Street.

Leon Schklar and his wife, Edith, arrived in Murfreesboro in 1941. They leased the one building (A-211) in which to establish an auto parts store. The name of the business was to be Standard Auto Parts. That was to be a busy, prosperous, and expanding undertaking. Soon Leon leased the 213 address next door. He was open six days per week and made himself available on Sundays. The Schklars bought these two properties (211 nd 213) in the late 1940s. By the late 1960s, Leon and Edith owned the four adjacent stores (211, 213, 215, and 217).

In the meantime, Leon had added another building onto the rear of the 211 and 213 building. That became a shop in which to grind crank shafts and to repair alternators and starters. The two sons of Leon and Edith, Norman and Maury, joined the business during the early 1950s.

Leon passed away in 1985. From the single operation in 1941, his business now covered more than one-half of the 200-block on West Main Street. Norman and Maury were quite interested in the communication and electronic business, so they closed the forty-seven-year-old auto parts store in 1988.

The two sons sell and service telephone equipment, mobile radios, and computers. They also rent beepers and provide a live answering service.

EPILOGUE

The employment of the title - Mink Slide to Main Street - to show the contrast between the Square of 1924 and the Square of 1990 would have been inappropriate had it not been for the Main Street Program.

A pondering stroll up East Main Street and around the Square evokes a prideful admiration of the aesthetic beauty and grandeur of the court house centerpiece and the historically preserved revitalized buildings surrounding it. The merely economic and bare financial aspects of the former area have been significantly enhanced and highlighted by the flower plots, the brick street crossings, the park benches, the historic lamp post replicas and the honey locust and ginkgo trees.

At a meeting recently of a group planning a state-wide convention to be held in Murfreesboro, it was suggested and wholeheartedly agreed that the conventioneers should be given a tour of the Square. Murfreesboro has much to offer tourists and visitors. There are Oaklands, Cannonsburg, Middle Tennessee State University, Middle Tennessee Medical Center and now the Public Square which is all decked out for showing. In a few months, there will be the new Civic Center, the new Linebaugh Library and the new parking garage.

The quest to reach the Main Street pinnacle which the Square now enjoys has not been easy nor inexpensive. An Uptown Merchants Association was formed in the nineteen sixties with almost the same goals which the Main Street program fostered and attained in the late eighties. The merchants met regularly and were dedicated to the task of revitalizing the twenty-five block area of the Square. However, they lacked the day to day leadership which only a corporate entity such as Main Street could engender. The new leadership devised an architectural plan, aroused support for the concept, especially in city and county governments, and instilled in the merchants and property owners a spirit of cooperation.

This last thrust was perhaps the most remarkable result that the Main Street effort attained. The task was going to cost money, much of which would have to be paid by the property owners of which there were one hundred and twenty-nine. Each would be assessed $121.00 per linear foot of property frontage. A meeting was held, a vote was taken and the consent assessment passed with little opposition. The city and county had agreed to bear a substantial portion of the total cost of the project. Main Street was and continues to be on its way.

Within the twenty-five block area which comprises Main Street, there are two hundred and sixty-one small businesses and nine large businesses. The nine are considered large on account of their larger personnel employment. The spirit of cooperation and pride of achievement seems to have permeated the business owners, their employees and even the new customers who now appear on the revitalized scene. Much of this could not have happened had there not been certain property owners who felt that the adaptive reuse of old historical buildings as an alternative to new construction would be good business that offered significant profitability. The concept has appealed particularly to those who were vitally interested in preserving architecturally sound and historical old buildings which also preserve our links to the past.

The Main Street Program capitalizes on the unique character of the court house Square and surrounding area with the goal of transforming it into the cultural, social and professional center of Rutherford County.... in essence the hub of community life.

It would have been difficult for Ed Bell in 1938 to have imagined the new exciting revitalized face of the Square. He would appreciate it. However, he would not be excited. Nothing would excite Ed Bell. He would applaud the individualities of the participants around the Square. He would applaud the equality of opportunities that are even more numerous in 1990 than they were when he walked his beat from Main Street to Mink Slide fifty years ago.

The Main Street group claims accomplishments such as:

* $5 million low interest loan payment;
* $2.8 million invested in 78 renovations;
* $1.5 million public improvement project;
* $9.25 million City Center fifteen story building;
* $13.1 million for the civic plaza with an 800-space parking garage.

Jack Weatherford became Main Street's first chairman in 1985. Blake Tidwell became the next chairman and was followed by the present chairman, Gary Middleton. Since its inception six years ago, Dawn Eaton has been the ramrod of the project. She sits behind the desk where the buck stops. An observer has only to stroll from Mink Slide to Main Street to see and feel the results of her team's work and efforts.

Hopefully, this almost seventy year account of the store and shopkeepers, the bankers and professional people, the employees, the property owners, those who frequented the Square, the variety of businesses and the upward struggle from the Mink Slide of 1923 to the Main Street of 1991 will enhance our respect for the unique people and their architecture which we pridefully witness around the Square today.

Murfreesboro's Andrew Lytle in his *Wake for the Living: A Family Chronicle* wrote that historic buildings are more than mere relics for "architecture most substantially exhibits the soul of a society."

Hopefully, this account will provide a bridge of continuity between the horse and buggy days of the early twentieth century to the space and computer age of the last decade of this same century.

Hopefully, this account has emphasized the intrepid individualism of those participants in the market place about the Square and their ardent belief in the system of private enterprise. They would never have contemplated any other system. No other system would have ever brought the Murfreesboro Public Square from Mink Slide to Main Street. No other system would have brought the United States to the pinnacle of being the greatest nation on earth.

ABOUT THE AUTHOR

Charles Byron Arnette was born March 16, 1918 in Concord, a small village between Rockvale and Eagleville in Rutherford County.

Arnette began school at the Misses Eliza and Belle Ransom Private School on North Academy Street, attended Crichlow Grammar School and graduated from Central High School. He continued his education at Middle Tennessee State College, the University of Tennessee, Watkins Institute, Michigan College of Mining and Technology (as an Air Force cadet) and the University of Tennessee Extension in Murfreesboro.

In 1948, he married Sara Louise Kimery of Shelbyville. They have four children and eight grandchildren. C.B. and his wife operated Arnette Antique Galleries for thirty years, during which time they traveled extensively over Europe. Since retiring in 1986, they have continued to spend much time in travel.

C.B. has made one hundred and thirty-three trips to Europe, traveled to all seven continents, visited all fifty states in the Union, all of the provinces in Canada, circled the globe and recently traveled to Russia and through Siberia via the Trans-Siberian Railroad.

Arnette has served as President of the Tennessee Auctioneer Association, Chairman of the Board of Middle Tennessee Christian School, President of the Murfreesboro Antique Association and Vice-President of the Board of Directors of Stones River Manor. In June 1986, he was inducted into the Tennessee Auctioneer Association Hall of Fame. He has served as feature writer for the *Historical Review and Antique Digest,* a Tennessee publication.

Charles B. Arnette. Author of *From Mink Slide to Main Street.*

INDEX

A

B

C

D

E

F

G

H

J

K

L

M

N

O

P

Q

R

S

U

V

W

Y

Z